SAVING GARY McKINNON

SAVING GARY McKINNON
A MOTHER'S STORY JANIS SHARP

Biteback Publishing

First published in Great Britain in 2013 by
Biteback Publishing Ltd
Westminster Tower
3 Albert Embankment
London SE1 7SP
Copyright © Janis Sharp 2013

Image of Janis Sharp outside the Royal Courts of Justice, plate section page 2
© Getty Images

Image of Janis Sharp receiving Liberty Human Rights award, plate section page 5
© and by kind permission of Bill Knight

ISBN 978-1-84954-574-7

10 9 8 7 6 5 4 3 2 1

A CIP catalogue record for this book is available from the British Library.

Set in Caslon

Printed and bound in Great Britain by
CPI Group (UK) Ltd, Croydon CR0 4YY

MIX
Paper from
responsible sources
FSC® C020471

To Wilson, my husband, the love of my life, whose love, care, optimism and humour kept me going through the darkest of times. Without him life would have been infinitely harder, much less interesting and much less fun.

To my son Gary, a talented and extraordinary man who I love dearly and am proud to call my son, and to Lucy, whose light and laughter shone into his life.

CONTENTS

FOREWORD BY JULIE CHRISTIE

When the news broke that a young man from north London called Gary McKinnon was to be extradited to the United States for hacking into computers there and leaving behind him some rude remarks, I was as puzzled as anyone. What had he done that could not be dealt with by the British courts? Why was it so serious that years after the hacking the American authorities, all the way up to their Attorney General, were still pursuing him?

It gradually became apparent that the authorities were hunting him for a crime that, as far as I know, is still not on the statute books: causing the United States government deep embarrassment. In the meantime Gary, to his bewilderment, had suddenly to fight to remain in Britain and avoid the possibility of being locked up in an American penitentiary, labelled a national security threat. And anyone who has followed what has been happening in Guantanamo Bay over the last decade will know that once 'national security' is involved in the United States the chances of a fair trial – or even a trial at all – become minimal.

It was Gary's mother Janis Sharp who led the ultimately triumphant battle to halt the extradition. Without her courage and determination, Gary would undoubtedly now be behind bars – or not with us at all. In this book, Janis tells us about Gary's childhood and his curiosity about UFOs that led to his eventual hacking of the NASA computers, how she first learned of his arrest, how he came to be diagnosed as suffering from Asperger's, and how the efforts to save him slowly built into one of the most admired – and successful – campaigns for justice that many of us can remember.

The book paints a much fuller picture of Gary and of Janis than we have ever had before. It catalogues the highs and lows of the rollercoaster ride to halt the extradition. It also acts as a fine example of how to mount a campaign when all the odds seem stacked against you, and provides a fascinating insight into how politics, the law and the media work in Britain.

Janis Sharp is a remarkable woman. That someone should dare to take on the mighty authoritarian institutions that control our lives, with no prior experience of doing so, should be an inspiration to us all. As injustices grow in the wake of the 'war on terror', this book is essential reading, not only as a political thriller and a personal story, but also as an eye-opener to the way our freedoms can be threatened. Bravo, Janis!

Julie Christie
June 2013

CHAPTER 1

OUT OF THE BLUE

How did this happen? I mean, out of all the people in the world, why us?

It was 19 March 2002 when my son Gary McKinnon was arrested by the Hi-Tech Crime Unit. Ironically, I had said to my husband Wilson, Gary's stepdad, just months before: 'Isn't it amazing that Gary has reached the age of thirty-five without getting into heavy drugs or into trouble of any kind?'

I should have known then – once you start patting yourself on the back something happens to make you wish you had kept quiet. Maybe we had tempted fate into deciding we'd had life too easy.

Just hours before the phone call from Gary I was snuggled up in bed next to Wilson, thinking I could happily stay there forever.

It had been the same as any other morning – being woken by our dogs barking and Wilson bounding down the stairs to let them out.

Drinking tea and gazing through the patio window as the sun filtered through, I thought how much I loved life, loved watching the dogs running around in the garden, the fish swimming in the pond and the birds eating the berries from the tree. I was blissfully unaware that these moments of peace were about to be snatched away.

'Wilson! Let's take the dogs out.'

'OK, I won't be a minute,' said Wilson as he headed for the bathroom.

I switched on my computer, knowing that Wilson's minute means he disappears into a black hole and emerges half an hour later, book in hand, lost in the story he's been reading.

I'm still in awe of how via the internet I can access the most intricate details of virtually any subject from across the globe. I've always been good at absorbing information; having the library of the world at my fingertips is something I never take for granted.

'I'm ready, dogs out,' called Wilson, standing in the doorway all wrapped up and looking like a Viking Santa Claus as he absent-mindedly stroked his white beard.

'Have you got the keys and the phone?'

'I have,' said Wilson, still lost in thought.

'Then let's go.'

Dogs in tow, we walked through the trees, their branches held out like arms for woodland creatures to perch on and to shelter in, breathing peace into the atmosphere of nature's cathedral.

As Wilson told me in detail about the story he'd been reading, we were transported into another world, as our hounds ran like deer through the woods.

• • •

Arriving home we heard the phone ring, missed it. It rang again. It was Gary.

'Mum.'

'Hi Gary.'

'Mum, don't get upset. I've got something to tell you, but don't worry.'

'I'm worried, tell me!'

'I was arrested.'

'Arrested? What do you mean, arrested? Why would you be arrested?'

'For hacking into NASA … and the Pentagon.'

'What! NASA? The Pentagon? How could you have hacked into the Pentagon?'

I was gripping the phone so tightly the blood was draining from my hands as panic came in waves. I was wishing he would laugh and say he was joking, but Gary tells the truth – that's just the way he is.

The sinking feeling in the pit of my stomach was pulling me deeper and deeper and I instinctively felt this was way more serious than Gary realised.

'I was searching for information on UFOs. Don't worry, Mum. The police from the Hi-Tech Crime Unit are really nice; they're computer guys just like me.'

Oh Gary, they're not like you, and you need a lawyer.

'They told me they'd been monitoring my computer for months and as I hadn't done any damage I was looking at six months' community service. It's OK.'

I wanted to ask him how he could have been so stupid. I wanted to shake him and wake him up, but most of all I wanted to wrap him up in my arms to protect him: he was my son and an innocent to the core.

That's the thing about being a parent: your child is your child no matter what age they are. Their troubles are your troubles and you somehow find the strength to move mountains to protect them.

'I'll get you a lawyer, Gary.'

'I don't need one; I've told the Hi-Tech Crime Unit every-thing and they said they might give me a job after all this, as they need people like me.'

Oh Gary! Gary, this is America we're dealing with, this is Goliath.

I wanted to scream and tear my hair out at his naivety.

'I've always told you, if you were ever in trouble to ring me and I'd get you a lawyer. Why didn't you?'

'I didn't want to worry you.'

'You *have* worried me! Where are you?'

'I'm on my way home; they said they'll let me know when they want to speak to me again. I have to go.'

A wave of relief swept over me knowing that at least he was free: they didn't have him, he wasn't a prisoner, he was free.

It seemed ironic, as when Gary was younger he wanted to work for the police and I had talked him out of it. I was afraid of the violence in London and that people he knew might distance themselves from him, the way people often tend to do with the police. Now he had been arrested I started to question every bit of advice I'd ever given him. Maybe if I'd encouraged him to join the police he wouldn't be in this position now and would be working for the Hi-Tech Crime Unit instead of being arrested by them.

'Maybe' this, 'maybe' that, could have, should have, if only…

It's funny how when things go wrong we tend to keep going over the past, trying to work out how we could have avoided being in the place we're in now, even though we know it's too late to change things.

We used to say Gary was thirty going on thirteen. That annoyed him, but he's always been naive and young for his age, although clearly intelligent.

'What are we going to do, Wilson?'

'There's nothing we can do, we'll have to wait and see what happens.'

'We can't wait! This is NASA and the Pentagon we're talking about. How could Gary have hacked into the Pentagon? It's mad. Apart from anything else, surely Pentagon security has to be the best in the world?'

'You're pacing, Janis.'

'I never pace.'

'You do now.'

'Maybe Gary should go and live with his dad in Scotland for a while and they'll forget about it. I want him to be somewhere safe.'

'He can't, he's on bail.'

'I don't like this. If he got six months' community service that would be fine but I can't see it somehow.'

Wilson was calm. Wilson is always calm and I was glad of it at that moment as I had gone straight into panic mode. I wished my mum was still here – she always had good instincts and would have known what to do.

CHAPTER 2

LIFE BEFORE TECHNOLOGY

My mum, Mary May Macleod, was the heart of our family; and like the sun our lives revolved around her. Her eyes mirrored her soul. She had the most wonderful imagination and sense of playfulness and filled the house with music and laughter. She was half Irish and amazingly used to dream about our family's babies before they were born and before anyone realised they were pregnant.

It's said that many Celts have the gift of second sight and I know that in our family prophetic dreams are an accepted part of our lives. However, my dad, an engineer, had a practical approach to life and a fear of anything described as supernatural, so we were never allowed to speak about anything out of the norm when he was in earshot.

My dad was Donald John Macleod from Stornoway, the main town on the Isle of Lewis in the Outer Hebrides of Scotland. His family lived on a croft in an area that survived by self-sufficiency. They spun their own wool, fished in the sea, grew their own food and kept their own animals to provide a source of cheese, milk and eggs. My dad spoke only Gaelic when he first arrived in the big city of Glasgow in his teens. He was a proud, hardworking man who, in true Highland fashion, would not drink a drop of alcohol on a Sunday. He enjoyed cooking us all a healthy breakfast, and tried to encourage us to eat things like kippers, which to a child were pretty unappetising.

My dad was fascinated by the moon landing and had a passion for astronomy, taking us all out onto the veranda one night to view the passage of a comet, which was a magical moment for us.

My mum didn't know she was pregnant with me as her periods hadn't stopped, but she then had what the doctors thought was a miscarriage. They said no baby could have survived as she had lost everything, but unbeknown to them, there was a determined little girl still in there clinging on for dear life.

I was born dead, my mum had haemorrhaged and her life was in immediate danger. She was adamant that the doctors should attend to me first but they had decided it was too late for me and were working on my mum as a priority. Hearing my mum's pleas for her baby's life, a young nurse held me in her arms and refused to give up as she persistently tried to breathe life into my rapidly cooling body until finally I gasped for air. The last thing my mum heard before slipping into unconsciousness was the sound of her baby, crying. She said I was meant to be.

• • •

I was born in Glasgow as Janis Thomasina Macleod, the youngest of three children. We lived in a place called Gilshochill, not far from Maryhill.

One of the earliest and most haunting memories of my childhood was standing up in a metal cot in a children's home, holding onto the sides and crying and crying for my mum. Even now, just touching on the memory, tears well up, blurring the letters on the page.

My dad came to visit me in a children's home he had been forced to put me into temporarily when my mum was seriously ill in hospital and there was no one at home to look after me. He had my seven-year-old sister Lorna in tow.

My memory of this is vivid. I could hear the nurse's voice saying, 'She won't eat, and just stands in her cot looking at the door and won't stop crying.'

'Take her home, Daddy,' Lorna said pleadingly.

'I can't, I've got to go to work.'

'I'll look after her, Daddy.'

'You're too young, and you've got school.'

'But Mrs Clarke from upstairs will help me. Please, Dad. She needs to come home, we can't leave her here.'

My sister Lorna was fighting for me; she knew I was scared and she wouldn't give up until she had persuaded my dad, who thankfully relented and took me home.

The next memory I have of that time was when, months later, my mum, who had been seriously ill, came back home from the hospital and was standing in the darkened hall of our old ground-floor tenement flat in Glasgow. Lorna was holding me in her arms with her pigtails brushing my cheek and I remember I felt angry at my mum because she had left me and I clung to Lorna. Then I heard my mum's voice, warm and familiar but filled with sadness, saying, 'She doesn't remember me.'

I reached out, to be lifted up by my mum and held in the comfort of her arms. Home was home again and at the age of one I was back with my mum where I belonged.

Who knows how I can remember that far back, but I can. Maybe it's the memory of this traumatic childhood experience of separation from my family that led to me feeling even in adulthood that I had to be in control of certain situations.

I was incredibly attached to my mum; she was so different

from anyone I've ever known. When my sister, brother and I were little she used to spread thick polish on the floor and then tie rags onto our feet and we would slide around on the floor, laughing and singing and falling over and getting up again and sliding around some more until we had polished the floor to a high shine while having the most amazing time. She was brilliant at inventing the most ingenious ways of doing things.

In those days television was so new that it was rare for anyone in Scotland to have one and as children we mostly played outdoors. Some of our play was quite entrepreneurial. The older children would chop up wood while we younger ones tied the wood up in bunches, selling it door-to-door to get money to buy sweets or toys.

We occasionally went into the local chapel when it was empty and, regardless of anyone's religion, we would light candles and then ask God if we could take a few of the candles for our home-made den and some of the holy water in a small container. God always said yes, of course, and the few times the priest saw us he would tell us off gently, with a smile and sometimes with a wink. The doors of churches and chapels were always left open in those days.

The older children would boast to friends and neighbours that the holy water had spiritual powers, which we wholeheartedly believed. Some children would offer us sweets or sometimes, more appropriately, angel scraps in return for a few drops of the holy water with the magical powers.

Scraps were essentially like Victorian paintings of cherubs, children and animals printed on thin pieces of shiny paper that we'd keep in pages of books and then swap or trade with each other from our beloved den.

When it rained we played in our den and when there was thunder and lightning and the atmosphere seemed sinister, we'd sit inside our den with the candles lit, or in the enclosed stairway of the flats, and the older children would tell us ghost stories that scared the life out of us. We'd all either dissolve into fits of laughter or scream and run home as fast as our legs would carry us.

Getting caught in the rain and coming home soaking wet and sitting around the blazing coal fire while your wet clothes were drying was so comforting. Staring into the flames, I could see images of anything I cared to imagine, and I loved that.

We would put bread on the end of a very long, large metal fork and hold it over the fire until it was toasted. Before going to bed our mum would bathe us in a large tin bath in front of the fire, which was the absolute centre of our home.

In those days men in Scotland shied away from showing their affection towards their children. It was rare for dads to hug or to cuddle their children, but I used to sit at my dad's knee and he would dry my hair with a towel and I'd never want it to end. That was his way of showing his affection.

• • •

The older children used to teach the younger ones all the skills they had learned. Lorna taught me how to make tablet, a Scottish sweet a bit like fudge, only more brittle.

Fridges were virtually unheard of then, so we'd put the tablet out on the windowsill in the cold night air and leave it to set. It tasted good even if it was sickly sweet and bad for our teeth.

We also made toffee but managing to do it without getting your fingers burned was an art and gave a sense of self-satisfaction when you got it right.

My brother Ian was the eldest of the three and the quietest. Ian could draw well and tried to teach me but I was never any good. Ian once drew an excellent portrait of our dad sitting in his chair reading the newspaper. My dad didn't really react and didn't praise Ian, which I thought was a shame as the drawing was so good.

Whenever the weather was fine we would wander with our friends and have picnics in the fields and make buttercup and daisy chains. When it was cold we would roast potatoes over the glowing embers of a campfire the older children made. That taste is something I remember to this day.

We'd pick and eat wild blackberries and no matter how many we ate there were always loads left over to take home for our mums to make jam. Our clothes were saturated with bramble juice but we didn't care; it was fun and the juice washed out.

Some of the older people in the allotments would ask the children to help them with their gardening and would give the children carrots and turnips to munch on. They called the turnips tumshies, and we would eat them raw. Can you even imagine children wanting to eat raw turnips nowadays?

One day, when one of our group helped themselves to a turnip without being given permission, the man from the allotment chased us and we all had to run for our lives. It seemed exciting at the time and the relief of getting away safely made us giggle until the tears rolled down our faces.

My dad had an allotment and everything he touched seemed to grow to a huge size; he was forever winning prizes for his vegetables and flowers and we always had loads of fresh fruit and vegetables to eat. Perhaps it was because he was brought up on a croft in a pretty bleak part of the world, where unless you had such talents, survival would have been difficult.

Although I didn't inherit his green fingers, I did inherit my dad's love of the outdoors.

When I was little I felt like a free spirit, as much a part of nature as the deer that ran in the forest or the eagles that flew in the air. I wouldn't have traded my upbringing for the world.

Ever since I was a child I've cared desperately about neglected animals. When I was three years old I was playing in the back court in Glasgow. An old lady had put a litter of kittens in the dustbin and put a large rock on top of them and I could hear them crying. Neighbours were standing around looking and shouting at the woman, who was at her window, but no one was doing anything and I couldn't understand why the adults were all just standing there and wouldn't save the kittens.

The older children were at school so couldn't help me. I used every bit of strength I had to try to remove the rock but I couldn't budge it. I ran to the house and begged my mum to come and save the kittens, but a neighbour told her that it was too late: they were beyond help.

The kittens were hurt and crying and I was too small to help them. I was heartbroken and cried myself to sleep that night. I hated feeling powerless and wanted to grow up quickly.

I felt far too young when I attended my first primary school. I was five years old and dearly missed my mum, even though she would come up to school to see me at playtime and would pass me sandwiches through the railings.

I would sit at my desk gazing out of the windows, longing for the freedom of the outside. I wanted to run in the fields with the wind in my face, instead of being trapped in a classroom wasting my days away.

I always thought it strange that young children, geared to run and jump and laugh and play, were confined to a schoolroom and made to sit still at a desk for seven hours a day. To be at an age when you are full of the joys of life and bursting with energy, and then be forced to suppress that energy seemed odd to me. It was like being put in a straitjacket.

School was a shock to my system and I became quiet and shy when I was there. When my sister Lorna started secondary school I felt so lost and alone that I walked several miles to seek out her school. I have no idea how, at five years old, I could have found my way through miles of busy streets to a school I had never seen, but by sheer luck my sister was one of only two girls out in the playground when I arrived.

In those days I would sometimes see groups of children hanging around outside pubs their parents were in, waiting for money to buy a fish supper. It was a reflection of the times that even some very young children fended for themselves, usually going around in groups with siblings and friends, the older children always looking out for the younger ones.

Times in Glasgow were changing and when the old Victorian tenements where we lived were earmarked for demolition, we moved to a flat in a newly built development on the outskirts of Glasgow. My parents loved having a modern kitchen and a bathroom with hot running water and an indoor coal bunker, but my dad missed his allotment and we all missed our friends and tight-knit community.

I remember after we moved my mum and I heard a man singing in the communal garden of our new flat. Looking out of the bedroom window we saw it was a busker who used to make a living singing in the back courts of our old tenements; as the population moved, he was searching them out in an attempt to continue to make a living. He was a proud-looking man with a strong voice, and he held his cap over his heart as he sang. It was sad, as he was a really good singer, but apart from my mum I don't think anyone gave him money, and we never saw him again.

CHAPTER 3

THIS IS MUSIC

We had been brought up with virtually no technology apart from a radio, but about a year before we left our old house someone in the street got a TV to watch the coronation of Queen Elizabeth. We were all invited in, and lots of us sat in our neighbour's house watching the magical vision of TV for the very first time.

When our old community died I felt that a part of us had died too, but life, like Glasgow, was changing – as was the music.

My sister Lorna, who was almost six years older than I was and still charged with looking after me while my mum and dad worked, took me with her to the cinema for the first screening in Glasgow of the film *Rock around the Clock*. When we were in the cinema Lorna asked a few of her friends to keep an eye on me, and suddenly Lorna and other people in the cinema were dancing wildly in the aisles to this new music. At the age of eight I was witnessing the beginning of rock 'n' roll. It was incredible.

Lorna danced like a wild thing, but I wanted to learn how to play the music.

Lorna used to teach me to jive and would throw me over her back no matter how reluctant I was or how much I protested; I had no choice as she was bigger than me.

I used to skip lunch at primary school to run home and play my two favourite Elvis Presley songs, 'Big Hunk of Love' and 'One Night with You' on a Dansette record player. Headphones were unheard of then but I used to put my ear next to the little inbuilt speaker, cover my head with my coat and turn the volume up full so that I was enclosed in a world of music. I hated having to switch the music off to rush back to school again.

One day Lorna sewed the name 'Elvis' onto her top using sequins and rhinestones and I thought it looked amazing. She offered to do the same for me, but my mum said I was too young to go to school with 'Elvis' emblazoned across my chest.

I went to bed and when I got up in the morning my mum handed me my top and the large sequined words across the chest read 'Doris Day'. I could have cried. I looked at my mum and could see how tired she was. I knew she had been up all night sewing it for me and she so wanted me to like it. She had decided that Elvis on my top wasn't appropriate at my age and had sewed Doris Day's name on instead. She had no concept of how humiliating this would be for me to wear in school.

I couldn't bear to hurt my mum so I wore the top and sat mortified in school all day as my classmates teased and ridiculed me. I never wore it again.

Music wasn't just for kids – my mum adored Frank Sinatra and Irish music, whereas my dad's taste was more operatic in the style of Mario Lanza. He often sang in Gaelic, his native language.

Even though we sometimes got up to mischief, my mum never hit us, although smacking was common at that time. She herself had a difficult upbringing with an abusive father but she still had an amazing sense of humour and, like many people in Glasgow, possessed an optimism and a strength that carried her through the darkest of times. Even against the most daunting odds she believed that anything was possible, as do I.

I was independent and used to go out on my own and wander through the fields and the woods with my dog. One day when I was walking along the canal bank, two boys had caught a large fish from the canal and I watched it gasping for breath as it was dying in front of me. Seeing the fish struggling to live upset me so much that I gave the boys sixpence to throw it back in the water. Watching it swimming to freedom made me feel so happy.

• • •

I always felt different from other people and it was a huge relief when a new girl named Jean Connolly came to our school. We got on like wildfire and talked continuously, and both of us had an opinion on just about everything – which also caused us to argue at times.

We believed that we could change the movement of the clouds with the power of our thought. We'd cycle for miles and walk across fields barefoot with flowers in our hair, aspiring to emulate the romanticised lifestyle of a gypsy girl we had read about in story books. Our feet not being as tough as the gypsy girl's meant going barefoot didn't last long.

We also used to love playing in the fog that would descend on Glasgow at that time. The fog was so thick that sometimes you couldn't see two feet in front of you. It was like another world or a spooky film and we would call each other's names and then jump out and grab each other from behind, scaring the living daylights out of ourselves and dissolving into laughter. Coal fires were banned some years later, making thick fog a rarity.

Jean came from a big, warm family. Her dad was a lamp-lighter, who lit the gas streetlights in many areas of Glasgow.

When a fifteen-year-old boy who lived with his grandmother

was rendered homeless after her death, he went to live with Jean's family. This was Charlie McKinnon, who was destined to become a big part of my life.

Glasgow was full of warm-hearted people. Whenever you visited friends, no matter how much or how little they had, they would invite you to have dinner with them and always made you feel welcome.

From the age of eleven I attended North Kelvinside Secondary School, one of the best in the area. Although I was in the top girls' class and passed exams with flying colours, every stage of school felt like prison to me. School holidays were a huge relief and it was on one of these holidays I found a new love that would underscore my life.

One summer I went to Butlins with my family and this is where I first heard the song 'She Loves You' by The Beatles. I had never heard music like this before: it was new and energetic and optimistic and I was in love with this song. My friend Jean and I started going to pop concerts, which is where I first saw and heard another legendary band, the Bee Gees. We started to dress differently from the other girls we knew, trying to look like the girls in The Ronettes, who had the hit record 'Be My Baby'.

Some of the other girls from school said we looked 'gallus' in our black trousers and jackets, but we noticed at the school dance, when our parents made us wear party dresses, that it was girls who seemed prim and as though butter wouldn't melt in their mouths who were getting up to things that their parents might have been less than happy about.

Jean and I used to stand on the table using a hairbrush as a microphone and sing our hearts out, pretending we were on stage. Eventually we acquired an old tape recorder with a real microphone and we were able to make our own recordings.

Some of Jean's brother's friends formed a band, and one day I asked if I could try their electric guitar. I taught myself to play the riff from 'Peter Gunn', an instrumental song by Duane Eddy. The boy took the guitar back from me quite abruptly. At the time I thought it was because I hadn't played it well but when I got older I realised that it was probably because I had played it too well and too quickly.

Because I loved animals so much I wanted to be a vet and thought I would stay on at school to get the qualifications, but when I found out that part of the job would involve putting healthy animals down, I knew there was no way I could do it. So I left school just a few months before my fifteenth birthday. I decided to go out to work and earn my own money while I figured out what I'd like to do with my life.

It was 1963. Glasgow was bursting with energy and with an eclectic mix of musicians, artists, dancers, singers and writers. In May there had been anti-Vietnam War protests in Britain, and music was changing in line with the mood of the people. The world was changing and there was a sense of freedom in the air. I felt I belonged in this brave new world.

CHAPTER 4

BABY, IT'S THE FIRST TIME

One of my first jobs was at a clothes boutique in the centre of Glasgow. It was always busy and the other girls who worked there were full of fun. Occasionally, in a mischievous mood, they would drag their feet along the nylon carpet to build up a static charge in their fingertips and then touch the back of the neck of one of the unsuspecting young male customers, saying, 'Can I help you?' The boys would jump at the shock and then join in with our laughter. They never seemed to get annoyed at all.

I had known Charlie McKinnon since I was twelve years old and saw him regularly as he was living with my best friend's family. We fell in love when I was fourteen years old and got engaged when I was fifteen but I think I loved Charlie from the first moment I saw him. He was and is one of the kindest and most caring people I've ever known. He was a huge Elvis fan and an excellent singer, performing in pubs and always working hard at whatever job he was doing.

I saved up all my wages, as did he, and we bought a flat when I was fifteen years old, which was as unusual at that time as it is now.

We were planning to get married four days after my sixteenth birthday, and visited the man from the church to organise the banns. It's perfectly legal to marry at the age of sixteen in Scotland

and no parental permission is needed, which is why for centuries many young couples fled from England to Gretna Green, just over the border, where a marriage can be conducted by a blacksmith.

Gretna Green is still one of the world's most popular wedding destinations, hosting over 5,000 weddings each year. All the weddings are performed over an iconic blacksmith's anvil and the blacksmiths in Gretna became known as anvil priests.

Because the church official we had visited was worried about me being so young and was afraid that my parents might not have known I was getting married, he called unexpectedly at our house. The man explained his concerns about my age and my mum told him she had advised me that because of my age the marriage had a higher chance of failure but that in the end I made my own decisions. Charlie was a good person whom my mum and dad trusted and were fond of.

Charlie and I married four days after my sixteenth birthday, as planned. It was a freezing cold December day and Charlie's friend Jim, Jean's brother, who was the best man, had flu and collapsed in church during the ceremony. Fortunately he soon recovered and Charlie and I were married, with Jean as my maid of honour. Seeing the photos now, I look like a little girl dressed up as a bride.

We were married the year that hundreds of students demonstrated against the Vietnam War in New York's Times Square and twelve young men publicly burned their draft cards – the first such act of war resistance.

• • •

Gary was born just over a year later in 1966, the same year the Prime Minister, Harold Wilson, refused to send British troops to Vietnam. I was seventeen years old.

My mum had worried that because of my impulsive nature and my age, I might change quite quickly and want to follow another path in life, and in a way she was right. I went into hospital as a very young girl who was in love, happy with her life and about to have a baby, and I came home almost as a stranger, with a totally different outlook.

I looked around the one-bedroom flat that was home and saw it as dark and dull. I was upset because my pet bird had died and I thought that someone had forgotten to feed it. Above all, I felt as though I didn't belong there anymore. I felt guilty for changing but the change just happened.

When I went out to shops or to the park and saw other girls with their babies, I didn't feel a connection with them. Many very young girls had three or four children and this scared me so much that I decided then and there that I only ever wanted to have one child.

I also knew I couldn't live in the same place forever until I died, as many people did at that time. Just the thought of that terrified me.

When Gary was born he was healthy and well but wouldn't feed. The nurses were concerned about it but left me to deal with it and I was panicking. I don't remember how long it took or how I managed it but it seemed to take forever before I eventually succeeded.

I used to be fascinated just watching Gary for hours as he lay in his cot. It was amazing that this little life had come from inside me.

I initially saw Gary as a baby that I fed and cared for and was protective towards. I loved it when he gripped my fingers with his tiny hands but when Gary said his first words I was totally smitten – I realised that he was a real little person, and he was my little person.

Gary stood up in his cot one day, looked at us and said clearly, 'Mammy, Daddy.' He was about ten months old and from that day on his speech came on leaps and bounds.

Charlie made a brilliant dad. He had an amazing and very natural Glasgow sense of humour, like Billy Connolly, and he made everyone laugh.

Before Gary was born I had a dream about a baby with a mischievous face, auburn hair and freckles, wearing a nappy and running through puddles. I told my family about the dream but voiced doubt that any baby of mine would have auburn hair and freckles as I had dark hair.

Sometimes I feel as though life is scripted in some unfathomable way and then occasionally, just occasionally, little snatches of this great narrative are revealed in a dream or a moment of déjà vu.

When Gary was born he had downy black hair and blue eyes, but his eye colour changed from blue to green and as time passed his hair became a beautiful shade of auburn.

So gradual was the change that it was only when he was about eighteen months old that I recognised Gary as being the baby from my dream.

• • •

From the age of two or three, Gary was obsessed by space and used to lie in bed beside me, talking about the stars as we gazed up at the night sky through the bedroom window. He wanted to know the names of the planets and how far away they were, and seemed to grasp concepts of space that eluded me. He had an unusual way of seeing but often made an odd kind of sense. When he was about five years old he said, 'Mummy, was Noah's Ark a spaceship?'

'Well, I suppose it might have been, I hadn't really thought about it.'

'Well, do you think Noah just took seeds of all the different animals so that he could grow them later? Because there wouldn't have been enough room for all of the animals, would there?'

My marriage to Charlie drifted into friendship and it seemed that my mum was right. Many people who marry at such a young age often change so much that their lives take them down separate paths, causing the marriage to break down.

Gary was five years old when we separated but his dad, who is now happily married to Jeanna, has remained close to Gary and is a major part of his life. Jeanna and Charlie have three sons together and Charlie also has a daughter, giving Gary four siblings. Charlie was a huge part of my life and knowing he is happy makes me happy.

I met Wilson when Gary was six years old and quickly discovered that as well as being a musician, Wilson was into space, UFOs and science fiction. He used to live near Bonnybridge, a place that's often referred to as the UFO capital of the world. Naturally, Gary liked this idea and quizzed Wilson constantly on this subject.

We moved to London in 1972, where there were more work opportunities for musicians and artists like Wilson. There was already serious interest in Wilson's band Aegis, and a producer of note had arranged to record them in a top London studio.

We arrived in Muswell Hill in north London; a friend from Glasgow named Dougie Thomson was renting a flat there and we stayed with him for a few nights.

Fate can be quite amazing sometimes. While in Glasgow Dougie, who was a bass player, had once told us that he intended to quit his band, The Beings, and travel to London to get a job with either of his two favourite bands – The Alan Bown Set and Supertramp.

Dougie Thomson arrived in London and had been there for only weeks when he joined The Alan Bown Set; he had the advantage of knowing all their songs inside out. As if that wasn't amazing enough, a short time later Dougie went for an audition with his other favourite band, Supertramp, and again he knew all the songs, played brilliantly, got the job and became a key member of Supertramp.

It was coming up to Christmas and Wilson and I were searching for a place to live. We were standing outside Highgate tube station when a young guy with long hair and a cockney accent came up to Wilson and said, 'Hi man, I'm Johnnie Allen, we were at school together. What are you doing here?'

'We're looking for a flat.'

'Come back to ours, everyone is away on tour and you can stay there.'

Johnnie was working as the road manager for a band named Uriah Heep. He was just about to go off to Italy on tour, so we happily accepted and went with him back to the large Edwardian flat in Muswell Hill. Johnnie was pleased I was there as he thought I could cook Christmas dinner, including a large turkey he'd bought. He looked so disappointed when I told him I was a vegetarian and couldn't bring myself to cook the turkey.

The flat had lots of large rooms with high ceilings and French doors that led onto a beautiful garden. Johnnie told us we could stay as long as we wanted. He then left to go on tour and every time someone from one of the bands arrived home we had to explain who we were, which we dreaded as it was so embarrassing.

Eventually James Litherland, whose flat it actually was, arrived home. Jim had played and sung with the band Colosseum, and luckily he recognised Wilson as they had played at some of the same venues. Jim was kind and friendly and said it was fine for us to stay there until we found a place of our own, which we did very shortly afterwards.

Jim has remained a lifelong and very dear friend, and is one of the kindest and most caring people we have ever met, as is his wife Helen. Their son James Blake is now making his own mark on the music world.

The Vietnam War was on everyone's mind at that time and musicians like Crosby, Stills, Nash & Young played their part in exposing its brutality and helping to end it.

Through the efforts of people such as John Pilger, the photo of a nine-year-old Vietnamese girl named Phan Thi Kim Phuc running naked down the street, her body burning with napalm, was broadcast. The worldwide protests against the war and the outrage of the American people in reaction to this image were what finally led to the end of US involvement in the Vietnam War in August 1973.

• • •

In 1974 Wilson and I got married in Wood Green to the music of Pink Floyd – an edited version of 'Us and Them', extending the instrumental to last throughout the ceremony before David Gilmour's voice came in on the verse.

Wilson looked every inch the musician with his long hair and d'Artagnan-style moustache. An excited Gary looked beyond cute and my mum had travelled down from Glasgow to be with us.

I love London. I've loved it since the day we arrived here. I love the buildings, the history and the fact that when you stand in Westminster Abbey you are surrounded by the spirit of so many great figures you were taught about in school.

We continued to live in Muswell Hill and Gary attended Muswell Hill Primary School. One day while sitting at the kitchen table Gary asked us when the world was going to end and we reassured him that it would be around for a very long time. He was obsessed with the end of the world and kept pressing us for a date, and was agitated and upset that, instead of telling him when, we were trying to reassure him that it wouldn't be ending until long after we were all gone.

Gary then asked if I was going to die one day and I told him yes, everyone dies sometime. He dissolved into tears. He then asked if Wilson was going to die, if his dad was going to die and if his grandma was going to die, and he cried more and more when I told him again that everyone dies sometime but that it wouldn't happen until we were very old, which would not be for a very, very long time.

No matter how much I tried to comfort him, Gary was inconsolable. He missed his dad and wanted us all to be together; Charlie eventually moved to London to work and met his new wife Jeanna, which was great for Gary as he then had everyone he loved around him.

Although Gary was only six years old he had already been taught fractions and some French at Dunard Street School in Glasgow, and had started reading at the age of three. When he started at Muswell Hill Primary School the class was being given counters to learn how to count and *Jack and Jill* books to read – Gary was bored as the education seemed to be years behind his previous school. Although I was surprised at this, I quickly realised that the school excelled in English and was very good at giving children confidence in themselves and encouraging them to develop good communication and social skills, something Gary needed help with.

Gary became restless and would sometimes wander out of

school and come home, and I'd have to take him back again. He liked being at home, as he felt he didn't fit in at school and was becoming more and more unhappy there. Gary preferred the company of adults. His classmates bullied him for being 'different' and his Scottish accent also set him apart. There were basic skills and concepts that he found difficult to grasp and this was at odds with his obvious intelligence.

Gary had difficulty opening all sorts of things, but would take toys and locks apart to see how they worked – never putting them back together again. He also had difficulty following instructions and I used to think he was having us on. He would often get the wrong end of the stick because he took everything literally. His directness could also be misconstrued as rude and could sometimes make people feel awkward.

We only holidayed abroad once because of Gary's fear of travel and resultant meltdown when he was too far from home.

His was a literal world, a world of logic; outside of that world chaos reigned.

CHAPTER 5

FIRST LOVE

I started learning to play the guitar just before I left Glasgow and was obsessed with it. Wilson bought me a Fender Telecaster which I used to play almost every day. After I moved to London I started rehearsing in a King's Cross studio with other girls, who played bass and drums. Jackie Badger from Islington was the bass player, but we had difficulty finding a good female drummer until a young, slim, dark-haired American girl named Holly Beth Vincent walked in and played like a pro. This was our very first band and all three of us are still in regular contact with each other.

Holly eventually formed her own band, Holly and the Italians, and Mark Knopfler from Dire Straits became her boyfriend; a few of Dire Straits' hits were songs that Mark wrote about Holly, including 'Romeo and Juliet'.

My friend Jackie rang me one day and asked me to join a girl band she was in named Mother Superior, as they had lost their guitarist. I joined them on a tour of the UK; I had never played a gig before, but being thrown in at the deep end improved my guitar playing and, although daunting, it was an amazing experience.

I missed Gary and Wilson when I was touring and although

the band was getting great reviews, when the tour ended I decided to leave.

A few months later I answered an ad in the *Melody Maker* for a female guitarist. Miles Copeland rang me up and arranged for me to go to his house for an audition. Unfortunately someone told me that it wasn't a good idea and gave me lots of reasons, with regard to the music business in general, as to why I shouldn't go, so I didn't.

Miles Copeland rang back the next day to ask me why I hadn't turned up, and I was embarrassed and apologetic, and annoyed with myself. Some time afterwards Miles Copeland put the girl band the Bangles together; when the band The Police were formed, it was Miles who managed them, with his brother Stewart Copeland as their drummer.

I started writing songs and, rather than playing separately, Wilson and I decided to form a band together – named Axess, then renamed Who's George, and finally The Walk. We advertised for a vocalist but couldn't find one that we were happy with, so I started singing the songs I wrote.

We toured universities and played all around London – at Dingwalls, the Rock Garden, Camden Palace (now KOKO) and the Venue, among others. Our songs were played on the radio and one of my songs scraped into the charts and we had the occasional TV appearance.

At one of our Camden Palace gigs it was announced that Elvis Presley was dead. Charlie, Gary's dad, was there and was incredibly upset by this news. Everyone in the hall was in a state of shock and disbelief. A legend had died.

Gary had always loved music but wasn't interested in playing any instruments until he was about seven years old, when one day Wilson and I were in another room working out a song I had written. We heard Gary banging discordantly on the piano, suddenly followed by grand chords being played in a classical style. Wondering who else was there, we peeked into the room and saw Gary playing the piano with both hands, utterly absorbed.

'God, Wilson, can you hear that? That's Gary. Where did *that* come from?'

There was our little Gary sitting playing these powerful, dramatic chords that left us with our mouths open as we peeked from behind the door. We were enthralled and didn't want to leave, but we didn't want to stay either, or he'd become aware of us and stop.

We moved home shortly after this and didn't have a piano until a year or two later, so Gary used to go to a neighbour's house to practise. One day she came to our door and I invited her in.

'You really have to send Gary for piano lessons, Janis. I've been having lessons for years and without any guidance Gary can play much better than I can, so just think what he could do if he had lessons.'

Little did she realise that we had enough difficulty paying for our rent, let alone for piano lessons.

A year or two later we bought a grand piano from an auction for about £300. It cost us more to have it delivered than it did to buy. We spray-painted it white as I wanted it to look like John Lennon's piano in the 'Imagine' video. Gary, about nine years old at the time, taught himself to play the 'Moonlight' Sonata in a matter of days.

The first time we heard Gary sing was another revelation. He had just come home from a local community group he attended in Crouch End called Kids & Co. They wanted the children to learn a song to perform, so Gary asked us if we'd record him singing. I said, 'Right, what song do you want to do?'

'"She's Leaving Home",' Gary replied.

'The Beatles song? You know it's not the easiest song in the world to sing if you've never sung before.'

'But that's the one I want to do.'

'OK,' I said, thinking that this just wasn't going to work. Gary used to wander around with headphones on and when he sang along it sounded so awful we'd decided that as far as singing was concerned he was tone deaf. So when Gary started to sing 'She's Leaving Home' we were blown away by this deep, haunting voice that flowed effortlessly.

He was so modest and unassuming that no one realised what he was capable of. Unfortunately Gary was excluded from Kids & Co. shortly after that as he apparently didn't listen to or wouldn't follow their instructions. Becoming excluded from things was happening too often and would be difficult for anyone to take. I knew how hard Gary had been trying to fit in, to find his place in the world, but because he felt he was failing, he was becoming more and more isolated. To be so talented yet so undervalued by people seemed so damned unfair.

What is to 'fit in' anyway? To try to fit in is to try to become ordinary and be conditioned not to raise your head above the parapet or stand out from the crowd. If someone is 'different', why should they be expected to strive to become ordinary?

Encouraging people to manage their differences and to express themselves through whatever medium they can, and encouraging others to accept and value those differences, is surely what society should strive for. Whether that medium is music, art, computing, cooking, gardening or being good with animals, all are equally valid. We are all links in a chain that make our society what it is.

Not all who are different are talented, but many are. Michelangelo was by choice a solitary figure who slept in his clothes, shunned the company of his fellow man and had no interest in food other than as a necessity.

Great thinkers such as Isaac Newton did not fit in; the suffragettes were extraordinary women who rebelled in a way that shocked society.

If someone feels that they have never achieved anything, remind them that each and every one of us swam in the race for life and won that race, when competing with millions of other sperm, so each one of us is pretty amazing.

• • •

That Christmas we bought Gary his first computer, an Atari with a memory of 8K. There were no such things as hard drives then – well, no affordable ones anyway. Gary was fascinated by the computer and could quite happily have sat in front of it day after day. I was worried about him being cooped up indoors, but he would say, 'Mum, please don't tell me I should go out to play.'

When, in the spring, a neighbour told me about a school summer camp in Wales, I persuaded Gary to try it for a week as I thought it would be good for him to be out in the fresh air with other children. I watched his little face at the window of the train as it sped into the distance. Gary looked so small and alone, even though the train was full of children headed for the camp. I worried that I had made a mistake but, despite the trauma of the journey, the camp was a success. He loved the woods and the campfire, and met a young girl named Rachel Glastonbury. A few summer camps later I received a letter telling me that Gary was now excluded as they didn't have the time to deal with him. However, he and Rachel remained close and continued seeing each other – she became Gary's first love.

Rachel's brother Dan played various instruments and was

gentle and vulnerable; a few years later he took his own life at a time when he felt unable to cope. Rachel was very close to her brother and his death took a huge emotional toll on her.

Wilson and I were still pursuing our own musical careers; I was working on combining melodies with the power of rock. Peter Vince, one of the senior figures at Abbey Road Studios, liked some of my songs and arranged for us to record them there. In the Abbey Road canteen we met Paul and Linda McCartney with their baby boy, James, and their occasional babysitter, our friend Josie Betan, who also worked in Abbey Road. Paul and Linda invited Wilson and me over to their table to see the baby but we declined as we had a man from EMI with us, who was tipsy and star-struck and we felt, likely to impose on them. In retrospect I regret this, as we were all vegetarians and I'd love to have discussed animal protection with Linda. Ray Cameron McIntyre heard the songs we had recorded at Abbey Road and invited us to his home in Hampstead. He worked hard to help us as he loved the songs, but there were other people involved and we went in a different direction. However, we remained on good terms and worked on other projects together. Ray used to write material for the Kenny Everett TV show and he had a real feel for music and production. Sadly, he died of a heart attack some years later when he was just fifty-five years old.

Whenever I see the comedian Michael McIntyre on TV, following in Ray's footsteps, I think how proud his dad would have been of him.

We were contacted by manager Jazz Summers, who wanted to represent us, and he arranged a record deal for us with Mickie Most, who loved the songs. We went to RAK Studios and met with Mickie, but for various reasons we turned down the management and because of this we lost the record deal. In retrospect this was foolhardy of us – Jazz Summers was very successful and went on to manage Wham! and George Michael very shortly afterwards.

We were later offered a record deal with Warner Bros, who wanted to release an album, and the single was to be 'Stand Up', which was one of my more credible songs, which I was pleased about.

We were advised to use a music lawyer, which we duly did. However, after months of discussions, Warner Brothers said it was like negotiating with Led Zeppelin and pulled out. In retrospect we should probably have just signed.

I loved writing songs, but when a French record company wanted an artist called Sheila B. Devotion to do one of my songs, being naive and silly, I said I wanted to keep my songs for myself. They said in a shocked tone, 'But Sheila B. sells millions of records!', but being the fool that I was I couldn't be persuaded.

Chas Chandler, who was in the Animals, released another of our songs called 'I Can't Resist You', which we performed on TV. It got a lot of radio play and sold quite well. We were happy and having fun.

When we lived in Glasgow, a medium/spiritualist once told us we would go to London and should take every opportunity that came our way, but unfortunately we threw away virtually every one.

We should have taken at least some of these opportunities, as financially life would have been much less of a struggle for us. But then again, Wilson and I are happy.

CHAPTER 6

DREAMS ARE MADE OF CELLOPHANE

When Gary was sixteen years old he got a job in town and suddenly started losing his intellectual faculties. We were seriously worried. He was referred to a neurologist as it was thought he might have a brain tumour. The neurologist examined him and did various tests but there was no sign of a tumour. However, Gary wasn't improving and had collapsed twice on the platform of the tube, which was pretty dangerous. We had no idea what to do when we were told by the neurologist that there was no physical cause.

This was a constant worry for us but fortunately Gary's fainting fits ceased and his intellectual faculties returned. However, when he was under pressure, away from home or seriously upset, this mental meltdown would kick in again and we felt that this fragility could put his life at risk.

Gary wasn't very good at making or forming relationships. His first live-in partner was Tamsin. The first time we saw her, Gary was in his early twenties, singing at his first and only gig, fronting a really good band made up of some of his old Highgate Wood school friends at The Bowlers in north London.

Wilson and I were incredibly nervous, rooting for Gary as he walked on stage. He'd never performed before so we figured he must be terrified. The music started and we were shocked. Our son – this tall, slightly gaunt, quiet young man with a mop of beautiful dark auburn hair – was suddenly transformed in front of our eyes into a David Bowie-type singer/performer. Gary looked and sounded as if he had been performing all his life. He was amazing and the applause was rapturous. My sister Lorna was there with us and she filled up with tears when she heard him sing; we were all so proud.

That was when Tamsin caught my eye: watching Gary with such intensity and warmth in her eyes that I had a feeling even then that this young girl who shone out from the crowd with her yellow dress, dark tousled hair and huge smile was going to be a major part of Gary's life.

He never really approached girls or made the first move. So some months later some of their friends apparently decided to get Gary a little bit tipsy, to give him a helping hand in getting to know Tamsin better.

Everyone always described Gary as very difficult to get to know. He never opens up about himself, hates small talk and discusses only those subjects that spark his interest.

Getting Gary tipsy must have worked as he and Tamsin became a couple not long afterwards. For a long time they seemed happy – until Gary's obsession with his computer became even more fanatical.

One year there was a party on New Year's Eve at Gary and Tamsin's flat. We popped over to quickly wish them a Happy New Year before the party got into full swing. The living room was full of Tamsin's relatives, gathering together in a corner and looking a bit uncomfortable. I turned around and there was Gary sitting in the middle of the room with a large computer on a very large table, oblivious to what was going on around him.

Gary was becoming more obsessed with the reverse engineering of UFOs that he believed had taken place but was being suppressed. He thought the world was controlled by aliens and once asked, 'How can they be human? Humans would never treat other humans so inhumanely.'

I looked at him sitting at his computer in the middle of the party and knew I had to say something.

'You can't do this, Gary; you have to put the computer away,' I said quietly.

'Why?'

'Because it's smack bang in the middle of the room and is in everyone's way.'

'There's enough room for them to walk around it.'

'But they shouldn't have to. Tamsin's relatives have travelled from all over for this party and it's pretty off-putting for them having you sitting at a big table in the middle of the room working on a computer when it's supposed to be a party.'

'But it's my party too,' he said plaintively.

'Oh Gary,' I whispered.

Running my hands through my hair I was trying to think of how to deal with this tactfully without causing upset or arguments on New Year's Eve.

'C'mon,' said Wilson matter-of-factly to Gary, while moving the computer to one side. 'I'll help you to carry the table, you take one end and I'll take the other.' And Gary did. Just like that.

Wilson is gentle to the core, with a kindness and humour reflected in his eyes that is immediately recognised by children and animals. He's one of the most innocent people I've ever known and this, along with his intelligence and tenderness, is what I love most about him.

We walked out into the cold night air, and looked up at the

full moon, always a magical sign to us, as so many of our life-changing events have for whatever reason coincided with a full moon.

Shortly after this I started to write a drama, which became the independent film *Lunar Girl*. It's about a girl who is different and lives in a world of her own but is happy that way. Wilson produced the film. He used our music to create its mood, and also wanted to use our friends as the actors – but I wanted it to be as professional as possible and put an ad in *The Stage*. We were overwhelmed with the number of CVs, applications, videos and photographs we received. The postman brought them by the sack-load. I had to sort through thousands of photographs and letters and felt guilty that unless a stamped addressed envelope was included, we were unable to send the photos back as the cumulative postage would have cost us a small fortune.

I found it alarming that some very young teenage girls would offer to do virtually 'anything' to be in a film. So many people wanted to be famous rather than to be good actors and were willing to pay a high price for fame, which I not only found sad but dangerous. Fame was highly unlikely in this instance as it was an independent effort financed on a less-than-a-shoestring budget.

We hired a large rehearsal room in Jacksons Lane Community Centre in Highgate and the people we had shortlisted travelled from all over to audition. Jacksons Lane was perfect for us: it even had its own theatre and vegetarian restaurant.

We eventually chose a fifteen-year-old girl from Edinburgh named Charli Wilson for the lead role. Basienka Blake and Pete Gallagher got the other major roles; they had acted together in *Buddy*, a high-profile West End musical. All three were the best choices we could have made.

I used my credit card to finance the film and Wilson and I filmed it ourselves down at Covent Garden and along the South

Bank where kids used to skateboard. There was a lot of artistic graffiti on the walls – sadly later cleaned off for a visit by the Queen during her Golden Jubilee year in 2002.

We filmed in our house and garden and used our music and Gary's as the soundtrack. Gary also played a homeless person and I directed, although at the time I didn't have much idea how to. Luckily Charli was a natural and Basienka and Pete were incredibly professional and very helpful.

Although *Lunar Girl* was corny in some ways and we were learning as we went along, I loved how some of the scenes turned out. It was a steep learning curve into film making and Wilson and I used to sit up until the early hours of the morning editing the film. I was fascinated at how the whole feel and tone and even the storyline of the film could be altered by editing.

Amazingly, *Lunar Girl* was screened on TV many times, which I thought was awesome as we were musicians and had no previous experience of film making whatsoever.

We had no way of knowing then that 2001 was going to be our last year of happiness for many years to come.

Three things happened to me that in retrospect seem like warnings of what was to come and gave me the first inkling of the disastrous turn our lives were about to take.

There was the day in the summer of 2001 that Wilson and I were walking our two dogs, a collie cross and an Egyptian Pharaoh hound, on Hampstead Heath. Our collie was Mindy, a stray dog we had taken in few years before, and our Pharaoh hound was Jaffa, who we had rehomed. We had moved from the area ages ago but still occasionally walked our dogs on the heath because they knew it and it's a great walk.

The north side of the heath has several meadows linked to each other by narrow tractor-sized tracks. We had just left the first meadow and paused while the dogs sniffed around when

I noticed a man, probably in his twenties, approaching us. Everyone had to pass this way but he seemed to be walking purposely towards us as though he wanted to talk.

'What's her name?' he said as he stroked our collie rather than our regal-looking Pharaoh hound, which most people were drawn to.

'She's called Mindy, after Mork and Mindy,' I said, smiling.

'You're a musician,' he said in a matter-of-fact kind of way as he lingered and looked at me intently while continuing to stroke our dog.

'Yes?'

'You have a son who plays music and writes songs.'

'Yes, that's right.' How could he know that?

'Well, your son is going to be famous all over the world but for something other than his music.'

I was fascinated and was trying to think of what Gary could possibly do that would lead to him being known throughout the world if it wasn't for his music. He was stuck in a job with a computer company at that time and, believe it or not, was described as having 'unremarkable' computer skills.

I wanted to hear more from this softly spoken stranger who seemed to believe he had some kind of insight into our lives and was becoming more convincing by the second. He started describing other things about our lives that were uncannily correct and that he would have had no way of knowing. This was no ordinary man; he was only pretending to be ordinary.

'Do you have an email address I could contact you on?'

'No, I don't have a computer,' he said, looking back before disappearing into the woods.

I smiled and said, 'Well, of course you don't,' half expecting him to fade away as they do in mystical films.

The next warning came in a dream I had.

5 a.m., 29 January 2002

'Wilson, are you awake?'

'I am now,' he answered, screwing up his eyes as he tried to avoid the light.

'I had this dream; it was strange. My sister Lorna came to me and looked into my eyes and said, "Your life is going to change just like *that*," and she snapped her fingers. I asked her, "In what way is it going to change, good or bad?"

'She stared at me in a cold and serious way, not like Lorna at all, and repeated in a stern voice, "Your life is going to change just like *that*," and she snapped her fingers again.

'It was chilling. I know it means something.'

'Well, it probably means your life is going to change just like that. Try to get some sleep, Janis; we have to be up early.'

Sinking back into sleep I saw someone staring at me from the shadows. I recognised the face as belonging to Eleanor, my sister-in-law, but I had never seen her with such an intense look. With a fixed serious expression she ordered me: 'Look at Gary!' and repeated again but more urgently, 'Look at Gary!'

I woke up and realised I'd been dreaming. But I could feel my heart beating twice as fast as normal as panic rose to my throat, staying longer than it should have on account of a dream. Even after I found my voice, that gnawing feeling of anxiety didn't fade. I felt something was wrong and I phoned Gary to make sure he was OK but there was no answer and I panicked.

'Wilson, we have to go to Gary's, something's wrong.'

Fortunately Wilson listens to me. We got dressed, grabbed our coats and got into the car.

'Damn! Someone has parked in front of the drive; I hope he's going to move. The entire road is empty and he blocks our drive.'

The driver eventually moved his van, with irritating slowness. We drove straight to Gary and Tamsin's ground-floor flat in north London, which they rented from Tamsin's aunt, who lived upstairs.

I had a sense of foreboding as I rang the bell. No answer. I rang again. I waited and still no answer. I peered anxiously through the front window and caught a glimpse of movement. The relief I felt when Gary opened the door, still in his dressing gown with bleary eyes, hair sticking up and looking bemused as to why we were there so early in the morning, made me smile with a mixture of relief and affection.

Gary looked thinner; I hadn't noticed before and hoped he was eating enough. We stayed for a while. I looked around and everything seemed fine, but Gary looked troubled. Only much later did I learn that Gary had been up all night on his computer and still hadn't been to bed.

If only I'd known then, or somehow understood what the dreams meant, maybe I could have done something – like throwing Gary's computer out of the window.

I can't explain why dreams sometimes come true but they sometimes do.

• • •

Wilson and I had been thinking about fostering children and embarked on the cathartic and emotional process of being assessed.

The extent and type of questions asked makes you reach deep into your soul. It's like looking into a mirror and seeing yourself for the first time. You learn much more about who you are and why you are as you are and what experiences in your life played a vital role in shaping the person you've become.

Fostering was always something we knew we would do when we were a bit older as we believed that if the majority of families fostered at least one child there would be virtually no need for children's homes. The time seemed right and we decided to foster siblings to stop them from being split up, as happens all too often. We'd just been approved to foster when out of the blue on 19 March 2002 Gary was arrested and our lives were turned upside down. Our lives really did change 'just like that', as my sister had foretold in the dream, and in more ways than one.

Gary and Tamsin were arrested and held in custody for about eight hours. Gary was questioned by the British Hi-Tech Crime Unit and released on bail but was not charged. The Crown Prosecution Service (CPS) stated their intention to prosecute Gary. They also told him that as he hadn't caused any damage or sent any malicious codes the likely sentence would be approximately six months' community service. The fact that Gary had accessed Pentagon computers filled me with dread but when we heard nothing further, we began to dare to hope that no charges would be brought.

It was Easter Saturday. The Queen Mother had died just seven weeks after her daughter Princess Margaret. Her body lay in state in the Palace of Westminster, a grand and opulent building that, unbeknown to us, would soon become an all-too-familiar part of our lives.

CHAPTER 7

FOSTERING

One day the phone rang and we were asked to foster five young siblings. It was an emergency. The youngest was a tiny baby and as well as all the uncertainty in our lives about what was going to happen to Gary, I was doubtful about caring for an infant, as it had been so long since Gary was a baby that I'd almost forgotten what to do.

The social worker said, 'It's like riding a bike, you never forget.' We agreed to take all the children, as they would have been split up otherwise and we didn't want that to happen.

The social workers arrived with five small children, all aged under six years old. They looked pale and tired, and Mae, the eldest, looked up at Wilson and said, 'You'll have to go.'

It was quite late at night, so after giving them something to eat I took them up to their bedrooms. Jay repeatedly dug his nails into my arms, rhythmically, the way a cat does when it's purring. Jay was anxious and, struggling with speech that was almost impossible to understand, asked me, 'Will you look after us?' I reassured him that I would.

Mae was bright and chatty and wanted to help look after her younger siblings. She told me I wasn't putting the baby's nappy on properly and insisted on showing me how it was done.

Despite her liveliness, Mae's eyes had a sadness in them that touched my heart. Our world was rocked and another unforgettable parallel journey began in our upturned lives.

The next day we all went to the supermarket and after getting all the shopping Mae put her hands on her hips and said, 'You've forgotten something.'

'What's that?' asked Wilson.

'The beer,' said Mae with a small voice of authority and still with hands on hips.

'We don't drink beer,' said Wilson.

'You liar,' said Mae, with a cheeky glint in her eye.

• • •

Life was even more of a rollercoaster from that day on. Suddenly we had to get up through the night to feed the baby and then again at 6 a.m. and I would bath the children and change their nappies. Wilson made us all breakfast and later we'd take them out for a walk in the park or to the heath along with our dogs. Gary was brilliant with children and used to come along with us on some of the outings, which the children loved. Walking on the heath also gave Gary a change of scene while he was waiting for news from the CPS on whether or not they intended to charge him. However, there is no doubt that Gary underestimated the gravity of his situation at that point in time.

We took the children on long walks and to wildlife parks, danced with them and painted with them. Mae was the most amazing little girl. She was clever and articulate and always wanted to help. Wilson and I were run into the ground for the first six weeks but as time went on we lost weight and fortunately became fitter than ever.

After they were settled in, I searched the house for musical instruments for them to have fun with. Five little faces gathered around, eagerly looking up at me to see what I had found for them to play.

'OK, Jay, I've got some maracas for you to shake when we sing.' Jay took the maracas and beamed.

'Mae, you can play the keyboard, just hit this key in time with the song, or both of these keys together if you can manage it.'

'Like this,' said Mae as she flicked her dark hair back and gave us a demonstration.

'Yes, just like that,' I smiled.

'And Willie, you can bang on the drum and we'll all play a song for little Michael and baby Charlotte. Now which song shall we play?'

'"Old MacDonald",' said Jay excitedly.

'I know: we can sing "Wheels on the Bus". I'll teach it to you, Jay,' said Mae, scratching the side of her nose with her head tilted to one side.

Willie smiled and was happy just banging his drum.

'Stop, Willie, we haven't started yet,' said Mae.

I picked up my guitar and started playing and singing 'Wheels on the Bus' and Jay shook his maracas while Mae repeatedly played her note in time to the rhythm and sang along with me at the top of her voice. Willie banged on the drum while Michael beamed and Charlotte's eyes danced as she bounced up and down in her baby walker.

'Too loud, Willie, too loud,' said Jay, as he suddenly smacked Willie hard on the front of his head with a maraca.

'Jay, hitting is not allowed. If someone hits someone else, then the music has to stop, OK?' Jay's face fell.

'Willie, you've got a huge bump on your head. Come with me and we'll get some ice for it. Doesn't it hurt?' I said, surprised that Willie wasn't crying.

'That's nothing,' said Mae. 'He's been hit much harder than that.'

One of the reasons I thought it would be good to get the children involved with music is that it's a powerful tool in helping damaged children to overcome trauma. I've since learned that when you make music it lights up the medial prefrontal cortex, which is just behind the eyes and which links music, memory and emotion, and engages many different areas of the brain, including visual, auditory and motor areas. While still in the womb babies are able to respond to music, and learning to play an instrument at a young age has been shown to have a significant effect on the brain. So even something as simple as singing, dancing, shaking maracas, banging on a drum or clapping along to music is beneficial to a child's well-being. It just takes time – but watch out for those maracas.

• • •

I used to lie awake at night to make sure the baby was breathing properly; she was so tiny.

Whenever I couldn't hear her breathe I'd get up and go over to her cot just to make sure she was OK. Charlotte was a quiet baby, slept well and was easy to care for.

I'd look in on her brother Willie and he'd be asleep with one arm behind his head, which was so cute.

The children all caught measles and the doctors were worried about baby Charlotte and admitted her to hospital. I stayed there with her. Charlotte kept slipping and falling when she stood up in the metal hospital cot as it seemed to slope for some reason, so I took her into the bed on the floor that I was sleeping in. Fortunately she recovered but we both left hospital with a horrendous gastric flu we had caught there and which we passed on to almost everyone else when we got home.

When Jay's speech improved he told me about the bad man who had hurt him.

The horrific abuse inflicted on young children, often by their own families, never ceases to shock me. I'm just glad that this little family was brought to us in time to stop it escalating and damaging them even more.

Later discovering that one abuser had put a gun to another young child's head while forcing them to submit to sickening abuse made me overwhelmingly grateful that social services had got these five children to safety. Yet that abuser was never prosecuted. Due to the difficulty of young children giving evidence in court, people all too often get away with crimes against them and are left free to continue with their abuse.

Mae, Jay, Willie, Michael and Charlotte had more energy than any children we had known. Many might have classed them as hyperactive; we saw them as lively, energetic and mischievous. Our love of the outdoors gave the children an outlet for their energy. They loved life but not boundaries and initially swung on and pulled down curtains, pushed earth from plant pots into DVD slots, and Jay once pooed in the book of *Pooh*.

Gary used to play guitar and sing to the children. Baby Charlotte loved this and used to try to jump and dance in her baby walker.

Once, after coming home from a long day at the fair I told the children that they couldn't take the life-size blow-up aliens that we'd won into their bedrooms but in the morning the aliens were there large as life in their bedrooms and Jay said, 'Janis, the aliens just walked up the stairs all by themselves and when we told them they had to go back downstairs, they wouldn't; they just stood there.'

'Of course they did, Jay,' I smiled.

Looking after the children was physically hard, but emotionally rewarding. There were many happy and many sad times, always interspersed with the worry of what might happen to Gary.

The night five-year-old Mae told me she had been abused in her home, I had to fight back the tears as I held her in my arms and tried to help her to make some sense of what had happened to her. This little girl felt guilty and confused because although she hated the man who had hurt her, she liked this same man when he was being kind to her. She also constantly worried about her mummy, whom she loved, and was frightened because mummy was left with 'the monster'.

Mae asked me, 'Are people here good?'

I said, 'Well, lots of people who live in this area are really nice and are good people but you always have to be careful when you don't know someone, as it takes time to get to know and trust people.'

She looked up at me with big blue eyes filled with tears and said, 'Where we lived, the people were mostly bad but Mummy was good.'

Jay had no sympathy for the 'bad man' and wanted to become a superhero so that he could save his mummy and have the bad man locked up in prison forever.

These tiny children had more resilience than many adults. Despite all that they had gone through they started to blossom before our eyes – although only time will tell just how much emotional damage has been done.

Mae went to school and became one of the most popular girls in her class, and even directed her own plays. Because we had made an independent film she came to believe that she could do anything, and belief is everything.

As we were in a state of limbo, waiting to find out what was going to happen with Gary, having the children to care for helped me to stop permanently dwelling on the various scenarios that frequently popped into my head regarding Gary's situation.

• • •

Gary was interviewed by the police for a second time on 8 August 2002. This time he had a lawyer representing him. Tamsin had researched various lawyers and told Gary that Kaim Todner seemed the best bet. Gary rang Karen Todner, the managing director, and said, 'Do you do computer crime?' 'I could do,' answered Karen, who from that day on represented Gary with a passion and perspicacity rarely seen in legal circles. However, at that point we were still hoping that this police interview would be the end of the matter, but instead he was bailed until 9 October 2002.

Between those dates I suddenly got another call I didn't want to hear. The Crown Prosecution Service had told Karen that Gary didn't have to answer bail in October after all, as the CPS no longer intended to prosecute him – but that America might be seeking to extradite.

'Extradite!' At that moment I was plunged into a state of terror. Real heart-stopping terror, the kind that makes you want to grab your possessions and bundle your family into the car and head for the hills.

The Hi-Tech Crime Unit, who had been monitoring his internet activity, had told Gary that he was looking at a UK sentence of six months' community service for accessing Pentagon computers as he hadn't damaged anything and hadn't sent any malicious code, but now they were suddenly talking about America wanting to extradite! It didn't make sense. Gary was confident that they wouldn't be able to extradite him as he hadn't caused any damage. I wasn't. This was America we were dealing with.

In 2002, without prima facie evidence, i.e. evidence that can be contested in a UK court – and without proof of financial damage of at least $5,000 on each machine – extradition could not take place.

As confirmed by the Crown Prosecution Service, no evidence was ever presented by the US to the CPS to support their allegations of damage. Hearsay does not constitute evidence and is inadmissible as such in British courts.

In November 2002 our worst fears were realised when the US called a worldwide press conference to announce their indictment of Gary and their intention to request extradition to the US, where Gary would face a maximum sentence of ten years per count.

Suddenly six months in the UK had become sixty years in an American prison.

This was crazy. Gary hadn't murdered anyone; he'd tapped on a keyboard from his bedroom in north London. Why would anyone want to extradite him? Surely extradition was for fugitives who had fled from another country and the scene of a heinous crime?

Gary wasn't a fugitive, had never left the UK and had not committed a heinous crime. What was going on?

Everything was becoming more terrifyingly surreal by the second. I needed to wake up from this nightmare and find a way out; my mind was racing in search of ideas to save Gary. I also had to lose this fear that was taking hold of me. I needed to think straight. I missed my mum and was beginning to feel little in this big world, but I wasn't little anymore and couldn't allow myself to feel that way.

• • •

I remember dreaming in detail about my mum's funeral before she died. In the dream, the sun was shining and my mum was smiling at me and wanted me to speak to her friends. She died one year later and my world was shattered. Despite the dream, her death was an absolute shock and I just wasn't ready to lose her.

On the day of the funeral I watched my dream play out in front of my eyes. My brother Ian was standing in the doorway of the church, speaking to our mum's friends as they filed outside. I'm normally shy but because in my dream my mum had wanted me to speak to her friends, I made a point of doing so, and I believe that my mum was there somewhere watching me, just as she had in my dream.

As the funeral car we were in passed Gary's dad Charlie, without being touched the horn on the car sounded 'peep peep' twice, in a friendly way. The horn then peeped twice again as we passed the house Charlie, Gary and I used to live in. It was a friendly peep, the way people do when they pass someone they know. The chauffeur was very apologetic and said he couldn't understand how the horn could have peeped twice in succession without being touched, and my sister Lorna said, 'Don't worry; it was our mum letting us know that she's OK.'

The minister looked around at us as though we were crazy, which made me wonder about his beliefs. I mean, surely he believed in miracles?

• • •

It seemed ironic that I was brought up with virtually no technology and now my only child was facing the threat of extradition for a crime that would have been science fiction when I was born. There was no TV in Scotland, wireless was a radio and the internet hadn't been dreamed of. The web was something a spider made and hacking happened to trees.

How could Gary ever have realised that tapping on a keyboard and leaving a few virtual notes – including telling the Pentagon

that their security was crap – could lead to this? Totally disproportionate sentences which would be regarded as ludicrous in
the UK are all too often given in America, with no apparent
sense of perspective. We were scared.

Gary and Tamsin's relationship, which was already suffering,
wasn't helped when, after Gary's arrest, a journalist had gone
through every number in Tamsin's aunt's phone and rung them
all – her friends, her employers and even people she barely knew
– to try to get information on Gary. This was hugely upsetting
and embarrassing for Tamsin's aunt and could have cost her her
job but instead cost the journalist his.

2002 was the year of the Queen's Golden Jubilee and there
seemed to be almost as many headlines about Gary as there were
about the Jubilee. I had no idea then how much the media
coverage was going to help us in our fight to save him. People
tend to forget the good that the media often does in exposing
corruption and crime and in fighting for justice and fairness.
There are some damn good journalists out there.

However, the downside of the media attention was that
because of the publicity, despite his best efforts Gary could no
longer get any job in computers, but managed to get a job as
a trainee forklift truck driver which he then lost because his
employer was being bombarded constantly by phone calls from
the press trying to find out information on Gary. 'The biggest
military hack of all time,' they said, quoting the US prosecutors.

How could it be 'the biggest hack of all time' when Gary had a
basic home computer on a 28K dial-up connection and had
had no need to hack as there were apparently no passwords or
firewalls on the machines he was alleged to have accessed? As
computer expert Oxblood Ruffin said: You hack into a jungle,
you don't hack onto a bowling green.

Gary had left cyber-notes informing the Pentagon that their

security was crap and that he'd keep disrupting 'by leaving cyber-notes' until someone at the top paid attention and sorted it out.

Gary is a pacifist and genuinely believed that US security had been infiltrated by aliens. He stupidly left a cyber-note accusing the US of state-sponsored terrorism – in essence a cyber-peace protest that if scrawled on a wall few would have noticed. He also left a cyber-note that tied into some of the conspiracy theories that were prevalent on the internet at the time.

It didn't help that some of this happened after 9/11 when paranoia reigned and the news was obsessed with 'terror, terror, terror', which for some reason always reminded me of Violet, the little girl with the red hair in the TV series *Just William* when she threatened, 'I'll scream and I'll scream and I'll scream until I make myself sick.'

I still couldn't believe that Gary had managed to access NASA and Pentagon computers from his home computer. Although when one of the US prosecutors said in an interview that the computers Gary accessed were 'protected' by easy-to-guess passwords (including the word 'password') it became easier to understand.

It was heartbreaking that someone as nice as Gary, the boy who was fascinated by UFOs and aliens and who used to be afraid to travel on a bus, was now being destroyed by prosecutors treating naive computer pioneers as some kind of 21st-century witches.

In 2002 prima facie evidence that could be contested in a British court of damage amounting to $5,000 on each machine was required in order to make the crime of computer misuse an extraditable offence. The US alleged exactly this amount of financial damage in Gary's case but no evidence of the alleged damage was ever produced and no prima facie evidence was ever submitted to the CPS. We believe this is why the US did not officially request extradition from the UK for Gary until late 2004, as by then the 2003 extradition treaty had begun to be used and under this new treaty with America no evidence is required in order for the US to extradite anyone from the UK.

Gary was being threatened with being dragged from his home, his family and everyone and everything he ever knew, to be taken in chains to a foreign land. The terrifying prospect of a sixty-year sentence made it likely that he would die there and never set foot on British soil again.

One weekend when his dad Charlie was visiting us, I mentioned that Gary was young for his age in many ways and he said, 'I'm not, am I, Dad?'

'I'm afraid you are, son,' said his dad.

It seemed so unbelievably wrong that this unique and gentle man, our son, should find himself in a position worse than that of most murderers, rapists and war criminals. Gary had never hurt anyone. Could someone please tell me how this could be happening?

Gary never leaves the UK, rarely leaves north London and never goes on holiday, yet they wanted to drag him to a foreign land and incarcerate him in some godforsaken prison for sixty years. Well, he couldn't go, he just couldn't. Anyone thinking a computer geek should serve sixty years in a US prison, or in any prison for that matter, had to be crazy.

After the US indictment in 2002 and their announcement of their intention to extradite, the fear was consuming me. I'd wake up in the night sweating and in a state of terror, thinking that they might be going to take Gary at any second. I felt that we were the ones being terrorised by the government and not the other way round.

How could the CPS, who had intended to prosecute Gary,

suddenly tell us months later that they were not going to prosecute him after all, as they had been 'ordered' from the very top to stand aside to let America deal with him? Who ordered them? And this was despite the CPS having put in writing their dissatisfaction with the lack of any evidence from the US other than what they described as hearsay that would not be admissible as evidence in a UK court.

How could the CPS be allowed to cherry-pick like that? The same CPS prosecutor had just allowed Aaron Caffrey to be tried in Southwark Crown Court, where he was acquitted. Yet Aaron was accused of attacking and bringing Port Houston to a halt immediately after 9/11. Why wasn't Gary being tried in the UK like Aaron Caffrey and Mathew Bevan and every other alleged UK computer hacker before him?

That so many NASA and Pentagon computers did not have basic security installed that would immediately have flagged Gary's presence was shocking to everyone. Gary had embarrassed the US and for that he was to pay a high price.

David Burrowes, Gary's MP, found out at a later date that the cyber-notes Gary had left were one of the major reasons why America was relentless in its pursuit. They were angry because in the American ambassador's words, 'He mocked us.'

We felt that if we kept quiet and if Gary kept a low profile and avoided making their lack of security public, America might drop the extradition warrant and let it go.

It was Christmas 2002 and we were going to make this the very best of Christmases as our five little ones were looking forward to it so much and we knew that Gary would love to see their faces when they opened their presents. The children all helped to decorate the Christmas tree and Mae made a Christmas angel to put on the very top of it. We took them to visit Santa in Crews Hill in Enfield and real deer were there for the children to interact with. Christmas Day was magical and my Christmas wish was for Gary to stay here where he belonged and for the children to have a happy future ahead of them.

More than a year had now passed since Gary's arrest in March 2002 and on 5 April 2003 Karen Todner and Tracey Newport from Kaim Todner Solicitors and Gary's QC, Edmund Lawson, met with the legal attaché to the US embassy in London to discuss a document containing a proposed plea bargain. They were taken on a tour of the US embassy in Grosvenor Square. The building has nine storeys, three of which are below ground, and Karen said it had shops and cafés and was like walking around a city. However, no matter how impressive it was, Karen did not for one second lose sight of why she was there.

Extract from the notes of Edmund Lawson QC:
At face value it would seem to be an extremely one-sided document with not too much benefit to Mr McKinnon. Instructing solicitors understand that he would serve the totality of that sentence, minus fifty-two days per year and in a low-category facility. America have also indicated that they would be willing for Mr McKinnon to transfer relatively quickly to an English prison to serve his sentence here but that he would serve the actual time imposed by the American court as his sentence rather than, for example, half off for any sentence under four years as in England and Wales.

Mr McKinnon's initial view is not to accept this offer. He states he does not trust the American authorities to abide by the agreement.

When Miss Todner asked Mr [?] why they felt that the matters could not be dealt with in this country under the Computer Misuse Act, his response was that they did not feel that the sentencing authorities for offences under the

Computer Misuse Act were of sufficient severity to counter Mr McKinnon's conduct. Mr [?] in fact kept referring to the fact that 'one state' wanted Mr McKinnon 'to fry' and that should he contest extradition proceedings, they would be looking for an extremely lengthy sentence.

Although Karen had not told us about the 'fry' threat at this point as the discussion with the US was confidential, the fact that the plea bargain could not be guaranteed and that the proposed sentence was X number of years 'per count' was terrifying enough.

I started having nightmares about running through fields with Gary to try to reach a place of safety. In one of the dreams Gary was little and I was holding him under my arm as I was running through the streets trying to find a place to hide. People were offering to hide us but the security cameras had seen us going in so we had to leave again and keep running. I would wake up exhausted and unable to shake the feeling of absolute fear.

• • •

As time went on, we started to carry on with our lives as normally as possible under the circumstances. Gary was confident that the US would be unable to show evidence of any damage as he hadn't caused any and we thought that as so much time had passed, they must be going to drop the case against him.

We still had Mae, Jay, Willie, Michael and Charlotte with us and they needed all our day-to-day attention. Being so unbelievably busy looking after the children was a partial escape from dwelling on what we had no control over with regard to Gary's fate, inextricably linked to our own. But although the children filled my heart they didn't halt the fear that hovered there.

Breakfast time, bath time, bed time and all the happy chaos in between occupied us. The children loved nothing more than to curl up in bed while I read them a story: the same story night after night after night, as that was what they wanted to hear.

I invented cartoon characters, paving stones from famous London squares and weaved them into a story about a naive young paving stone named Lester Square exploring London with his friend Trafalga when they were out of their squares together. All of the children we fostered loved the stories and enjoyed singing and dancing, so I wrote and recorded the 'Lester Square' song, which they adored dancing and jumping around to.

Being an artist, Wilson couldn't resist drawing Lester and Trafalga and their friends from other London squares, bringing the characters even more to life for the children. Because they loved them so much we later decided to publish our first book: *Lester Square*. We were over the moon when Foyles bookshop sent us a letter congratulating us on how many copies we had sold through their shops.

Two companies rang us to say they were interested in making an animation of Lester. We were excited, but until we knew that Gary was going to be OK, we couldn't concentrate on any of our own plans.

The children were very settled with us. We did everything together and Mae and Jay got excellent reports from school. They were popular with their teachers and the other pupils and were constantly being invited to parties. We were very much a family.

The social workers came to visit one day to tell us that now the children were doing so well, their behavioural problems resolved, they were looking for people to adopt them and were intending to advertise them in the *Be My Parent* magazine. Although I always knew this time would come, I had put such thoughts to the back of my mind. Logically I knew that the children would be going to people who were younger than us, probably people who couldn't have children, but the thought of it cut my heart like a knife.

Taking photos of the children for the magazine was one of the hardest things. The children had no idea what the photos were for and we felt as though we were betraying them, as they sat together on the floor, smiling and looking up at us with trusting eyes.

We wondered if we'd be allowed to adopt the children, but because of the uncertainty of Gary's situation, I doubted it would be feasible.

It was a hot summer's day and we took the children to Paradise Wildlife Park, an adventure-park-cum-wildlife-centre. The children dashed straight into the large paddling pool. Willie was singing as they were splashing around and that made us laugh, but it was a bittersweet moment as I could no longer imagine life without them.

We decided to go on the helter-skelter and the older children got themselves into sacks and whizzed down. Charlotte wanted to go on it too, so I took her up and we both went inside the sack and I had my arms tightly around her to keep her safe. As we started going down, my right arm was pressed hard against the side and suddenly I was in agony as it was tightly dragged all the way down until we reached the bottom. Every second of the friction burning and tearing caused excruciating pain. I desperately wanted to tuck my arm into the sack but I couldn't move it for risk of letting Charlotte go for even a second – I instinctively protected her, no matter what.

When we got off at the bottom, my skin was raw and bleeding and layers of skin had been totally removed. I was in agony.

We went to first aid but because of health and safety they are no longer allowed to give any cream or medication to members of the public for burns or injuries, which seemed absurd – what's the point of having a first aid centre when they can't give first aid? We hurried straight home so I could put gel from our aloe vera plant onto the friction burn to relieve some of the pain, which it did almost immediately.

The phone rang and it was Family Placement to say that they had found potential adopters for the children. When we told the children they would be leaving us they were distraught. They cried all night and told each other that they were staying and that the others were going because they were naughty.

Mae was extremely rude to one of the adopters when she spoke to her on the phone. I had never heard Mae sound so rude and angry. We knew how much the children were hurting and tried to reassure them that they would be loved. All of the progress the children had made started to fade before our eyes as their survival mode kicked in.

The chosen couple visited the children at our home and I liked them immediately. Difficult though it was for us, I felt that the children really would be loved and that comforted me. We were raw but the woman planning to adopt seemed caring and sensitive to our feelings and during an official meeting without the children, we cried together.

The time was drawing closer for the children to move to their new home. Wilson and I took them on holiday and Gary and my sister came along too and we all had the best time ever. We swam, sang and cycled and Mae won a children's dance competition.

'Janis, let's sing a song,' said Jay.

'I'd like that too,' said Mae, holding the end of one of her pigtails to her mouth.

'Which song shall we do?'

'"You Are My Sunshine",' they said in unison.

I knew this was going to kill me. It was the song I sang to baby Charlotte and to Mae, and to Jay, Michael and Willie. Halfway through I had to stop and leave them to carry on singing. I told the children I had something in my eye but Mae followed me through to the other room and through tears, said that she didn't want to leave and wanted us all to run away together so that no one could find us. It was heartbreaking.

We did our best to prepare the children for the move and told them how much we liked and trusted the people who were to become their parents. The day the children were leaving was one of the hardest days of our lives. The one consolation was that we liked the people who were adopting them, but saying goodbye and watching them drive away was devastating. The man was going to be the main stay-at-home carer as the woman worked and I knew that Mae was desperately keen for the woman to be at home with them.

Watching them drive away tore us apart and I knew that as well as being sad, Mae was angry with me for letting them go.

For the next few weeks Wilson and I would find ourselves beginning to cry when we were in the car or walking through the supermarket. We worried about the children constantly.

That's the thing about fostering. When the children leave or are adopted, the chances are you might never see them again and it can feel almost like a bereavement. Foster carers aren't officially allowed to grieve but of course they do. They are human beings and naturally worry about the future of the children they have cared for and who have lived with them as part of their family.

It is very difficult for foster carers to raise concerns about a child's welfare after the child has left their care. Foster carers are basically expected to know their place and rocking the boat is done at your peril.

Because of the secrecy of the family courts, even although many years have passed I could be prosecuted for voicing certain details of children we've cared for. However, I'm now going to raise some general points.

Although this does not relate to children we have fostered, children in the UK are allowed to be fostered and adopted by people who belong to cults, and apparently even by people who worship Satan, whether or not the birth parents object. Satanism is a long-established officially recognised religion in the UK and was recently upheld as such by our courts.

While watching the Nicky Campbell Sunday TV show *The Big Question* on BBC1, I was surprised to see a man who apparently performs in porn shows say he is also a foster carer. I doubt this would have been allowed in the past but times have changed.

I consider myself to be reasonably open minded and tolerant. However, when it comes to children I believe we should always err on the side of caution.

When situations arise where foster carers have what they regard as legitimate concerns about the welfare of children they have previously fostered, they should surely be allowed to spend a day with the children to speak to them on their own, or in the presence of an independent social worker, as it could put minds at ease and ensure the children's safety.

No system is infallible. In one case a birth mother went to court to try and prevent the adoption of her children, when out of the blue an arrest warrant was issued for her. If she did not attend another court at exactly the same time as the adoption hearing was taking place in a different court, she was to be arrested. The young mother, although terrified, bravely went to court on her own to fight for her children. At the very last minute someone managed to sort out the error that had occurred. The arrest warrant for the children's mother was deemed to be a 'mistake'. This happened to the same mother again some months later when she was again wrongly imprisoned for days while in the midst of fighting for her children. The secrecy of the family courts can make it almost impossible for genuine cases of injustice to come to light and it is inevitable that there will always be some such cases.

Ironically the insight we gained into the workings of the system was akin to a rehearsal for what was to come in Gary's case, and was partly responsible for some of the decisions I took that I believe played a major part in saving Gary.

CHAPTER 8

SNATCHED

Gary and Tamsin separated in 2003. Gary was living a hermit-like existence and rarely ventured out until he met Lucy from Leicester in late 2004. Lucy was down to earth, easygoing and attractive, with blondish hair and a ready smile. She put Gary at his ease. He was comfortable in Lucy's company and it was good to see him looking relaxed for the first time in years.

Lucy lived in Leicester but worked in London for a charity five days a week. She and Gary started to see each other. They had a lot in common, including a love of children, cats, music and cooking. Eventually Gary told Lucy about the US indictment just in case it ever reared its head again, although by then more than three years had passed since Gary's arrest in 2002, so we were sure it was going to be dropped. I mean, they couldn't just decide to try to extradite him more than three years after his arrest, could they?

Suddenly, on 7 June 2005 the phone rang: it was Gary.

'Mum, I've been arrested.'

'Oh no, Gary, no!' I screamed. 'Where are you?'

'I'm in Brixton Prison.'

I could hear the fear in his voice.

'What's wrong, Janis, what's happened?' said Wilson anxiously.

My voice was breaking and I could hardly speak. I was trying to hold it together as absolute terror struck my heart.

'Gary's been arrested, he's in Brixton Prison.'

Saying the words out loud made it worse somehow, as though an invisible veil shielding me had been ripped away, forcing me into a stark reality I wasn't ready to face.

It reminded me of when, months after my mum died, I had to fill out a form that involved writing down that my mum was 'deceased' and I couldn't do it. I mean obviously I knew my mum was dead, but somehow having to write down that word was the most traumatic thing, as the finality of her death hit me and I was forced to accept the painful reality I thought I had faced but hadn't.

Actually saying the words 'he's in Brixton Prison' tore through my heart. I couldn't even voice the thought of the word 'extradition' as that would make it real and my mind couldn't deal with it right now.

I could hear Gary's voice in the distance.

'Two men jumped out of a car when I was walking along the road and asked if I was Gary McKinnon. When I said yes they arrested me and bundled me into a car. They said they were the extradition squad and brought me to Brixton Prison. The guards are taking me to court in the morning.'

Gary was trapped; I wanted him out. I wanted to run with him to safety but they had him, he wasn't free anymore.

'When the extradition squad stopped you, you should have said no you weren't Gary McKinnon. Why didn't you ring me? I could have done something!' I screamed.

'You couldn't, Mum.'

'Are you in a cell on your own?'

'No, I'm with a Scottish man.'

'What is he in prison for?'

Gary fell silent.

'What is he in prison for, Gary?!'

'He's accused of murdering someone but I've told him my mum and dad are Scottish.'

'Oh, that's all right then.'

'What do you mean?'

'I'm being sarcastic, Gary, ignore me. How did they know your address? Surely they should have contacted Karen, your solicitor, first and arranged for you to go into the police station instead of pouncing on you in the street and bundling you into a car?'

'I'm sorry, Mum.'

'It's not your fault. How can they be allowed to arrest you three and a half years after the fact? How can they?!'

Wilson took the phone.

'It'll be OK, Gary. We'll see you in court tomorrow and your lawyer will sort it out.'

'Someone else wants the phone. I have to go in a minute.'

'OK. Take care, Gary, we love you.'

'Love you too.'

I couldn't move. This deep, dark, pervading fear was invading the hollow space in my heart at an unsafe speed, ruthlessly forcing happiness to eject without my heart having a chance to prepare for the effects of being plunged into darkness.

'Oh Wilson, how will Gary survive in Brixton Prison? What if he's extradited? This can't be happening.' I was stifling the sobs that were rising to my throat. 'Are we suddenly living in Nazi Germany? He's a computer geek, for God's sake, a computer geek! If he'd rung us we could have done something.'

'We couldn't, Janis, what could we have done?'

'We could have crashed into their car and got Gary away and I could have hidden him.'

'We couldn't, Janis, you're not thinking logically.'

'I am thinking logically, he can't go there, he'd never survive, you know that!'

'I know that but the Americans have sat on it for over three years and how are they going to explain that to the judge? The courts won't extradite him and he'll get bail until it's sorted out, it'll be OK.'

'What if he doesn't get bail? And even if he does it will probably be about £100,000 and we couldn't afford anything like that in a million years.'

'You're panicking, Janis.'

'I'm panicking, I am, I'm panicking. Will you go and see to the children, Wilson? I need to try and get myself together and I don't want them to see me being upset.'

'OK. Don't worry, Janis, it'll be OK.'

We were now caring for a group of five young siblings and I was fighting hard to remain calm.

Losing control was rare for me but this heart-stopping fear left me clutching at the air in desperation for something or someone to appear out of the blue and to make everything OK again.

'I wish you were here, Mamma, I'm scared and I don't know what to do.'

• • •

The 2003 extradition treaty wasn't supposed to be used retrospectively, so how could our courts allow this? The US had been sitting on Gary's case since 2002 when they issued an arrest warrant and announced their intention to extradite, yet the CPS hadn't made them produce prima facie evidence as they were obliged to do at that time. Instead, the US had been permitted to wait until 2005 before getting a UK arrest warrant for extradition, by which time the 2003 UK–US treaty was being used by the UK and evidence was no longer required to extradite any British citizen. However, the treaty was still not ratified by the US. How could this be allowed? They could never justify a three-year delay in court, surely?

I wasn't able to see Gary until the next day, when he was brought to Bow Street Magistrates' Court. We had never been there although we knew the area well.

We passed the beautiful sculpture of the ballet dancer glinting in the sunlight as she sat pensively, with head bowed, outside Bow Street Court, as though sensing the worry of the troubled people filing past her before they walked through the imposing courtroom doors into the dark and dismal foyer full of desperate people.

The contrast of walking from the light into the gloom and seeing unfortunates huddled with their lawyers in darkened corners of this Dickensian scene was chilling. It's one of those places you don't want to go into and can't wait to get out of.

The inside had panelled wooden walls and smelled old and musty, the way those historic buildings do. It was a place of wigs and hierarchy and sombreness. I wore a long black unbuttoned coat dress, with black trousers and top underneath and I was now feeling the heat on this hot June day. Presumably because of my black clothes, I was mistaken for a barrister when I was in the foyer and security allowed me to go through first.

Old school friends of Gary's were there and journalists were everywhere. This was the first time I had met Lucy and it was under the darkest of circumstances. I removed my long black coat as I walked into the courtroom, and could feel the eyes of the journalists on us.

Gary hadn't arrived and I was worried. Had something happened to him that they hadn't told us? Had he been attacked by the man sharing the cell?

Eventually Gary arrived very late because the prison guards had forgotten about him. It was unbelievable: they had actually forgotten about him and had to get another van to collect him from Brixton Prison to bring him to the court.

I had visions of hijacking the van and rescuing Gary and getting him to a place of safety. You have an absolute duty to protect your child and if you leave it too late and they are carted off to a land that has a judicial system that thinks Guantanamo prison camp is acceptable, or that locking a prisoner up in solitary confinement for up to forty years is not torture, or that putting a man to death after decades on death row is not barbaric, and where male rape in prisons is so endemic that suicide becomes the only option for some – then what does that say about you as a parent or as a human being?

Would anyone simply allow their child to be extradited without putting up the fight of their lives, if they realised for just one second what was at the other end? Of course they wouldn't.

Gary walked into the court and slouched forward as he stood in the dock, the way you do when you're wishing the ground would open up and swallow you.

'Stand up straight, Mr McKinnon,' the judge ordered in sergeant-major-style voice.

Gary stood to attention as instructed. It was hard sitting there watching, as he looked so vulnerable.

The journalists all laughed when they heard that Gary's passport was years out of date and had been issued to him when he was at school, as he never travelled. The judge banned Gary from using the internet, which seemed crazy as the US and the CPS had left Gary on the internet for three and a half years after his arrest in 2002, proving that they regarded him as no threat whatsoever, and Gary had not abused that trust.

I was convinced bail was going to be £100,000 or more, which we could never afford. Gary was chewing his nails and staring down at the floor.

His barrister asked for bail and explained we were not wealthy and, unbelievably, the prosecutor, a kind woman, didn't object and the magistrate set bail at £5,000.

She didn't object! This was the best news I'd heard since Gary was arrested. He was going to be bailed, he'd be free again and as long as he was free he'd be OK. I just had to fight to get the truth out and to keep him free. I could do that.

The judge ordered the next court hearing to take place on 27 July 2005.

I was ecstatic and so relieved I almost ran out of the courtroom.

Outside in the sunshine I could breathe again. Looking up at the sky I wanted to spin round with my arms outstretched and get lost in the dizziness, the way you do when you're a child and you and the sky become one.

The bail money had to be paid in cash and we only had a few hours left to raise it. We ran around using cash cards and credit cards but daily limits on bank cards meant we were still well short of what we needed and the banks were closed. We drove to Enfield and borrowed money from close friends who don't trust banks. Cash is king, they said, and that day it was.

I could barely believe that at virtually the last minute we had managed to get the whole amount together, but the bail office at Bow Street Magistrates' was closing so we had to run to have any chance of making it in time.

We got there too late and my heart sank as I realised it was past closing time. We walked up to the door anyway and were taken aback when it suddenly opened. The young women who worked there had waited for us to arrive with the money so that we could collect Gary from Brixton Prison and take him home.

This was the start of people we didn't know going out of their way to help us and I was so grateful to them as I didn't want Gary to have to spend another night in a prison cell.

We drove to Brixton. They had already released Gary, who was waiting outside the prison for us when we arrived. He was free, they didn't have him, and he was on his way home.

Next day we were sitting at the kitchen table looking through the newspapers and there was a horrendous photo of Gary on the front pages. Media headlines shouted CYBERTERRORIST and CRIMINAL MASTERMIND, which anyone who had met Gary knew was the furthest thing from the truth.

'That photo doesn't look anything like you, what have they done?' I was looking at one of the worst photos of Gary I'd ever seen.

'I was in the police van and the photographers were pressing their cameras against the high blacked-out windows and flash-bulbs were going off non-stop. They were banging against the van and shouting "Gary! Gary!" I was low down on the floor of the van and I realised the photos would be in all the papers and I didn't want to look like a criminal, so I looked up and I tried to smile. Huge mistake, eh?'

'It's not your fault,' said Wilson as he looked at the papers.

'The photos were taken with wide-angled lens through tinted windows and it's the fish-eye distortion that's made you look odd, that photo looks nothing like you. It might have been designed to make you look sinister to make the story seem more dramatic.'

'Please don't get involved, Mum, or I'll look silly, needing my mum to speak up for me when I'm thirty-nine years old,' said Gary worriedly.

I decided that if it all went smoothly I'd keep a very low profile but if things looked as though they were going to go badly, I would step in.

Gary was articulate, of that there was no doubt, but he was vulnerable and young for his age and could easily misjudge the mood or motives of others. He tended to get the wrong end of the stick, causing him to respond in a way that could be misinterpreted. Many people thought Gary was aloof, when in fact he was quiet and lacked confidence.

I was hugely relieved that Gary was free again and I knew I had to keep him free. To do that I had to learn everything about the extradition treaty and about how everything works inside and outside the courts. I initially stayed away from the meetings he had with his legal team as he wanted to prove he could do this on his own and I didn't want to embarrass him.

Gary started giving interviews and every time I read them I would want to curl up and die. He was being asked by journalists to tell them what he had done and how he had done it. They understandably wanted a story but Gary's freedom and very life was on the line and I don't think he realised that he might be making things worse for himself. However, I quickly discovered that people liked Gary. From young guys and girls to old white-haired ladies and men, who invariably described Gary as that lovely young man.

I remember the prosecutors giving interviews where they were irritated as they felt that Gary was being portrayed as some sort of choirboy, but Gary was just being Gary, and his gentle nature, honesty and naivety were transparent to many people.

It was 27 July 2005 and we were due back in court for the second time. I wore the most conventional thing I owned but also wore my favourite yellow platform shoes.

Wilson and Gary usually wore casual clothes but today they were both dressed in the way that every Celt is taught by their parents to dress for such a sombre occasion: in smart suits.

It was a warm, wet day in London as we again walked past the ballet dancer, her head still bowed as the rain washed over her body. Stepping back through the dark, heavy wooden doors of Bow Street Magistrates', the intoxicating atmosphere of oppression in the air drained hope from the hearts of the hopeful.

Photographers and journalists congregated outside and Gary was nervous. He always carried a small bottle of water when he was going in and out of court and I think that holding the bottle somehow helped him to stay calm.

We met Gary's QC, Edmund Lawson, for the first time. Impressive and intelligent, he was also a showman who without effort commanded the attention of everyone he spoke to both inside and outside the court. Edmund had a warm personality and a great sense of humour.

This was the first chance I'd had to speak to Karen, as after the previous court hearing we had left immediately to try to raise the bail money.

Karen was young with blonde hair. A bit different from other solicitors, she wore trendy clothes and fishnet stockings. She was caring, intelligent and down to earth and thankfully didn't seem intimidated by anyone.

We went upstairs to the courtroom, to find most of the seats already occupied by journalists but we all managed to squeeze in.

The prosecutor hadn't turned up, so we sat around for a long time until we were informed that the prosecutor was going to be late, then sat around a while longer until the judge appeared.

'Sit where you are, Mr McKinnon, as you will become cramped in the seat in front of me,' said the judge, referring to the dock.

A compassionate judge – this seemed like a good start.

When the charges were read out they sounded damning. The US government appeared to have dropped the charges relating to intrusions into US universities that had been listed in the original indictment. The US universities had subsequently announced that no damage had taken place. Instead the prosecutor now concentrated only on government facilities. Emotive names such as Pearl Harbor and references to 'after 9/11' were used, making it sound as though Gary had single-handedly controlled the entire American military machine from his home computer in his bedroom in north London. It was ridiculous. Gary's knowledge was deliberately being overrated – or perhaps it's just that the prosecutors were computer illiterate and had no idea of the reality of what Gary had or hadn't done.

The majority of the judges seemed ill equipped to understand, as, I believe, were some of the prosecutors whose information the judges were relying on. If Gary had been capable of bringing the US military to its knees from his very basic home computer on a dial-up connection, then God help the planet.

I didn't like where this was going. Everything was escalating out of all proportion and I knew then they were going to try to crucify Gary. The Official Secrets Act was mentioned despite the fact we'd been told that no classified information was involved, as the networks he had allegedly wandered through were non-classified.

Surely instead of spending a fortune on prosecuting people they should spend it on securing their systems against a real attack from an unfriendly country with sophisticated equipment?

Gary seemed to me like a scapegoat for incompetence more than anything else. They tried to make him sound like an expert, which he isn't. As Gary said, he's a phisher, not a hacker. Real hackers use much more sophisticated methods and they don't leave silly cyber-notes.

Part of Gary's bail conditions in 2005 were that he was not allowed to use the internet, but this judge said Gary could use

the internet for work providing he gave the police and the courts
his IP address. Unfortunately the kindly judge didn't understand
that if Gary returned to his previous job working in networks
there would be hundreds of different IP addresses, as every
computer has its own one.

Gary's QC, Edmund Lawson, said he was concerned that
they might be planning to try Gary in a US military court, using
national security as a reason, and he raised this with the judge.

'In that case I can't send him,' announced the judge.

'*What?*' My ears pricked up. This was amazing. The judge was
going to refuse to extradite!

At that point Edmund asked the judge for a private word in
the back and they disappeared through a doorway. When they
re-emerged the judge didn't mention refusing extradition and I
couldn't understand why. Later on the US provided an unsigned
diplomatic note which supposedly gave an assurance that a military tribunal would not be used – but as the note was unsigned,
there *was* no assurance.

At the following court hearing the prosecutor suddenly raised
part of a conversation that took place in the US embassy and
was looking pleased with himself, when suddenly Gary's QC
jumped in and said that an American prosecutor had announced
that he'd like to see Gary fry.

The prosecutor looked shocked and a bit worried and said
something to the effect that Edmund Lawson wasn't allowed to
bring that in as it was part of a privileged conversation.

'Oh yes I can,' said Edmund excitedly. 'You just brought in
part of that same conversation and have therefore opened it up,
allowing me to bring it in.'

'Fry'! I couldn't believe what had just been said. Well, Gary
couldn't go. Anyone thinking someone should 'fry' for computer
misuse had to be crazy.

Edmund Lawson was a hero, unafraid to confront the court with the truth and to challenge authority when it was in the wrong.

• • •

The judge by his own volition changed Gary's bail conditions so that Gary only had to sign at the police station twice a week, as opposed to every evening. This was in spite of the prosecutor's protest that if it were possible they'd have liked Gary to sign at the police station every few hours.

I couldn't understand why, but the judge also ruled that Gary's address was to be made public. He had been told that Gary had previously lost a job because of the publicity and the journalists camping on his doorstep.

The case was postponed until 18 and 20 October so that an expert lawyer from America could come over with an affidavit which, we hoped, would help. Clive Stafford Smith was also going to give evidence for the defence, about the torture and inhumane conditions that he said existed in the US.

There were so many photographers outside that everyone who began to walk out into the street turned back and walked inside again. Gary's solicitor Karen Todner spoke to the press and one photo was agreed to. A friend got a taxi so that Gary could leave quickly. We didn't realise then how important it was for the press, the photographers and the media to be involved, or what an essential part of our lives they would become.

• • •

With the stroke of a pen David Blunkett for Tony Blair's government signed the rights of British people away so that without evidence, and without having set foot in another country, we could now be carted off like slaves and taken in chains to a foreign land with a foreign culture, whose judicial system and sentencing bears scant resemblance to our own.

What other country would remove the rights of their own people in this way? America certainly wouldn't. The 2003 UK–US extradition treaty was entirely one-sided, as no US citizen has ever been extradited for a crime committed while they were physically on American soil.

Since the treaty came into effect, British judges seem to be impotent in extradition cases, and appear to be rubber-stamping extraditions rather than trying the cases themselves, even when the accused had never left the UK.

It seems that the extradition of computer geeks – and subsequently even of students accused of copyright infringement – is being requested by the US simply because they now can.

On 14 February 2006 Clive Stafford Smith gave compelling evidence for the defence. We thought Gary had a good chance of winning his case. However, on 10 May District Judge Nicholas Evans in Bow Street Magistrates' ruled that extradition should take place. On 4 July Home Secretary John Reid signed an order for Gary to be extradited. Karen launched an appeal against Reid's decision and simultaneously appealed against the decision of the district judge on the basis of passage of time, human rights and abuse of protest.

A crowd of young computer guys who were outraged at what was happening to Gary filmed themselves on 5 November, Guy Fawkes Night, making LED throwies at home and then walking with them in their hands towards Bow Street Magistrates' Court. When they reached the court they threw hundreds of home-made sticky LEDs – little batteries with magnets and light-emitting diodes – which then stuck onto all the metalwork of the court building, including railings, drainpipes, lights, above the door, on the red telephone boxes outside the court and on anything made of wrought iron.

Passers-by joined in and it was a visually spectacular Sticky LED Bow Street Light Show protest in support of Gary, filmed and set to music by computer guys who believed that what was happening to Gary was completely unjust.

They made a little speech and then shouted 'Free Gary' at the end of the protest. The first comment written underneath the video when posted on YouTube said: 'Just wanted to say you have our support here in the States. Americans stand behind Gary, and he did a very American thing. FREE GARY.'

• • •

On 3 April 2007 Lord Justice Maurice Kay and Justice Goldring dismissed Gary's appeal. However, the pressure to induce a plea of guilty on the basis that substantial benefits would be withdrawn if one was not forthcoming, plus the threat to refuse repatriation, was described by the judges as an anathema. They gave Gary leave to appeal to the Law Lords on this basis.

On 30 July 2008 Gary was devastated when the Law Lords dismissed his appeal against Jacqui Smith's decision to extradite. Karen remained as determined as ever and applied on 7 August to the European Court of Human Rights for interim relief.

The constant cycle of high hopes turning to dust makes everything you reach for feel like a mirage. Life takes on a surreal quality. I felt as though we were constantly trying to run up a downward escalator, never quite managing to reach the top.

Karen immediately arranged for us to have a legal conference at the barristers' chambers to discuss our options. While walking through the new tunnel walkway in King's Cross, which has an Orwellian science fiction-type feel to it, Wilson told me about a dream he'd had. His dream was of us walking along this same tunnel and in this dream, when we approached the bend in the tunnel, a Home Secretary who was female looked at us with a smile and wanted us to know that she was singing our song. This seemed a good omen and, although it didn't fit with Jacqui Smith's decision on Gary, Wilson's dream made me feel more optimistic.

The conference with Gary's legal team was full of positivity and they were as determined as ever to see Gary tried in the UK. When we got home I decided to write a statement to the court but couldn't keep my eyes open and kept falling asleep in the front of the keyboard. I was totally drained of energy. It's easy to lose your sense of time when you're exhausted and constantly under pressure, but when you're fighting for your child somehow you manage to get up each day, put one foot in front of the other and carry on – because you have to. I've also found that some of the best ideas spring into your mind when you're dog-tired and find yourself staring into space. Inspirational thoughts are like revelations that invigorate the soul. Suddenly the tiredness is gone as your mind races with ideas, endowing you with a new-found energy that puts you back into fight mode.

The European Court of Human Rights announced on the morning of 28 August their refusal to even consider Gary's case, while simultaneously deciding to take on that of Abu Hamza.

I submitted a statement I had written to the court. Despite my signature, the judges refused to consider it – they said it had clearly been written by a lawyer, which it had not.

Gary's legal team then asked me to submit evidence for the court swearing that I alone had written my statement, with no input from a lawyer – which was the truth of the matter.

One of the younger lawyers suggested that he could write it out for me. I laughed and pointed out that it would be a bit silly for him to write an oath in which I'm swearing that I wrote my own statement, and he said, 'Oh, right.'

In my oath, I pointed out to the judges that by thinking I wasn't capable of writing my own statement they were basically underestimating the intelligence of mothers. I then added mischievously that it was hardly rocket science and that I had the benefit of having access to the internet, the library of the world.

CHAPTER 9

PARANOID REALITY

Tracey Newport, one of Gary's lawyers, had evidence on his laptop relating to conversations that took place with regard to the statement from a US official that one state would like to see Mr McKinnon 'fry'. Suddenly the laptop containing this information was stolen from his car. This was a bitter blow to our case and, rightly or wrongly, we started to suspect that it was no ordinary theft.

A file containing the notes of a meeting Karen had in the US embassy, also relating to the 'fry' statement, mysteriously disappeared from Karen's office and this seemed just too much of a coincidence.

We started to become paranoid. Someone who worked for Gary's lawyers was worried about being followed by someone from the FBI who was involved in the case: wherever she went, this man seemed to be behind her and she felt very intimidated by him.

It later transpired that Gary's QC, Edmund Lawson, had his own notes about the 'fry' threat, but few were aware of this.

It seemed that our phones were also being monitored. One day, having just hung up after a phone conversation with a friend on our landline, the phone rang and, when I lifted it up, I heard a recording of our whole conversation.

Another time two of my friends rang me separately and were both able to get through at the same time – we had a three-way conversation on the landline. It was increasingly feeling as though we were living more in some kind of spy film than in reality.

• • •

16 June 2008 was the date of Gary's appeal to the House of Lords.

Gary's QC, Edmund Lawson, seemed to have disappeared off the face of the earth. Whenever we asked where he was everyone was vague and spoke about him maybe being in Hong Kong or elsewhere. We couldn't understand what had happened.

A QC named David Pannick was keen to take Edmund Lawson's place and to represent Gary in the Lords on a *pro bono* basis and as he was well respected, we agreed that he could act for Gary, but we were extremely disappointed in not having Edmund Lawson as we believed that he would have won Gary's case.

Civil liberties campaigning group Liberty was also intervening in the case, represented by the legendary Edward Fitzgerald QC.

The case was to be heard in the morning and I had to get up very early to do a radio interview before we left. We climbed into the car and turned the volume up loud, and for ten precious minutes could sink into a world of sound. I don't know how I could survive without music, it's such a release, such an escape from worry, even if only temporarily.

We jumped onto the train in the nick of time and even managed to get a seat. It was a hot day – I knew I shouldn't have worn a jacket.

We arrived at King's Cross train station twenty minutes later and ran down the escalator and onto the tube. A strikingly dressed woman with dark hair and a red coat kept staring at me. She was tall and slim and wore shiny black platform boots and looked as though she might be the head of a fashion company or something – she stood out from the crowd.

'You're Gary McKinnon's mum,' she said, as a statement rather than a question.

'Yes, I am.'

'Well done to you. Keep fighting and don't give up. This is England and not America and if your son has to be tried anywhere it should be right here in an English court.'

'That's what we're fighting for. We're in court today.'

'Good. Gary's got the entire country behind him. An American would never be extradited to Britain if the boot was on the other foot, we all know that. Your son has embarrassed them by showing up how abominable their security is and the Yanks don't like to lose face. Our government are wimps; let's hope they have a spine among them. Good luck,' she said, putting her hand on my shoulder before she stepped off the tube.

'Thank you,' I smiled.

'She's right, Wils; let's hope they've got a spine among them.'

'I doubt it but I hope so. This is our stop.'

We got off the tube and ran along the road. When we walked inside the court the session was just beginning. It was a dark, depressing room with a large painting on the wall and that familiar musty smell hanging in the air.

Despite the huge press presence, we managed to get space to sit down on one of the hard, uncomfortable benches.

The Law Lords were on stage, exuding an air of superiority while deciding on virtual life-or-death decisions to be passed on British subjects, in this case on my son.

It was as though time had stood still again and we were back in a Dickensian world reminiscent of the hanging judges of years gone by. Although Britain thankfully no longer has the death penalty, Gary was facing what he believed was a sentence worse than death.

Who are these people, these Law Lords smiling and acting mildly amused, as though it's some kind of game? How dare they think that it's fine to send one of their own countrymen to be dragged like a slave to an alien land he's never set foot in, and for a ludicrous number of years? This was no laughing matter.

Had Gary murdered anyone? No!

Had Gary raped anyone? No!

Had Gary sold secrets to anyone? No!

Had Gary made any money from anything he did? No!

Had Gary hurt anyone? No!

Did Gary believe in conspiracy theories? Yes!

Did Gary post a peace protest in a cyber-note accusing the US government of state-sponsored terrorism? Yes!

Had Gary left cyber-notes telling them their security was crap? Yes!

Had Gary embarrassed them? Yes! – and therein lies the crux of the matter.

• • •

The court was in session and David Pannick QC started delivering Gary's case.

Maybe I got that wrong … he didn't sound as though he was acting for Gary.

'*Is* he Gary's QC, Karen?'

'Yes.'

'That's scary.'

'I know what you mean,' said Wilson.

The more I heard, the more I could feel my heart sinking.

'Is this the barrister everyone raved about?'

'I believe so,' said Wilson solemnly.

Why do the Law Lords keep referring to Gary serving a possible ten-year sentence in the US – surely they know it's ten years *per count*?

Lord Phillips must have read my thoughts. 'Was it ten years per count? Is that where the sixty years came from?' he boomed. I was thankful that at least one of the Law Lords finally seemed to acknowledge this.

It was Lord Brown's turn now. Oh no! Lord Brown was trying to equate Gary's computer misuse with aviation crime. Good God, Gary had never been charged with any such thing. Was this an ingenious attempt by Lord Brown to try to justify the sixty-year sentence suggested by the US?

How could a judge, whose job it is to be independent, strive to make a case to justify a life sentence for a British computer nerd who had never hurt anyone… if that's what he was trying to do?

'Didn't Lord Brown work with the Americans at GCHQ at one time?'

'I think he did,' said Wilson, tugging on his beard.

'Right. That might explain it.'

That Lord Brown could basically suggest without any evidence whatsoever that Gary's computer misuse 'may' equate with crimes against shipping or aviation, when even the CPS had been given no evidence of any such thing, was morally wrong as far as I was concerned.

I mean, anyone could suggest that anyone was guilty of anything but when that person is in a court of law is it right that the judge deciding whether or not you should be extradited should publicly announce suggestions of serious crime with no evidence to back those suggestions up? Especially when, due to the very nature of the extradition treaty, the accused is not even allowed to defend himself in a British court against any allegations? Besides, the CPS had admitted that they had received no evidence from the US, only hearsay.

In addition to this, Gary had no lawyer present during his first police interview in March 2002. After his second police interview in late 2002, the lawyer representing Gary had written in his notes words to the effect that Gary wasn't right in the head.

Gary was eccentric and clearly vulnerable, and he paid a high price for his naivety and openness and his attempts to be ridiculously helpful when he was arrested.

• • •

I continued to be confused and worried by David Pannick's performance but I still wasn't prepared for his answer when Baroness Hale asked him if he regarded what the judges in the High Court had described as threats that amounted to anathema as incentives or threats. Mr Pannick replied, 'Incentives, M'Lady.'

I couldn't believe what I was hearing. How could threats such as those made against Gary if he didn't accept a plea bargain possibly be described as incentives?

Will the courts start to describe blackmail as an incentive to keep a secret?

We raised QC Pannick's performance with Karen and she said she didn't know what was wrong with him, as he had a good reputation.

I was overwhelmed with outrage and worry and wished that Edmund Lawson was there. Where he when we needed him?

I looked at the Law Lords, who were supposed to be listening to arguments in order to make a judgment; rightly or wrongly, I believed that their minds had never been open to argument or reason. It seemed to me that the decision had been made and the only reason they were there in front of us was to attempt to publicly justify extradition and even possibly to attempt to justify a life sentence being given for a non-violent crime.

The reality is that our judges and politicians rarely refuse the US any demand they make.

Thankfully Edward Fitzgerald, acting for Liberty, spoke up for Gary. Although he hadn't prepared an in-depth response we were very grateful to have Edward there.

We were later informed by other barristers that David Pannick QC had claimed that his performance in the Lords that day was down to him feeling tired. But that didn't explain why he had ended Gary's case early, by turning down the following day in court that had already been arranged for Gary's defence.

Could someone please explain what the heck was going on?

• • •

Some months afterwards we discovered that Gary's original QC, Edmund Lawson, had died suddenly, apparently of a stroke. We were shocked and saddened, all the more so because Edmund left young children.

We were nervous waiting for the judgment to come through and weren't optimistic because of what we perceived as the shambles in the Lords.

Every time I saw an email from our solicitor Karen on the computer, I was actually scared to look at it.

On 29 July, Karen informed us that the judgment was due to be announced on the following day and that she wasn't allowed to tell us the result until then. Gary, Lucy, Wilson and I were waiting for Karen to call us when we heard the judgment being announced on BBC TV. The lords had ruled against Gary. What a way to hear such a devastating decision. The Law Lords upheld the decision to extradite and dismissed the appeal.

It was no surprise to me as I was convinced that the Law Lords had made their decision before even hearing the case. But you always cling to the hope that good will prevail, and hearing that we had lost floored us.

Gary was devastated, as he thought this was the end. I rarely cry in front of anyone and tried to wipe the tears away, but they were coming too fast for me to hold back and we all cried together.

When I managed to compose myself and look at how this was destroying Gary, my sadness was replaced by anger. I told Gary he wasn't going anywhere and that it wasn't the end: we would win his freedom. What was happening was wrong and just about everyone knew it.

When a sentence of six months in the UK can become a sentence of sixty years in the US, it is patently clear that our justice systems bear scant resemblance.

Duncan Campbell wrote in *The Guardian* after the hearing in the Lords in 2008:

'The difference between the American system and our own is not perhaps so stark as the appellant's argument suggests,' said Lord Brown of Eaton-under-Heywood in his ruling.

... Well, who knows what news gets through to Eaton-under-Heywood these days, but if Lord Brown and his four colleagues had done some cursory research on the current state of the US criminal justice system they would know there is a very stark difference between the way [Gary] could be treated by the US courts and how he would be treated here.

There may be much wrong with the British criminal justice system but, compared to the lottery that is the American judicial process, there are a number of sober differences. For a start, here you would not find yourself in jail for fifty years for stealing $160 worth of video tapes, or for twenty-five years for smoking marijuana. Nor does the UK operate a Guantanamo Bay where the most basic legal principles have been abandoned as part of a post-9/11 panic. And there is no guarantee that, if tried in the US, McKinnon would not be confronted by some grandstanding, publicity-seeking judge deeply offended that a chap in a flat in north London can leave a message saying 'your security is really crap' on the Pentagon computer, as McKinnon did. After all, one American official in this case has already said that he would like to see him 'fry'.

In the beginning we had such faith in the British judicial system. OK, the American system allows plea bargains, where convicted people can get their sentence reduced if they testify against someone else that the authorities want put away, lengthy solitary confinement and the threat of ridiculously huge sentences, often to pressure someone into taking a plea bargain whether guilty or not ... but not *here*, not in the UK?

A disappointment as catastrophic as this was like the floor collapsing with Gary on it. He rarely showed his emotions and could appear calm on the outside, even when he was dying inside, as he was now.

Gary had arranged to give an interview with Ben Scotchbrook on ITV's *London Tonight* the following day. Gary was devastated and broken but people who didn't know him couldn't see that. They saw him as confident and self-assured, but nothing could have been further from the truth and we were seriously worried about him. However, I spent hours persuading him to go ahead with the interview as I thought it might help. Anyone who knew Gary could see that he was honest, naive and open, so I thought maybe viewers, including politicians and maybe even the American authorities, would see that too.

CHAPTER 10

NOT AN UGLY DUCKLING (A SWAN)

The following day Gary agreed to go to the TV studio and do the interview as promised. The studio sent a car to take him there and Lucy went with him to support him.

Wilson and I switched on the TV in time to catch the beginning of Gary's interview. As it transpired, it was one of the most important interviews Gary ever did, and agreeing to it, even when he was severely traumatised, was in retrospect one of the best decisions Gary ever made.

Ben Scotchbrook: There must have been occasions when you got into a military computer ... a NASA computer, and you thought, 'How on earth did I do this?' What went through your mind when you got that far in?

Gary: I was amazed at the ... well, not even the level of security, there was no security. In their indictment they say I left the networks open to further attack, but the networks were completely open to attack ... I never had to break into them ... it was like logging on ... it was like username with no password.

Ben: Did it not occur to you that these guys are the most formidable military force in the world? They came up with the concept of shock-and-awe warfare and you thought 'I might leave a bit of egg on their faces'?

Gary: Not so much egg. I used to leave messages. I was absolutely shocked at the lack of security. I left messages on almost every system administrator's desktop, which in a perverse way I hope was helpful because at least it was me there … it wasn't al-Qaeda.

Ben: Let's look at one of the messages you are said to have left. 'US foreign policy is akin to government-sponsored terrorism these days' … 'I am Solo' … 'I will continue to disrupt at the highest levels'. That message was left in the aftermath of the September 11 attack in 2001. What on earth were you thinking?

Gary: It's what's called Hactivism, like hacking as a form of activism, and the disruption is the announcement of your presence there and how ridiculous their security is and also, if you know your history of US foreign policy, in a lot of really credible people's opinion it is…

Ben: But at best you made them look stupid, at worst you must have sent terror through the network. Don't tell me you were just doing it to, eh, point out the fact that their passwords weren't very good.

Gary: I don't think you send terror through a network by leaving a note on someone's desktop.

Ben: But you accept now that you were asking for trouble. This wasn't just fiddling at the edges; you were into the heart of the American military and NASA.

Gary: Yeah, it was incredibly cheeky and incredibly stupid … but the chance to leave messages to very high-up people … I couldn't resist it at the time.

Ben: So here you are on the brink possibly of being extradited to America, you're told by American officials that they want to see you fry, according to your defence and you're … you've got the opportunity to say 'I'm sorry, it was a stupid, stupid thing to do', and yet you're still making comments about American foreign policy. That doesn't strike me as very level headed.

Gary: Well, should I be quiet in my political opinions?

Ben: No, but I would concentrate on the apology; most people would think you might concentrate on the apology.

Gary: I've shown remorse on many occasions. I'm hugely disappointed at the moment and hugely angry with my government, so I'm in a bit of a different mood.

Ben: What do you think your actions achieved, in the cold light of day?

Gary: I found what I was after. I found evidence of UFOs and the fact that NASA covered them up and I confirmed that with a photograph.

Ben: What did you see in the photograph?

Gary: It was a very exotic craft. I only saw about two-thirds of the picture. It had no seams or rivets. It didn't look man-made at all.

Ben: Well, you got what you were looking for; now you may get what the American judicial system is looking for. Can you give us some sort of idea specifically of what you fear might happen to you?

Gary: I've seen a letter from one of the official parties in the Department of Justice and they say 'we will reserve the right to prosecute Mr McKinnon under the enemy combatant law ... the military tribunal ... military order number one'. That's frightening. That's either a completely secret trial with no right of appeal and no right of press awareness, or it's Guantanamo, which I thought was ridiculous but I've been advised I'm accused of allegedly directly attacking American military networks. Whereas most, if not all, of the people in Guantanamo haven't been proven to be guilty of anything.

Ben: How frightened are you?

Gary: Pretty terrified ... but I'm also very angry.

Ben: Was it worth all this?

Gary: No, not at all, but when you think in Britain ... I mean, all I've done is log on to computers. All right, I've left really cheeky political diatribes and, OK, it happened to be the computer of the world sup— the world's only hyper-power, but I haven't hurt anyone, no one's terrorised, no one's murdered... Sixty years in prison? I mean that guy who's in The Hague [Radovan Karadžić] is going to get twenty-five and what's he accused of? Murdering thousands. There's a huge imbalance.

Ben: If you had American officials in here now, what would you say to them?

Gary: Gi'e us a job ... I'm serious. I'd gladly work for them. I think someone should work for them because every year, the government accountancy office comes out and gives the same report ... the same damning report. They're under federal guidelines for strict computer security and it's wide open. Every report is the same.

Ben: You wouldn't say sorry?

Gary: Oh, I already said sorry many times. I said sorry in writing. I've said sorry through my solicitors when I've had face-to-face meetings with them. I've offered to work for them. I've been sorry for six years, and now I'm very angry with my own country for throwing me to the dogs.

Gary was so traumatised by the interview that he refused to do any more. Lucy scolded Ben Scotchbrook for his harsh questioning, but Ben was a nice person who hadn't realised how much it had affected Gary and had only been doing his job.

I thought then that I shouldn't have talked Gary into doing it.

He was far too traumatised for such an ordeal. But I am so glad now that I did: after the interview was aired, Gary's solicitor's office was inundated with people ringing and writing in to say that he had Asperger's syndrome, a form of autism. Initially the receptionist apparently hung up on some of the callers until a young lawyer named Dinkledine picked up the phone during the receptionist's lunch break and took the information seriously.

We'd never heard of Asperger's and, like most of the general public, thought that autism meant you had low intelligence and could barely speak. We had never heard of high-functioning autism, but Mr Dinkledine and Karen Todner insisted that Gary should be assessed and, despite our misgivings, we eventually agreed.

Karen arranged for Gary to be assessed by Dr Thomas Berney, a consultant developmental psychiatrist and a leading expert in the field. We also took Gary to see Luke Beardon, who did not officially diagnose him, but said that in his opinion Gary had Asperger's syndrome.

Gary was already severely traumatised and now we were telling him that he might have autism, which was upsetting him even more.

The tests on Gary were long and intensive and took several days. Dr Berney gave Gary puzzles to solve and spoke in depth to our entire family, to Lucy and to Gary's ex-partner, Tamsin. It was another of those cathartic questioning sessions which compels you to look deep inside and to analyse everything.

After assessing all the data, on 23 August 2008, Gary was officially diagnosed as having lifelong Asperger's syndrome, a pervasive developmental disorder. When the doctor explained the effect it has on behaviour, perception of the world, and comprehension of some very basic things, I was astonished at how much it explained. I couldn't believe that I had never heard of Asperger's. So much of Gary's behaviour, problems and misunderstandings – even the meltdowns that caused his intellectual faculties to totally fail – were at last understandable.

Riding on her chariot at lightning speed, within days Karen provided the European Court on Human Rights (ECHR) with this medical evidence to show that extradition would be disproportionate and to ask them to take on Gary's case.

The very next morning – 28 August – the ECHR refused to even consider taking on Gary's case. Yet on the same day the ECHR took on Muslim cleric Abu Hamza's case and halted his extradition on terrorist charges. How would they even have had time to look through the brand new medical evidence on Gary that Karen provided them with?

We were now all feeling paranoid in the extreme, as the authorities could literally come and snatch Gary for extradition at any point. The unrelenting state of fear we were in waiting for the hand on Gary's shoulder made me acutely aware of the terror slaves were subjected to when being dragged from their homes, families and the land they were born in.

At one point, in the corridors of the court, the prosecutor said that a plane would be arriving – possibly even as soon as that night – to extradite Gary. I was trembling, but still determined that it wasn't going to happen.

Contrary to popular belief it was not only black people who were kidnapped and sold as slaves. The same thing happened to Scottish and Irish people as recently as the seventeenth century. Human beings were kidnapped, betrayed and sold by their own people and sent to American colonies and plantations.

Tens of thousands of these white slaves were children, which is where the word 'kidnapped' comes from. According to the Egerton

Manuscripts in the British Museum, the law enacted in 1652 allowed judges to ship Scottish people to a foreign colony or plantation.

This law was repealed when a British Bill of Rights came into force in 1689 and that same Bill of Rights, which disallows cruel and unusual punishment, is still in force today but is being ignored by our courts.

CHAPTER 11

JOURNEY TO UNDERSTANDING

A man who worked in antiques offered to hide Gary for the next few years. The next few years! We knew JC on a casual basis but didn't know him well, yet he was prepared to do this for Gary. JC was Jewish and understood better than most the absolute terror we were living in. We had always known he was a good man, but such courage and compassion overwhelmed us. Men with that kind of courage are thin on the ground. I'll never forget what he was prepared to do to help us, but I knew I couldn't allow him to put himself at risk. His kindness and bravery made me cry.

For Gary, living on the run would have been a terrifying prospect. I knew he would never survive as a fugitive; he just wasn't made that way. We had to win his freedom legitimately if we were to have any hope of saving his life and returning to some sort of normality.

Karen wanted Gary to have another medical opinion to confirm his diagnosis and to strengthen his case to be tried in the UK. Autistic rights campaigner Nadine Stavonina de Montagnac, who had two autistic children, was one of the first people who immediately recognised that Gary had Asperger's syndrome. Nadine was warm and intelligent and extremely helpful and knowledgeable. She told us that Professor Simon Baron-Cohen, Richard Mills, Dr Berney and Professor Digby Tantam were renowned leaders in this field.

Karen always engaged the very best of experts for Gary and never once compromised on that. Nadine helped us to get an urgent assessment and Karen arranged for Gary to be assessed by Professor Baron-Cohen at his clinic in Cambridge on 8 September 2008.

When Wilson and I took Gary to be assessed he was terrified of suddenly being snatched. I figured that the police would have to contact Karen first and she would make sure that things were dealt with properly. I didn't think anyone knew our address, so they wouldn't be able to snatch Gary without warning. Would they? Now that thought was in my head I couldn't shake it.

Taking Gary there was the most terrifying thing as we got it into our heads that Gary might suddenly be arrested there and then, and we knew we had to have the assessment done before any arrest took place – we felt that having both Dr Berney's and Professor Baron-Cohen's reports could help to save Gary from extradition.

Gary was unshaven and looked tired and rough. I hadn't been taking care of myself either – my hair needed a wash and I looked tired beyond belief.

Wilson was shattered too and was driving us to Cambridge. The drive was fraught with anxiety and our minds were focused with a healthy measure of paranoia. Wilson drove with his eyes as much on the mirror as on the road, constantly watching to see who was behind us. Several times a suspicious car seemed to be following us only for it to finally turn off, but, as Wilson pointed out, a proper tail involved more than one vehicle for the very purpose of not raising suspicions, so we remained worried.

A car eventually did appear to lock onto us, starting from a few cars back and now matching its speed to ours. If we slowed, it slowed. If we sped up, it did likewise. Every turn we took, the car behind took too, and Gary was in panic mode, while I was trying to think of how we could escape if we were cornered.

We desperately needed this assessment done at all costs.

I asked Wilson to take a different route. He waited until the car was close behind, then on the next roundabout did two full circles, bringing us behind the car where we could then follow, see where it went and avoid it. Wilson eventually convinced me that we were no longer being followed, if we even ever had been, and Gary agreed, so we continued to Professor Baron-Cohen's premises, which turned out to be an old building in large grounds surrounded by trees.

We arrived there looking dishevelled and afraid, like deer caught in the headlights.

As we pulled into the huge driveway we saw two big vans parked there with blacked-out windows, one of which was an armoured security van. I was terrified, convinced that it was the Americans waiting to pounce. We drove up the side and stopped out of sight of the vans and Wilson went in first to find out if everything was OK. Simon Baron-Cohen and his assistant were really nice, and reassured Wilson that the vans were just delivering and not collecting anything or, more importantly, anyone.

While Gary was being assessed, Wilson and I were continually checking the drive and surrounding area, shooting furtive glances around to make sure that no one was lying in wait to kidnap Gary.

Cambridge is a beautiful English university town steeped in tradition. It is the home of Grantchester Meadows and has the most magnificent historic architecture set in the most stunning surroundings, with settlements dating back to Roman times. Happy, carefree students cycled along quaint narrow roads, surrounded by street markets and cafés. In stark contrast, we were trapped in fear. I felt that everyone could see we looked hunted; it's an animal thing that one human being picks up from another. I glimpsed concern in the eyes of some passers-by.

When Gary's assessment was eventually completed we felt, for whatever reason, as though a weight had been lifted. We had hope, which is all a human being needs to keep going. We drove back to our house and, once again, we waited.

• • •

Professor Baron-Cohen's report conclusively diagnosed Gary as having Asperger's syndrome and deemed him at risk of suicide. That was the thing: Gary had told Professor Cohen intimate things that he had felt unable to tell us. Some of those things confirmed the risk to his life and as we hadn't known, Karen didn't know, so hadn't been able to use it in evidence.

Asperger's syndrome is a condition that is often masked by intelligence. This makes it much more difficult for other people to understand why some people with autistic spectrum disorder can often find it so difficult, and sometimes impossible, to grasp some basic concepts, while understanding the most complicated of things.

When Gary was a toddler, whenever I took him on a bus he used to scream continually and throw himself around. Nothing would calm him but as soon as we got off the bus he was quiet again. He was afraid of travel.

At the age of nine Gary would buy books on body language and study them and I couldn't understand why. I now I realise that he couldn't understand what the various expressions on people's faces meant and he was trying to learn it all by himself.

Gary took everything literally; so much so that it tended to cause confusion.

Gary's mental breakdowns when we took him on holiday as a child and in his early teens were likely to have been induced by his fear of travel and his inability to be far from home and familiar surroundings.

Gary's collapse on the platform of the tube when he was sixteen years old and the loss of his intellectual faculties was probably because he had left his local surroundings on his own for the first time ever, to start work in town, causing him to go into meltdown.

His obsession with computers which had caused his downfall was also an Aspie thing. Gary's world was a literal world, one of logic and obsession, and the logic of computers made perfect sense to him.

If we hadn't been living in such intense fear we could have taken comfort from the knowledge we had just acquired. It was like a jigsaw puzzle that had fallen into place. We always knew Gary was vulnerable and eccentric and different in many ways – but we were different and our unconventional lifestyle included many very eccentric friends. Gary was just Gary, more fragile and more vulnerable and more eccentric than many eccentrics, and we loved him.

ASD wasn't recognised by the World Health Organization until Gary was around thirty years old, so it would have been impossible for him to have been diagnosed as a child or for me to have known anything about Asperger's at that time.

Surely Home Secretary Jacqui Smith would now refuse to extradite Gary. The doctors' reports made it crystal clear that Gary's obsessions and search for the truth were connected to his ASD. He had no clue that he might face extradition for accessing US computers, given that the 2003 extradition treaty hadn't been written and no one else had ever been extradited from the UK for computer misuse – even in other cases deemed by the judges to be significantly more serious.

On 13 September 2008 we got more bad news. Jacqui Smith refused to stop the extradition and, just to finish Gary off, she refused to give him fourteen days' grace to allow the new medical evidence to be considered.

I couldn't understand how this crucial medical evidence could just be dismissed out of hand by the government, but Karen flatly refused to give up on Gary and said defiantly, 'I'm putting the new medical evidence in anyway and Jacqui Smith will just have to consider it.'

I was so glad of Karen's fiery nature and of the fact that despite awesome odds she fought and managed to keep Gary here until we could eventually win his freedom.

• • •

For the first few years I said barely a word in public, respecting Gary's wish not to make him feel silly by having his mum speak up for him. But when the situation became bleaker and bleaker, embarrassment was the least of our worries.

Gary was shutting down and deteriorating mentally at a rapid rate, unable to tolerate the constant stress and rollercoaster of emotions when hopes raised were continually crashed to the ground.

Duncan Campbell from *The Guardian* asked me if I wanted to write a piece in the paper's 'Comment is Free' section. So on 22 September 2008 I did just that. I wrote about Gary and extradition and how just the threat of it destroys lives.

Among the mostly positive responses, loads of negative and even abusive comments started to appear, many from people sounding American. One of those posts retained a link that someone had accidentally included in their post. I was amazed to discover that the link was to a website exclusively for American prison officers, soldiers and police, and that my *Guardian* piece was posted on the front page of this US website, from which most of the negative comments seemed to be emanating.

I was genuinely shocked at this and at just how far the US prosecutor's PR machine goes, that they apparently even have comments flooding our system, in an attempt to combat supportive articles written on someone they want to prosecute.

In September 2008 I arranged a protest to demonstrate outside the American embassy in London. If it's inside the Serious Organised Crime and Police Act (SOCPA) area, you have to inform the police of the names of the key protestors, the steward you nominate and a rough estimate of the numbers expected, so that they know how many PCs are needed to police it.

Because ARM, the Autistic Rights Movement, was joining us, police with experience of autism were also used. The Autistic Rights Movement made huge, impressive banners that looked like solid stone. The demo was well attended and gained a lot of TV coverage. It was both a plea to President Bush and a protest against what was happening to Gary via the UK's horrendous extradition treaty.

Gary was in a deep depressive state and there were serious and justifiable concerns that his life was at risk. He believed that death was preferable to being removed from everyone and everything he had ever known.

I felt as though I was wandering through a wilderness and calling out for help but no one could hear me. So many things had happened that I believed should be more than enough to change the government's mind, but they all led to nothing. Government hearts seemed cold and untouched by the cruelty being inflicted by outlandish threats. I needed to make my voice heard and to fight harder to make people aware of what was happening.

On 29 December 2008 I was looking through the newspapers online and discovered that Duncan Campbell had made Gary one of the 'Brits who stole the show this year' in *The Guardian*. This was amazing.

As if that wasn't enough of a boost to our spirits, Nadine had been in contact with Peter Howson, the famous Scottish artist, and in January 2009 Peter unveiled his impressive and powerful portrait of Gary, leading to extensive press coverage all over the country.

Suddenly people were coming on board from all directions to help us, and at a time when we most needed it.

The Home Office in the then Labour government wrote to Karen asking her to ask Gary's supporters to stop writing to them, as the volume of mail was stopping them getting on with their work. I couldn't believe the cheek, and let's just say that my heart didn't exactly bleed for them.

Gary's life was under threat and they were upset because they had received too many letters in his support?

It felt to me as though Gary was on death row and we were fighting to prevent his execution. In Gary's case extradition would have meant execution, but by Gary's own hand.

Before I opened my eyes in the morning my heart was filled with dread that Gary might not have made it through the night. The unrelenting fear of losing him and working 24/7 on fighting for Gary was physically and mentally exhausting.

I once fell fast asleep during a conversation with my friend Pauline on the phone and woke up with her shouting down the phone, 'Janis! Janis! Wake up, Janis, you have to go to bed, you have to sleep.'

I also regularly fell asleep in front of the computer in the early hours of the morning and Wilson would come down to take me up to bed.

Wilson was wonderful and without him by my side, life would have been infinitely harder. Wilson is gentle to the core. He fed me and made me endless cups of tea and understood that sometimes when I seemed irritable it was because I was beginning to crumble and was fighting hard to keep it together.

Wilson helped give me the confidence I needed to do what I was doing. I was shy and hated talking on the telephone, rarely answered the door and had never spoken on TV. Suddenly I had to do so many things that I wasn't prepared for and didn't know if I could do without falling on my face, but I couldn't afford to fail.

Wilson held me in the night when silent tears were falling and rubbed my back until I drifted into sleep. When I woke at an unearthly hour every morning, he would get up at 5 or 6 a.m. to make me tea and toast and to help me to find the information I was searching for on the internet. We've been married for thirty-nine years and together for forty-two and still love each other deeply.

Wilson is an artist and a musician and has a great sense of humour. He always tries to keep everyone happy and has helped to pull Gary from the abyss in the darkest of moments.

I remember thinking that what was happening to Gary was the worst thing ever, and then our neighbours called at our house and told us that their fifteen-year-old son had had an accident when he was jumping on a trampoline. Three friends had fallen on him, and because of the way they had all fallen, he was permanently paralysed.

I felt so sad for this family, whose lives were changed forever. The couple were going to have to employ a full-time nurse, which they could ill afford, but that wasn't the point. Their son was paralysed! The hopes that he and his parents had had for his future were gone in an instant, because of a freak accident that had occurred totally out of the blue. There was nothing I or anyone could say to lessen their pain.

'What would we choose, I wonder, if the choice was your son facing extradition and a possible sixty-year sentence but with a tiny glimmer of hope, or your son being safe in his own country but being permanently paralysed?'

'Where's the choice?' he answered.

'Where's the choice,' I agreed.

As we stood at the door to say goodbye, I watched them walk away slowly, shoulders bent, reflecting the weight of their hearts.

CHAPTER 12

PRESIDENTS AND PRECEDENTS

My heart was heavy too. Who knew what lay ahead for us? No alleged hacker had ever been extradited for computer misuse and the first person was not going to be Gary, it just couldn't be.

I received numerous emails about Gary every day. I'd even got some from classical musicians and cryptologists asking if it was right that Gary had cracked the 'Dorabella cipher'. I discovered that this was an encrypted letter written by Edward Elgar to Dorabella Penny in 1897. It seems that Penny never deciphered it and its meaning remains unknown.

I didn't know where the rumour had come from that Gary had cracked this code. I was asked to ask Gary whether, even if he hadn't cracked Elgar's code, he would take the time to try. They seemed to have no idea of what Gary was going through.

The Dorabella cipher, consisting of eighty-seven characters spread over three lines, appears to be made up from twenty-four symbols, each symbol consisting of one, two or three approximate semicircles oriented in one of eight directions (the orientation of several characters is ambiguous). A small dot appears after the fifth character on the third line.

I think just about everyone believed that Gary would not go anywhere in the end and, somewhere inside, I believed that too but I knew I had to keep fighting. We were desperately hoping that Barack Obama would win the American election as we believed that he would be a more compassionate President and might drop the extradition request.

When we switched the TV on to find that Barack Obama had indeed won the presidential election we were overjoyed. This was a true landmark in American history. Barack Obama would be the first ever black President of America and he could change the world for the better if he wanted to. I hoped he had the courage to do just that.

Melanie Riley, who had done the PR for the NatWest Three and who also ran the Friends Extradited campaign group, was committed to seeing the introduction of 'forum' in extradition cases, to allow people who were in the UK when the alleged crime took place to be tried here instead of being extradited.

In my very first contact with Melanie I argued with her about a demonstration she had organised, a protest by businessmen in support of the NatWest Three, who were fighting extradition to the US. I didn't know Melanie then but I sent out emails to Gary's supporters asking them to come along to the demo, as I felt that by joining forces we'd be better able to fight the extradition treaty. Melanie contacted me in panic mode, asking me to tell Gary's supporters not to attend as the demo was for businessmen only.

I wasn't happy about this but as I got to know Melanie, I understood more about her methods and realised she was caring and compassionate and was working extremely hard on trying to achieve forum.

I had been doing interviews for various newspapers and had got to know a lot of the journalists. The media would generally contact me at home, via Karen, or via the Free Gary website, which was run by the amazing Mark.

Melanie Riley rang me in January 2009 and asked me if I would do an in-depth interview with Lucy Bannerman of *The Times*. I met Lucy, a young Scottish woman, in the Cock & Dragon pub at Cockfosters. She was easy to talk to and there was a photographer with her who took lots of pictures. It's hard to smile or to look serious to order, so it never really feels or looks natural, but that was the least of my worries.

After the interview was published it got a huge reaction. Lucy Bannerman rang me to say that ITV had seen the story and wanted me to do a TV interview. That made me nervous but Lucy said, 'You're articulate and it could help Gary, so it's worth doing.'

I had no idea of how I'd come across on TV but knew that I couldn't let Gary down and had to do my best to put his case across well.

In the meantime Melanie approached us about arranging a press conference on 15 January 2009 at Gary's barrister's chambers in Doughty Street. I had reservations, especially about whether Gary would be able to cope with it, but we eventually agreed.

Karen Todner and Ben Cooper from Gary's legal team, Gary's MP David Burrowes, Professor Simon Baron-Cohen, Mark Lever from the National Autistic Society, James Welch from Liberty, Nadine Stavonina, Gary and I were on the panel. The press conference was packed with journalists from all over the world plus all the British newspapers and TV stations.

Melanie was right. It was well worth doing as it raised the profile of Gary's case and the extradition treaty even further.

I had emailed all the journalists I'd had contact with and when Alex Thomson from Channel 4 walked in an hour early because of a mix-up in times, he said, 'You sent me an email asking me to come to a press conference.'

'Yes,' I said embarrassedly, as I had to explain to Alex that it wasn't due to start until an hour later. This extremely tall, charismatic man with the warm, open smile wasn't at all annoyed and waited patiently. I've since discovered that he has a son with autism and I've been amazed at just how many people I've met from the media who have an autistic child.

It was much harder to speak off my own bat to an audience of seasoned journalists than to answer questions in an interview. My leg was shaking, but Gary was as articulate as always. However, when asked by one of the journalists how he felt, Gary said, 'I might appear calm on the outside but inside the fires of hell are burning.'

Gary had said that he couldn't look into his own eyes in the mirror when he was shaving, that he felt as though he was walking through a world that was about to end, and that there was a veil between him and the world he was living in. The psychiatrist told me that these were all dangerous signs.

The press conference was well organised and an old friend of Gary's named John Tayler who worked in PR was helping Melanie and paid for a buffet out of his own pocket. We especially appreciated his thoughtfulness in including the vegetarian food.

At the end of the press conference there were lots of interviews with journalists from all over the world. Everyone hung around afterwards chatting and eating and drinking and it was a good atmosphere with lots of positivity. Melanie was so right about the wisdom of doing a press conference – it had been an undoubted success.

• • •

The judicial review of the decision to extradite Gary took place on Tuesday 20 January 2009, the same day that George Bush officially handed over the presidency to Barack Obama, which I hoped was a good omen. Gary's lawyers had fought against fierce government opposition to get this date.

It seems that the QC acting for the Treasury solicitors argued against any sort of judicial review, and had apparently been demanding that if there was a 'JR' it should take place on 2 December.

Mark, who set up and ran the Free Gary website, reported that more public money was then wasted on legal fees, and the already overburdened court system slowed down, by a hearing in front of a judge to try to overturn Karen's rejection of the 2 December date. I've always wondered why the prosecution were so fixated on this specific date and I felt pleased that they failed – their desperation worried me. We were up against some very experienced prosecutors and every move they made was purposeful and with the intention of winning.

ITV rang me to ask me to do a TV interview on 21 January 2009. It was with Fern Britton and Phillip Schofield on ITV's *This Morning* show. They sent a car for me and Wilson came too, although he preferred to keep a low profile and didn't want to be interviewed.

I was nervous. Even when Wilson and I played gigs in music venues I never spoke between the songs, but I knew that I had to do this and do it well.

The people who worked in the green room were nice and everyone tries to put you at your ease. They have lots of tea and croissants and fruit, in case anyone hasn't had time for breakfast. They took me in to have my makeup done but I told the makeup artist that I didn't really want any added, so she kept it to a bare minimum.

I couldn't believe that I wasn't nervous while talking on TV, but it was because I was so busy fighting Gary's corner that I didn't think about myself at all. I knew all about the extradition treaty and how it wasn't supposed to be able to be used retrospectively, yet it was. When the interview was over I felt I had done OK.

Fern Britton and Phillip Schofield interviewed media lawyer Mark Stephens at the same time as interviewing me. I thought that Mark Stephens had been brought in to give the US point of view but I was amazed at how well he put Gary's case across.

Mark was saying that instead of the US concentrating on catching the likes of al-Qaeda they were instead wasting time and money in pursuing Gary McKinnon for years on end, which in his opinion was a ridiculous waste of resources.

You tend to find that one interview leads to another. Russia Today asked me to go into their London studio to do an interview with Moscow on 22 January, and they sent a car to collect us.

On the way there the car took detour after detour. Wilson had fallen asleep and I was feeling panicky and was trying to wake him up quietly, as I was worried about where the driver was taking us.

At one point we ended up almost back at the same place the car had been driving along half an hour before. I started becoming convinced that they were going to kidnap us and hold us hostage to try to get hold of Gary to use him in some way. I was sweating and scared and wanted out of the car, but it was driving too fast.

Then we got a phone call telling us that we were being taken to the TV studio for an in-depth interview as it was too late for the live link to Moscow. The car drove into a back yard that looked like the kind of place on TV where people are murdered or kidnapped, and we were transferred into another car. I could hear my heart thumping loudly in my ears.

Suddenly the car stopped and we were taken through a door into a reception area. I was wondering if it was a Russian MI5-type building, but it turned out to be the building for RT TV and the relief was overwhelming. I also felt silly for letting my imagination run riot, but because the US were going to such lengths to pursue Gary, I thought that the Russians might also want him for some reason and might be kidnapping us to get to Gary.

Fear can make you irrational and paranoid.

I've also since discovered that some of the drivers sent by the TV studios either don't know their way around London very well or take illogical detours.

It turned out to be a good week for us. On 23 January, Justice Maurice Kay ruled that the diagnosis of Asperger's syndrome was unequivocal and that, combined with other medical evidence, a judicial review against the Home Secretary's decision to extradite was justified.

This was a massive relief: it not only gave us more time to fight, it also made us feel more optimistic about a good outcome.

I started crying in court and Karen started crying too, and Ronke Phillips from ITV *London Tonight* news said, 'Why are you both crying? Have you lost?'

Through tears of relief I said, 'No, we've won a judicial review.'

Karen and I were laughing and crying and Ronke was beaming as we headed out of the court to do TV interviews.

We lived for days like this. No matter how bad things got or how hopeless they looked, something always came up at the last minute to keep us going.

On 26 January Boris Johnson wrote an article in the *Telegraph* in support of Gary. It was written with typical Boris humour and made me laugh out loud, but Boris is clearly more intelligent than many people realise as he was one of the few to understand exactly what Gary had done and how he had done it.

Boris wrote:

Gary McKinnon believes in little green men – but it doesn't make him a terrorist.

Way to go, Mr President. It is good news that he is getting rid of Guantanamo and water-boarding and extraordinary rendition. There is one last piece of neocon lunacy that needs to be addressed, and Mr Obama could sort it out at the stroke of a pen.

In a legal nightmare that has lasted seven years, and cost untold millions to taxpayers both here and in America, the US Justice Department is persisting in its demented quest to extradite 43-year-old Londoner, Gary McKinnon.

To listen to the ravings of the US military, you would think that Mr McKinnon is a threat to national security on a par with Osama bin Laden. According to the Americans, this mild-mannered computer programmer has done more damage to their war-fighting capabilities than all the orange-pyjama-clad suspects of Guantanamo combined...

In their continuing rage at this electronic lèse-majesté, the Americans want us to send him over there to face trial, and the possibility of a seventy-year jail sentence. It is a comment on American bullying and British spinelessness that this farce is continuing, because Gary McKinnon is not and never has been any kind of threat to American security. He had only one reason for fossicking around in the databanks of Pentagon computers ... Mr McKinnon believes in UFOs, and he is one of the large number of people who think that there is a gigantic conspiracy to conceal their existence from the rest of us.

I am not so brave as to claim that UFOs do not exist. The Astronomer Royal, Sir Martin Rees, has said he believes in life forms on other planets, and no decent empiricist could rule out the possibility.

It may be that David Icke is right, and that the world is run by giant lizards in disguise. Perhaps supersized saurians have been sent, in preparation for the great lizard takeover. Maybe political lizards will hail the arrival of the lizard mother ship as it perches on the mountain top.

All this is certainly theoretically possible, just as it is possible that there really was an accident involving an alien spacecraft at Roswell, and that there really is an extra-large teapot in orbit around Mars. It is just that I happen to think it vanishingly unlikely, and we have a word for people who persist in believing in alien abduction. They are cranks, and they do not deserve to be persecuted and have their lives ruined.

Gary McKinnon wasn't even a proper hacker. He did something called 'blank password scanning', and because these military computers were so dumb as to lack proper passwords, he was able to roam around their intestines in search of evidence of little green men. He was so innocent and un-furtive that he left his own email address, and messages such as 'Your security is crap.' And yes, since you ask, he does think that he found evidence that the US military is infiltrated by beings from the planet Tharg. He even knows the names and ranks of various non-terrestrial officers, though unfortunately they have been deleted from his hard drive.

It is brutal, mad and wrong even to consider sending this man to America for trial. He has been diagnosed as having Asperger's syndrome, for heaven's sake. How can the British government be so protoplasmic, so pathetic, so heedless of the well-being of its own people, as to sign the warrant for his extradition?

We treat a harmless UFO-believer as an international terrorist ... The British government is obviously too feeble to help
Mr McKinnon.

It is time for Barack Obama to invest in some passwords
that are slightly more difficult to crack.

It is time for the new President to let our people go. To
persist with this extradition is so cruel and so irrational that
the only plausible explanation is that beneath their suits the US
Justice Department and the UK Home Office are occupied by
a conspiracy of great green gibbering geckos from outer space.

Radio and TV stations were ringing up for interview after interview, one of which was with Richard and Judy.

I remember feeling a bit nervous when I walked into the
studio, as I wasn't sure what to expect. Michael Jackson's sister
La Toya was on the programme and Richard and Judy asked her
if she felt that President Obama would be a better president. La
Toya said she absolutely believed that he would be.

I added, 'Apparently he's also appointed somebody who's
going to reveal the truth about UFOs.' La Toya looked at me
and smiled and went on to discuss her brother, whose music and
dancing I loved.

I spoke about Gary and said that now that President Obama
was in power I had hope that Gary would remain in the UK.

Judy, referring to Gary, then said: 'Like a lot of people, and
goodness knows we've heard a lot of them, he did believe
that September 11 was a conspiracy and he foolishly put that
message—' and Richard interjected, 'on the very place that was
actually "bombed".'

This made me smile to myself as I wondered if Richard even
realised that he had just said the word 'bombed' when referring
to the Pentagon. I wondered if he also believed some of the

conspiracy theories that Gary believed in, that were circulating on the internet.

On 26 February the Crown Prosecution Service announced that it would not bring charges against Gary in Britain. This meant that the US extradition request would remain live and Gary's life was under imminent threat.

It was as though all of the help that had suddenly appeared out of the blue was a mirage that had tricked us into believing that hope was tangible, but our oasis of safety had faded and we were left stranded again.

It was the weekend and on Sunday 1 March I was wide awake at 6 a.m. I opened and closed the doors of the kitchen cupboards searching for the honey I was sure we had. Then I found it, hiding in the corner, but the jar was almost empty. I realised that the cupboards were bare as I'd forgotten to buy almost all of the things we needed. But there was just enough honey for two slices of toast.

I love honey and I like bees and worry about how they're dying off here. I'm sure pesticides must be at the heart of it and it can't help that everyone is obsessed with weeding out the wild flowers that the bees thrive on.

I sat drinking tea and watching the birds through the patio doors, thinking how absolutely free they looked. It must be the most amazing feeling to fly through the sky and feel the sun on your back, to soar above the clouds and be able to fly thousands of miles away to a warmer climate.

No waiting in queues to be searched or manhandled or strapped in a chair on a metal machine that is sprayed with disinfectants that can make you ill.

To build a flying machine is truly amazing, but to fly like a bird, that must be something!

I switched on the computer and looked at the newspapers

online before starting to write to MPs and to anyone I thought might help us, and there on the screen was an article in the *Mail on Sunday* with Sting and Trudie Styler saying they had written to Jacqui Smith to plead for Gary.

I couldn't believe it; we so needed this. I read it again. The rollercoaster of emotions leaves you feeling dizzy. I think fate plays some cruel games for its own amusement, but I thought, surely fate has to be on our side, because every time we think we're at the end something new comes up.

My friend Josie rang me and started shouting down the phone excitedly, 'Sting and Trudie are in the *Mail on Sunday* talking about Gary!'

'I know! I'm just going to buy the paper.'

I grabbed my jacket and ran down to the paper shop. I've never been star-struck but have always had huge respect for people who use their position or celebrity status to help others. I was so grateful to Trudie and Sting for doing this for my son, and for highlighting the horrendous one-sided extradition treaty. I knew that this could really help us. We hugged and hoped and I was so happy that I put the Stereophonics on and turned the music up loud and danced around the room, singing 'Dakota' at the top of my voice. There was a good feeling in the air that was unmistakeable, and anything seemed possible.

On 16 March 2009, human rights campaigner and former Middle East hostage Terry Waite publicly called on the US to drop their charges against Gary. This wonderful man who had been held hostage, and endured the mental trauma that comes with that, cared enough about what was happening to Gary to come out to plead for his freedom from the terror of extradition. We were overwhelmed by his support and grateful to Melanie Riley for highlighting Gary's case when discussing the extradition treaty.

Legally the US has to prove someone is a fugitive before extradition can happen, but our courts ignore this. Gary did not meet the definition of 'fugitive' and when the judges spoke about 'returning' Gary to America, Gary said: 'How can they return me to a place I've never been?'

In April, another fighter for justice, legendary Oscar-winning actress Julie Christie, wrote to Home Secretary Jacqui Smith:

I am writing to express my deep concern about the case of Gary McKinnon, who currently faces the possibility of extradition to the United States to stand trial on computer hacking charges. I know that already more than a hundred MPs and peers have urged you to act on this matter and that many others, such as Terry Waite, Boris Johnson and Lord Carlile, have also made appeals to you to intervene on his behalf. My understanding of your role is that it is, amongst other things, to protect the citizens of this country, particularly the most vulnerable ones. Surely this must mean that you stand up for Gary McKinnon, who has already made it clear that he is prepared to plead guilty to offences in this country, rather than submitting to a demand from the United States, particularly in the light of all we now know about their treatment of prisoners accused of anything resembling a political offence?

I very much hope that you will make it clear, either now or at the end of the legal proceedings currently underway, that Gary McKinnon will not become yet another victim of the American criminal justice system because this country did not have the courage to stand up to bullying demands.

I felt a force of good was gathering pace and driving the fight, not only for Gary, but for the hard-won rights that British people had died to attain, that had been so brutally stripped from us by our own government, leaving us all at the mercy of foreign powers.

On January 2009 we won permission in the High Court to seek a judicial review of Jacqui Smith's decision to uphold her original decision to extradite despite the new medical evidence and Asperger's diagnosis.

Alan Johnson became Home Secretary on 5 June. On 9 June 2009 Gary's QC, Edward Fitzgerald, and barrister, Ben Cooper, put in submissions, including that Ms Smith 'under-estimated the gravity of the situation'.

It was on 3 July that a definitive game changer occurred. Karen told us that the *Daily Mail* was taking up Gary's case as their new campaign and that this was the best chance we had – it would propel Gary's case to the forefront of the news and the *Daily Mail* tended to win their campaigns.

I was over the moon. This was the very newspaper that ran hugely successful campaigns in support of the Gurkhas and to bring the murderers of Stephen Lawrence to justice. Now, how good was that? Paul Dacre, the editor of the *Daily Mail*, had decided that Gary's case would be an honourable issue to devote a campaign to and arranged for his team to come to our house and spend time getting to know us.

Everyone said, 'Oh, the *Daily Mail* will tie you up so tight that you won't be able to move. They'll demand exclusivity and won't allow you to speak to any other newspapers.' As it turned out, nothing could have been further from the truth. There were no conditions or restrictions put on us by the *Mail*, and the other newspapers continued to support Gary.

This was the first time we met Michael Seamark, a tall, slim, immaculately dressed man who was to oversee the *Daily Mail's* campaign. Michael was intelligent, warm and easy to talk to and we liked him immediately.

Journalist Allison Pearson came to our house that day too. Allison is blonde, attractive and sharp-witted, with excellent observational skills. She wrote the first feature on our family for the *Daily Mail*. Allison is a very natural writer and everything she writes just flows. The result of her interview was an excellent two-page spread with detail and humanity and an in-depth explanation of Gary's plight – and of what the prolonged threat of extradition was doing to our family.

The attention-grabbing headlines and ongoing dramatic stories by Michael Seamark and James Slack were first class and really hit the mark.

All of this led to more TV interviews, which not only raised the profile of Gary's case but, much to the delight of the National Autistic Society, also raised the profile of Asperger's syndrome and helped to educate people about autistic spectrum disorders.

CHAPTER 13

I AM NOT A NUMBER

It was 4 July 2009, American Independence Day, and I had arranged to hand a petition, and a letter signed by prominent people, into 10 Downing Street. Trudie Styler had arranged to come along to help us to highlight Gary's case.

I was just deciding on my most conventional clothes, a black jacket and trousers, when the phone rang. 'Is that Janis Sharp?'

'Yes.'

'Do you know that you're coming in to have tea with Sarah Brown, the Prime Minister's wife, today?'

'No. I knew I was coming in with a letter and a petition but I didn't know I was having tea with Sarah Brown.'

'You are indeed and Sarah is looking forward to meeting you.'

When I came off the phone and told Wilson who it was, all I kept saying was, 'How did they get our telephone number?'

'It's the government, Janis; they can get anyone's number in the blink of an eye.'

I wasn't fazed that I was going to 10 Downing Street – but I was grateful to Sarah Brown for her compassion, which gave me hope. I've never felt humbled by hierarchy but have always been impressed by the extent of someone's humanity and their courage to stand up for justice. Respect is something that has to be earned and where you are on the ladder of wealth, fame or position doesn't come into it. It's a spiritual thing – not religious, but spiritual.

Among other things, I respect Trudie Styler and Sting for fighting to protect the rainforest; David Gilmour and Polly Samson for their commitment to building homes for the homeless; Julie Christie and Duncan Campbell for using their voices and eloquence to stand up against injustice; and Melanie Riley, Karl Watkin, Trudie Styler, Michael Darwyne, David Bermingham and Gary Mulgrew for their fight against injustice and determination to change the 2003 extradition treaty.

When Wilson was driving me into Downing Street to have tea with Sarah Brown and Trudie, we initially we made good time but once we got near Fleet Street the traffic ground to a virtual halt. I was feeling a bit nervous as I was running late and we eventually reached No. 10 with one minute to spare. By the time I got out of the car and ran across the road everyone was waiting and they were all panicking and rushing me through the gate while the photographers were taking photos.

I'm a last-minute kind of person, but I usually get there in the nick of time.

Trudie looked elegant and glamorous, dressed in white. We went in the front door of No. 10. The policemen inside take your mobile phone and any camera if you have one and your belongings are kept safe in little lockers in the wall of the large foyer.

We walked up the elegant staircase of the Prime Minister's residence, which is the same staircase that Hugh Grant danced down when he played the part of the British Prime Minister who stood up to the American President in the film *Love Actually*. I hoped that our PM was about to do the same for Gary. For a moment I imagined Gordon Brown dancing down the stairs and through the rooms of No. 10 just as Hugh Grant had done, and it made me smile.

We walked into a large light and airy living room and it occurred to me then that it must seem odd living here – like living in the office. Gordon Brown would effectively be on call all the time and I imagined that Sarah Brown and the children would find it difficult to get much privacy.

I was really looking forward to having tea, as it helps me to relax. The newspapers were keen to know what was going to be said and what I would be given to eat but the only thing that mattered to me was what No. 10 had in mind to help Gary. I hoped this meeting could somehow lead to Gary being tried here in the UK and I was sure they had something up their sleeve.

Sarah Brown was standing in the living room and looked more elegant and attractive in reality than in her photos, which don't always do her justice. She was slimmer than I expected and has pale porcelain skin and hair that is a lovely shade of auburn. She walked forward to greet me and her eyes reflected an honesty and compassion that put me at my ease.

I sat upright on the edge of the large sofa and Trudie sat next to me. She and Sarah Brown seemed to know each other quite well.

Several advisers walked in to join us. I was hoping and praying that they had secretly come up with some grand plan to sort everything out for Gary.

I poured out my thoughts and ideas and related other cases where British computer hackers had been accused of considerably more serious crimes against the US than anything Gary had done, yet they had been tried in the UK and at worst received a very mild sentence.

I also pointed out that Gary was accused of accessing the

computers prior to and during 2002 – before the extradition treaty was even written, years before it began to be used by the UK, *and that it wasn't allowed to be made retrospective.*

The advisers were making notes as I was speaking.

Sarah said, 'Do you realise you're up against some very formidable people?'

'Yes, I do,' I replied. I was, in fact, all too well aware of this.

I also knew that an adviser existed who was nicknamed the 'smiling assassin' by politicians.

I went on to speak about Gary having Asperger's and being suicidal, and about him preferring death to forcibly being taken from everyone and everything he had ever known.

'Gary can't go there and that's all there is to it,' said Trudie assertively.

Trudie is no shrinking violet. She is elegant, articulate, intelligent and compassionate, and went on to speak up for Gary at length.

'Contact the American ambassador to try and get his help,' said Sarah.

Glancing at Trudie with eyes full she added, 'It's very difficult.'

We said goodbye and Trudie and I walked out into the sunshine. I had been feeling optimistic but was worried about Sarah's suggestion that we should contact the American ambassador: surely 10 Downing Street was in a significantly better position to do that than I was?

The photographers were waiting outside and were all shouting, 'What did she say, Janis?' 'Did it go well?' 'What did you get to eat, Janis? Strawberries? Cream scones?'

I was evasive and just smiled.

I later privately told Michael Seamark from the *Mail* that I felt the meeting had gone well and as far as tea was concerned, we hadn't been given any. There was only water.

'Water! Well, I can't write that,' said Michael, and we both laughed.

Wilson and I drove home, happy in the knowledge that both influential and powerful people cared enough about Gary to meet with us and to hopefully find a solution. I also thought that it being Independence Day could mean that the UK government might be about to prove that the UK was truly independent from the US.

Just two days after my visit to Downing Street, Lord Carlile, the Home Office adviser on terror laws, stated in the newspapers, 'Extraditing Mr McKinnon would be cruel and unconscionable when he could be prosecuted in the UK.'

I was truly heartened by his words. That he would say this publicly I thought was politically very brave. I had never met him but he seemed to genuinely care about what was happening to Gary. I later learned that Lord Carlile apparently has a grandson who is autistic.

• • •

We had a court hearing for a judicial review against both Jacqui Smith and the Crown Prosecution Service on 14 July 2009. Gary's lawyers were making a bid at the High Court to try to legally force the CPS into allowing a trial in the UK, challenging a refusal by the Director of Public Prosecutions to sanction a trial in this country.

We were back in the Royal Courts of Justice. I had been here too many times to expect justice in a US extradition case, but hoped for it nevertheless.

This seemed to be Gary's last chance. Would he ever be free? Or was he doomed to carry on living in this twilight world, this surreal limbo he had been confined to for the last seven years?

We walked through the vast space of the great hall, which, although cathedral-like, held none of the hope of sanctuary that could once be found in such places. We approached what should be an impressive flight of stairs but it was a cold unfeeling place. Somehow, in extradition cases, you can't help but feel that the decision has already been made and that the job of the judges is to find a plausible justification for it.

The court where Gary's case was being heard was further up a smaller flight of stairs which brings you out among a collection of glass-cased costumes and hanging wigs, none of which do anything to raise your spirits. But perhaps that's the idea, like the hard uncomfortable benches – nothing is designed to make you feel at ease.

There is a wide passage with arched stone recesses that each have an oak table and bench where barristers and clients congregate to discuss their cases.

Watching over this area sits a large bust of a judge made entirely out of metal hangers, with the hooks pointed outward like a halo around the figure.

The ominous use of hangers, 'things that hang', to make this judge's image, also did nothing to raise my spirits. I thought he must be the infamous 'hanging judge' but I was wrong. Ben Cooper, Gary's barrister, told me that the figure was that of a good man.

The case that day was a judicial review into the decision of the previous Home Secretary, Jacqui Smith: in particular that she did not take proper account of the impact that extradition, a pre-trial detention of indeterminate length and a prospective sixty-year sentence would have on his mental health.

The day's hearing also included an additional judicial review into the decision of the Crown Prosecution Service not to proceed with a UK trial. For the first time we had been presented with an internal CPS report on the original evidence the American prosecutors had offered to justify their request for extradition.

Prima facie evidence had been required in 2002 before the extradition treaty had been signed, but the CPS confirmed that no evidence to back up the US allegations had ever been presented to them. The report, written by a CPS lawyer, dismissed the US submissions to them as hearsay and inadmissible. The report also questioned the lack of detail, and questioned whether proper procedures relating to the standard of evidence had been followed. It was a damning report on the quality of the American submissions by the very Crown Prosecution Service who acts on behalf of the American prosecutor in extradition cases.

We were presented with that report only days before this hearing, normally far too late to have a defence expert go over the details. Fortunately, I had heard of Professor Peter Sommer of the London School of Economics, one of the leading forensic computer experts in the world. I managed to get his contact details the night before the court case, and Gary's solicitor Karen formally instructed him.

Professor Peter Sommer literally sat up all night to produce a detailed analysis of the CPS report – and his own disparaging report on the lack of normal security measures in place on the computers which Gary had allegedly accessed.

He stated that the financial damage claimed by the US appeared to be for basic security that should have been installed in the first place but wasn't. Had it been installed, it would have flagged up Gary's presence.

Professor Sommer had dealt with the CPS on other occasions and knew the police officers involved. He could not understand why they had not quizzed the US about the lack of evidence provided and why Association of Police Chief Officers (ACPO) evidence standards appeared not to have been followed.

Gary was at home hiding from the world, not being able to face being back in court. But Edward Fitzgerald needed Gary there to explain to him the intricate technicalities of exactly what he had done. Edward is renowned for his ability to deliver complex arguments in a skilled manner.

I rang Gary, and Lucy answered. Gary was upset and wouldn't come to court; he was scared witless. Karen said he had to come – Edward needed him to be there. Eventually I managed to persuade Gary that there was no choice. Lucy accompanied him but he was clearly terrified, and even walking through the gauntlet of press was a huge ordeal for him.

Gary sat in court with Edward to try to explain exactly what he had done, but it had been so long that he could barely remember, so started to try to think what he might have done and how he might have done it. I mean, more than seven years had passed!

Ironically we were there in court to try to prove that Gary was guilty of computer misuse, as this could have allowed him to be tried in the UK.

Gary had admitted from the very start, in March 2002, to a summary section 1 computer misuse offence, but even a summary section 2 or section 3 computer misuse offence, deemed more serious, carried only a sentence of six months when Gary was first arrested in 2002.

The court rose as Lord Justice Sir Stanley Burnton and Justice Wilkie took their places on their dais in the no. 1 court, looking down over the massed media presence. Many young journalists having to sit on the floor made the court look more akin to a student 'sit-in' at a university.

The benches were filled with our barristers and solicitors,

the Home Office's barristers and solicitors and the Crown Prosecution Service's barristers and solicitors, each with a large pile of legal folders, and with friends and interested parties.

The judges appeared to be enjoying the ramifications of Gary's case and seemed amused that someone was applying to the court to be allowed to be prosecuted rather than the usual fight against it.

Throughout the hearing, the noises the judges made were promising. In spite of previous disappointments, you never fail to hope.

During the discourse, when they referred to the House of Lords attempting to justify the disparity of sentencing by suggesting that hypothetically an offence against the Maritime and Aviation Act could have been a possibility and could have led to a life sentence, Justice Burnton said 'and pigs might fly', and so did my hopes.

My heart was soaring with the possibility that we had found a fair judge and a brave judge, whose mind was not already made up beforehand.

After hearing of several other hacking cases which had occurred at the same time or prior to Gary's – all of which were tried in the UK and all of which resulted in acquittal or a small fine or a low sentence – the judge agreed with Gary's QC that most of those cases were deemed much more serious than Gary's.

When Justice Stanley Burnton read the CPS report and when the CPS admitted that they had been given no evidence by the US, just hearsay, Justice Burnton said, 'Do you know how embarrassing this would be for the CPS if Mr McKinnon was ever to be tried in the UK?'

The barrister for the CPS responded, 'Yes, M'Lord.'

I could hardly believe what I was hearing. Was *this* why the CPS was refusing to prosecute Gary? Fear of embarrassment?

Gary's QC, Edward Fitzgerald, fought hard for Gary to be

tried here. Watching him was a revelation. Edward's style had no abrasiveness or attempts to dominate. He didn't raise his voice for dramatic effect, or try to act as though he was in a Shakespearian play. There was no arrogance in the man, just a genuine sharpness of mind and a quest for justice.

Edward approached the judges at close quarters and looked into their eyes as he implored them to see sense. No ivory tower would allow the judges to hide, or escape from the honesty of Edward's heart and mind, as he spoke to them in such an intimately persuasive manner that all present felt as though they were privy to a private conversation.

Lord Justice Burnton eventually turned to Edward and, referring to the absence of evidence, said: 'In that case he can go on a plane and he'll come straight back again.'

'But that's not what would happen,' said Edward. 'That's not how it works in America.'

Simon Baron-Cohen had also written a strong report on the effect extradition would have on Gary which concluded:

I have a real concern that he would not survive a term of imprisonment. I am stating this as strong assertion because to put a vulnerable adult who has a disability into a situation of imprisonment when that adult has [stated] that suicide would be preferable, to avoid the suffering that he fears he will experience in a prison, is a decision that should carry with it some responsibility for any consequences. The courts, for example, should not be able to claim that they were unaware of the risks prison might pose to Mr McKinnon if he suffers a complete psychiatric breakdown or commits suicide. The courts should have it on their record that if they order him to be detained, it is in the full knowledge that this outcome is a serious and dangerous possibility.

Justice Burnton described the professor's words as 'going beyond his remit'.

Every British judge seems to choose to ignore the fact that America often inflicts what we regard as outrageously disproportionate sentences for crimes that would carry a significantly lighter sentence here, if sentence there was.

Edward Fitzgerald referred to one such case, where a young British woman named Chantal McCorkle, married to an American and living in America, ran a business with her husband telling people about buying repossessed property, refurbishing it and selling it on for profit. They promoted it with a video saying 'you too can have a lifestyle like this', and a TV ad that showed luxury houses, cars etc. that they supposedly had, but didn't, as it was just an advert.

When someone officially complained that they didn't make money, Chantal and her husband were charged and found guilty of 'infomercial fraud', apparently because they used actors and didn't actually own the houses featured in the commercials.

The American court sentenced Chantal to twenty-four years in prison. She was put in leg irons in a secure American prison, because, being British, she was considered a flight risk. Her husband, being American, served his sentence in an open prison.

After ten years in prison Chantal, known as 'goody two-shoes' to all her friends, asked to serve the remainder of her sentence in the UK and was told no, that her crimes were too serious!

Edward Fitzgerald had visited Chantal in America and shortly after he raised her case during Gary's hearing, she re-applied and was repatriated back to the UK, where she served a short time in prison and was then given parole. She is now safely back with her family. But all that time in prison may have deprived her of the chance of motherhood, a heavy price to pay for a non-violent crime.

Lucy was also approaching the age of forty: her biological clock was ticking and Gary would never agree to be an absent father. I am still hoping that they too haven't been deprived of the chance to have children.

When the hearing ended Trudie Styler stood at Gary's side on the steps of the court. Hundreds of flashbulbs went off as Gary clenched his teeth, waiting for it to be over.

CHAPTER 14

CHANGE THE WORLD

On 15 July 2009, I was invited to do an interview for BBC's *Newsnight*. I was pleased as it was a serious news programme with credibility. Jeremy Paxman popped his head into the room I was waiting in beforehand and said, 'I hope you won't be so nervous that you won't be able to speak.'

'Of course I'll be able to speak.'

'Well, that wasn't the case with Vivienne Westwood when I interviewed her. After a very long silence on a live show, she asked if we could start again.'

'Well, I'm not a fashion icon,' I smiled.

The producer then spoke to me at length to gauge that I was capable of fighting Gary's corner. She then spoke to the other guest who was being interviewed alongside me – an ex-CPS prosecutor. The producer stressed that he was to remember to say all the things that he had said he would say and not to hold back.

We then went on air alongside Jeremy Paxman.

The ex-CPS prosecutor made an experienced and pretty ruthless opponent and stated several times that Gary should be extradited. I was confident I could deal with all his points as by that time I knew the extradition treaty and the treatment of other accused hackers inside out.

Jeremy Paxman intervened to argue on my behalf much of the time but I felt frustrated as I believed that I could have held my own in this instance – but maybe everyone thinks that. My opponent was making disingenuous remarks, and Gary's life was at stake. I was in fight mode.

In the green room afterwards I had a heated debate with the ex-CPS prosecutor and told him that extradition without evidence that could be contested in a British court was wrong and that the US does not extradite Americans for crimes committed while they were physically on US soil. Jeremy Paxman was standing leaning against the door watching us with his arms folded during the off-air debate and eventually said, 'I almost feel sorry for this man.'

I have to say, I thought Jeremy's sympathies were a tad misplaced, as I was a mother whose son's life was on the line, and the prosecutor was a man who argued in court for a living.

The prosecutor looked embarrassed and, I thought, possibly even ashamed after I debated with him. I think that I might have made him realise not only the personal cost to people fighting extradition, but the cost to their families too. I also think and hope that I made him realise the unfairness of this one-sided extradition treaty we had with the US.

When I got home all the Free Gary supporters on Twitter were tweeting their anger at the ex-prosecutor and telling me 'Well done'.

The next morning it was back to racking my brains trying to think of what else I could do. I had written many times over to every MP in all three main parties and to the Prime Minister and to Barack Obama. I needed to do something else to raise the profile of Gary's case even further.

I began to stay up writing to politicians until 2 a.m. and would go to bed and then wake up at 5 a.m. with my mind racing and thinking of what else I could do. I researched other cases where extradition had been refused and studied extradition law.

I've always believed that knowledge is power and I hoped that the pen really was mightier than the sword.

• • •

When I went over to see Gary, he looked stiff and withdrawn. His teeth were clenched, his hands were held in fists and he was in robotic mode. I could see the absolute tightness of his mind and body. He wouldn't answer the phone and was angry that anyone was ringing him. He didn't want to speak or to see anyone and although I could usually bring Gary round to a point, he was slipping further and further away. He once told me that when he was very stressed, he felt physically tiny and everything and everyone around him was far away until he actually became like a dot in the room.

I put my arms around him but his body stiffened. I was trying to bring him round and to keep him here but he was trying to stay inside himself, in a place where no one could reach him. He was rigid and the veins in his neck were straining. I could see his eyes were full. I didn't know if he was about to lose control or to collapse in a heap on the floor but I had no intention of leaving him, that was for sure.

Gary was fading before our eyes and the terror that he might take his own life was ever-present. We were living on a knife-edge with no respite.

I couldn't relax as I had to stay on top of everything. I was playing chess with the grand masters, people in power who'd had years to learn what I was trying to learn in record time, but come hell or high water I was going to do it. There was no choice.

There were times I'd lie in bed feeling helpless but then suddenly I would feel this power surging inside me and I felt strong and knew I could do it.

I knew I had to make it bigger than just me.

We're musicians, and if I could get famous musicians to help us they could get the attention of the most powerful people in the world. Musicians are known for fighting for just causes.

An old friend, John Davies, was a neighbour of David Gilmour of Pink Floyd and also knew him socially so I contacted John and he agreed to pass on a letter to David.

Then, out of the blue, I suddenly remembered that when we'd met our old friend Joe Winnington years ago in Muswell Hill, Joe had said, 'Guess what? My sister Polly has just got married to David Gilmour.'

'Wow!' we said. 'How amazing.'

Wilson and I had married in Wood Green with the music of Pink Floyd's *Dark Side of the Moon* playing during the ceremony. I had also read that David Cameron's favourite album was *Dark Side of the Moon*, so this was all sounding promising and everyone knows that David Gilmour is a really good man.

This was almost too good to be true, plus Joe had known Gary since he was six years old! This had to be another stroke of destiny.

I sat down and wrote a letter to David Gilmour explaining Gary's situation, and I wrote to Joe, who we hadn't seen in years. Joe rang us as soon as he got my letter, telling me they had been following the case but that he had no idea that it was the same Gary he had known as a child as he hadn't seen us for years.

I decided that if we could get a song to President Obama from people in David Gilmour's league that the President would at least be made aware of Gary's plight – and then, surely, he would help us.

Graham Nash gave me permission to slightly change the lyrics of his song 'Chicago (We Can Change the World)'. This was a famous song about injustice and the Chicago Eight. As Obama cut his teeth in Chicago it would be perfect.

When Crosby, Stills & Nash were later playing the song 'Chicago' at Glastonbury, Graham Nash got a rapturous response from the audience when he spoke about and championed Gary during their set. He also did interviews in support of Gary and said:

I think the US government are being heavy handed.

If you open the Pandora's Box of the digital world you'd better watch out what happens. You've got no control. The toothpaste is out of the tube and you can't get it back in.

You have this autistic guy sitting in his apartment in London tapping away, looking for UFOs and flying saucers.

I fear they'll throw Gary into a US jail and we'll never hear about him again. If we bring enough attention to the case, they'll have to give it up.

It's a preposterous situation so I say f*** them – I want to help Gary.

Our friend James Litherland, a great musician who's played with the best, added his acoustic guitar and vocals to a backing track that Wilson had recorded, and Jim also arranged for gospel singers he knows to add their vocals to the track.

On 23 July 2009 we emailed the backing track of 'Chicago' to David Gilmour, who was in the midst of leaving to go on holiday with his family. Unbelievably, David took the time to add his vocal then and there. I can never repay him for that.

I decided to write to Bob Geldof and to follow up my letter with phone calls to his office asking him to add his vocals to the track. It was so hard for me to do this as I avoid the phone whenever possible – for some reason, whenever it rings it makes me jump. It was also incredibly hard to get any response from Bob Geldof's office, but I hassled them continuously and eventually he obliged, adding so much to the track.

Chrissie Hynde of the Pretenders also came on board, which was amazing. Being American it was courageous of Chrissie to do this for Gary, and huge respect to her for that.

Sir Paul McCartney also agreed to add his voice, as did Dennis Locorriere (ex-Doctor Hook), and Skin from Skunk Anansie. However, by then the boat that David Gilmour's Astoria Studio was on needed its hull rebuilt, unfortunately preventing further recording from taking place.

The Orb also did an excellent version of the song which is featured on their *Metallic Spheres* album, which David Gilmour plays guitar on. David and The Orb's Alex Paterson donated royalties from it to help fund all aspects of Gary's campaign and for his psychiatric treatment (e.g. to the Maudsley NHS Trust and also for his current ongoing therapy with Professor van Deurzen).

We also arranged for part of the royalties from the song to go to human rights organisations such as Liberty, and autism charities such as the National Autistic Society, ART and Research Autism.

We can never repay David Gilmour and Alex Paterson for all they have done for our family when we were at the lowest point.

David and his manager Paul Loasby arranged for the song to be recorded and filmed in RAK Studios in St John's Wood and, knowing that Gary was also a musician, they asked Gary to add his voice, which he did.

The entire day in the studio was incredibly well organised and Paul Loasby ensured that interviews could take place in comfortable surroundings, with TV crews placed in unobtrusive positions that didn't crowd Gary at all.

It was strange being in RAK again, as this was the very studio

Wilson and I were in many years before when we were offered a record deal that we foolishly lost by not signing with the manager who arranged the deal. Our lives were becoming more surreal by the day.

Gary wore a plain grey shirt and on the way to the studio I was looking at shops we drove past in the hope of finding him something special to wear, as the recording would be filmed. I got Wilson to stop the car at the one and only shop that looked the least bit promising. All of the clothes were underwhelming and extremely overpriced. Gary didn't want anything that would make him look dressed up, so I chose the only T-shirt I could find that looked good.

When we got to the studio there was nowhere to park so Gary and I went in ahead while Wilson drove around for ages looking for a parking space.

As soon as we saw Chrissie Hynde with her Animal Liberation T-shirt we were at our ease. I told Chrissie that I'd been a vegetarian since I was nineteen years old and Gary had been a vegetarian for his entire life, and Chrissie said with a smile, 'I knew I was backing the right people.'

Chrissie Hynde is shy but she was amazing with Gary and took the time to speak to him and to put him at his ease. She was lovely.

Gary was nervous. He didn't wear the T-shirt I'd bought and initially stood so still that he seemed almost frozen. He barely moved during the recording but his rich, deep voice added so much to the song and it was good to see Gary playing the piano again, even if only very briefly.

The studio had allowed some TV stations to attend the session – including Russian, German and American ones – and we did interviews with them all. I was worried about doing one with CNN in case of bias, but the interview was a fair one.

I'll be forever grateful to David Gilmour and Polly for all they've done for us; and to Paul Loasby for his first-class organisation of the event; and to Joe, a dear friend who came through for us in our time of need, despite not having seen us for years.

We got home and switched on the TV and there it was, 'Chicago', the song in all its glory. What was wonderful and totally unexpected was that Chrissie Hynde and David Gilmour – who rarely give interviews – did so in support of Gary.

We were watching and listening intently as David said:

> No one on the side of officialdom seems to be doing very much to help this chap Gary. He's being done by a law that was put into place for terrorism post-9/11, and this guy just isn't a terrorist. You know it's mad to sort of treat him as if he's a fully blown terrorist sort of chap. He's just a simple guy who's taken things a little bit too far and we should just let our own justice system here in England deal with him in whatever way they see fit. He doesn't need to be carted off to America to face the sort of sentences that have been bandied about in the press.

The song was aired on TV stations throughout the world and people could donate whatever they could afford to download the song. It was produced by Chris Thomas and, in another coincidence, a young Gary had helped to look after Chris Thomas's two children at summer camp. When Warner Bros offered us the record deal that we didn't sign in the end, Chris Thomas was their chosen producer.

After Gary's arrest every waking moment was spent trying to make sure he'd be safe. I hadn't written a song for ages, but when I was finding it hard to cope I'd turn the music in the car up really loud and get lost in it. Music was my therapy.

CHAPTER 15

LICENSED TO KILL

On 25 July 2009 I looked through the morning papers and read that the Labour MP Andrew MacKinlay had resigned and was going to stand down at the next election because of Gary. He believed extradition could and should be refused by our government, and what was happening to Gary was the final straw for him.

Now, when a man stands up and is willing to throw his career to the wall to help another human being, you know that man is a good man. It can never be taken with a pinch of salt when a career is ended on principle and few have the courage to make their mark by doing something so spectacularly selfless.

Totally out of the blue, things kept coming up for us. Searching through the papers I saw that Gordon Brown had spoken out for Gary and expressed sympathy for what was happening to him. This was good and, as Nicky Campbell said when he interviewed me on his BBC 5 Live radio show, Gordon Brown was the Prime Minister, he could refuse to extradite if he wanted to.

We were hopeful but I knew that, for whatever reason, our government are afraid of upsetting the US, whereas the US are not even the tiniest bit afraid of upsetting our government.

On 31 July we arrived again at the Royal Courts of Justice to hear the decision on Gary's judicial review. The streets outside were thronging with press and TV crews from all over the world. This exceeded even the huge media presence we were now used to.

Wilson and I sat down in court; Gary was at home with Lucy. The clerk of the courts appeared and said, 'All rise.'

We all rose, as Justice Stanley Burnton and Justice Wilkie made their entrance and took up their positions on their dais, overlooking those assembled below. Despite the judges having seemed to be on side at the hearing, I knew inside that they were going to rule against Gary, and they did.

Instead of crying I felt angry for having been taken in by their sympathetic approach at the previous hearing.

The court atmosphere was electrifying as journalists hurried out to ring their editors and the world's media were clamouring for interviews. I walked out of the court in defiant mood and, in front of hundreds of TV cameras, preached the injustice of this iniquitous extradition treaty that had never been intended to be used against someone like Gary. The prosecutors may have believed they had won but the mood of the country was against them and morally they had lost.

I was giving endless interviews and felt like a piece of rope in a tug of war.

'This way, Janis ... no, over here, Janis ... look up ... look down ... our crew are just across the road ... come this way ... no, we're next, our satellite van is just here ... no, we're next...'

And then I heard Melanie Riley's voice. 'Do you want some help, Janis?'

'Yes please, Melanie,' and she got the media to line up, told them whose turn was next and whipped everything into shape. The relief I felt was incredible.

The last interview I did was with Keir Simmons from ITV's *News at Ten*. Keir could see I was waning, so he hired rooms at the Waldorf Hotel, just yards away, and ordered tea, coffee, scones, sandwiches, cakes, drinks and even lunch if I wanted. It was so good to just sit down and to have tea and something to eat in this quieter atmosphere.

Keir had the computer switched on; he called me over and said, 'Look. Gary is trending worldwide on Twitter. Out of everyone in the entire world, Gary is leading and is the number one trend on Twitter.'

• • •

A few days later, Keir and his colleague proposed the idea of flying me over to Washington to raise Gary's case at the White House. I realised that meeting with influential people in the US and doing interviews there might help Gary, but I was worried it could become a media circus which might backfire on us.

When I told Gary about it he said, 'No! Don't go! They'll blow the plane up, they'll kill you; you can't go.'

Our lives were so surreal that virtually nothing would surprise me. I decided not to go, which made Gary happy.

The following week yet another offer of help appeared. This time it was from an Edinburgh-based Scots entrepreneur named Luke Heron, who said that if America's biggest problem was Gary supposedly having caused damage of around $700,000 (£470,000), he would write a cheque for that amount there and then, if it would end the matter.

Lord Popat also offered to help us, which was incredibly kind of him. Lord Popat is a Conservative life peer, born in Uganda, who immigrated to the UK at the age of seventeen with only £10 in his pocket.

In September 2009 Karen submitted an appeal to the newly opened British Supreme Court. This really was Gary's last hope.

In a bid to garner further political support, with the help of Matthew Downie from the National Autistic Society I attended all three party conferences and Matthew and his colleague accompanied me. We met with Chris Huhne at the Lib Dem conference in Bournemouth on 19 September, a beautiful sunny day. Chris Huhne had joined with David Davis and Michael Meacher just ten days earlier to form a cross-party delegation to persuade the Home Secretary to refuse extradition – unfortunately to no avail.

What was striking about the Lib Dem party conference was that there was no security and you could wander around more or less wherever you wanted to. The conference was held in the historic Highcliff Hotel, situated above the promenade. The relaxed atmosphere made it feel almost like being on holiday as we sat out on the terrace overlooking the sea and, just for a minute, I could become lost in the dramatic views across the channel.

It seemed odd to think that a decision that changed history was taken by politicians in this same hotel, overlooking this same seascape, in May 1940, at a time when German troops were pouring into Holland and Belgium.

Labour met at the Highcliff Hotel for its first conference of the Second World War and the committee voted unanimously that Labour would not serve under Chamberlain. That decision led to Neville Chamberlain resigning and recommending Winston Churchill, who was then appointed Prime Minister by King George VI.

Chris Huhne was friendly and interesting to talk to. He was keen to help and although there were no fixed ideas on how he could do this, his 'Freedom Bill' held real promise and we knew we had solid support from the Lib Dems. Chris Huhne suggested I should become an MP and I said that I'd scare them if I did.

I met with Keith Vaz at the Labour Party conference in Brighton, also a fantastic setting, with the sun shining again.

In stark contrast to the Lib Dem Party conference, the security for the Labour conference was massive, with a very large police presence. However, this coincided with a happy and relaxed atmosphere in Brighton. Everyone was cycling along the promenade, as the road is flat and perfect for bicycle rides.

Keith Vaz came to meet us, bursting with ideas and with a very upbeat and positive attitude. He had an incredible network of influential people both in the UK and in the US, including Jesse Jackson.

Keith Vaz was one of only ten Labour MPs who voted against their own government and insisted that the 2003 extradition treaty with the US should be reviewed and forum added as previously promised.

Mr Vaz informed us that the Home Affairs Select Committee, which he chaired, had already arranged to raise concerns about the extradition treaty and we discovered later that the majority of this excellent cross-party group were also in favour of Gary being tried in the UK.

I then met with Michael Meacher at the Labour conference. Michael is a very principled MP and is one of a minority of Labour MPs that I recognise as being socialist, in the way that Tony Benn was.

Michael had teamed up with Chris Huhne and David Davis on 9 September 2009 to champion Gary's case and also appeared on the BBC's *The One Show* with me.

Matthew Downie from the National Autistic Society (NAS) was well organised and an absolute dynamo. I could imagine

Matthew being in a powerful political position in the future. He also suggested he might be able to arrange for us to be offered the use of Alexandra Palace in Muswell Hill if we wanted to arrange a concert in support of Gary.

Next on the list was the Conservative Party conference in Manchester on 7 October 2009, where I met with shadow Home Secretary Chris Grayling. The place was buzzing and I somehow felt that the Conservatives were going to win the election this time round.

The conversation we had was friendly and productive. Mr Grayling said that, as Home Secretary, he would review all the medical evidence and would do all he could to have Gary tried in the UK if the Conservative party was elected. I said, 'You say that now but once in power when you are Home Secretary, the same government advisers will give you the same advice and will say you have to extradite.'

'No,' he said. 'Ministers decide and I will decide.'

Dominic Grieve raised Gary's case in his speech at the party conference, and said:

> And can somebody tell me how counter-terrorism will be served by extraditing Gary McKinnon to the United States for hacking into government computers in search of UFOs?
>
> Ministers say they can't block his extradition.
>
> They can't override the law.
>
> But we have proposed a change in that law, sitting in the House of Lords right now, that would prevent the McKinnon case ever happening again.
>
> Why hasn't the government accepted it?
>
> When will Gordon Brown wake up then stand up for the rights of British citizens?
>
> Our extradition laws are a mess.

They're one-sided.

A Conservative government will rewrite them.

Mark Lever from the NAS is another amazing man and he and his colleague Mathew Downie had arranged for me to do a speech at the Conservative Party conference NAS fringe meeting on autism, vulnerable people and the law.

Shortly before I sat on the panel along with Gary's excellent MP, David Burrowes, we got a phone call from Gary's barrister, Ben Cooper, to say that the Supreme Court had ruled against even hearing our appeal to review the medical evidence. This was in spite of them having agreed to allow Ian Norris's appeal, which was given on the same point of law as Gary's! Due to his mental health issues, Gary should have had more rights for his appeal to be heard under that point of law.

Ian Norris had worked his way up from the shop floor to become managing director of Morgan Crucible. Despite winning his case in the Lords, he was subsequently extradited to the US for obstruction of justice relating to the crime of price fixing, despite the Lords ruling that price fixing was not a crime in the UK at that time.

I had to ring and tell Gary the devastating news that the Supreme Court refused to even hear his appeal. I didn't want him to read it in tomorrow's newspapers. I knew that Gary would be distraught and might give up; I was away from home and afraid of what he might do. I spoke to Lucy first to make sure she was there with Gary to support him, but she was also distraught and I couldn't console them.

I joined the panel and as I started to deliver my speech at the conference I felt warm tears beginning to fill my eyes and I thought, 'No, Janis.' I hoped no one noticed and hadn't heard my voice beginning to break.

I remember seeing Mathew Parris in the audience before every emotion inside me came pouring out in a speech that magnified my anger, anguish and heartbreak.

Matthew Downie from the NAS was standing at the back listening intently and said afterwards that the speech was one of the most emotive and riveting he had ever heard.

Emotion transmits to other hearts and minds and I just hoped that some there felt the same as Matthew – and were influential enough to help Gary.

I wasn't allowed to mention the court's decision to anyone as it wasn't to be officially announced until the next day, but Matthew Downie knew by my reaction and my side of the telephone conversation I had with Gary's barrister.

• • •

The following day when I spoke outside the Royal Courts of Justice I was distraught, angry and ready to explode. I could feel this power and fury flowing through my blood and I knew that no one was going to take my son. I was in fight mode. I felt Gary was betrayed by our own courts and by our own government. I wouldn't allow myself to be shocked into silence by people in power who thought it was fine to betray their own citizens with a one-sided extradition treaty they'd been fooled into believing was intended only for terrorists.

At times like this the words flowed from within with no thought required. The feeling is akin to playing guitar when doing a gig and your mind wanders and the notes come pouring out, creating a heartfelt solo that leaves you wondering where it came from.

Despite our courts and politicians pointing to Ireland and France as examples of countries with the same treaty *both*

Ireland and France had included the right to refuse to extradite their own nationals. It seems that having a 'special relationship' isn't all it's cracked up to be.

I was worried about Gary. I could see his demons were taking hold of him. His mood was odd and his mind wasn't with us. When I got home something made me look on the internet at something Gary had asked me to order some weeks before. I don't know why it came into my head but it did. I looked through all of the things I had ordered and there it was: potassium chloride. The definition on the internet read, 'a metal halide salt composed of potassium and chlorine'.

It sounded harmless enough. I carried on reading until I came to the words 'uses of potassium chloride'. My heart almost stopped as I read the words 'used in medicine in lethal injections'. A chill ran through my body.

I was shaking as I carried on reading and came to the words 'potassium chloride is used in the US to execute people on death row'.

I could hear torturous muted screaming sounds like a wounded animal and realised that the cries were coming from me, as I sat hugging my knees to my chest, rocking backwards and forwards.

When I was able to speak, I rang Lucy, told her what I'd found and asked her to search the flat. Lucy rang back crying when she had eventually found the potassium chloride and disposed of it. This substance was licensed to kill. How on earth could something used to execute healthy people be described as medicine and be so easy to obtain via the internet? I mean, people could take their own lives with their families left believing they had simply had a heart attack. Worse still, a murderer could execute his or her victim(s) with this substance, leaving only evidence of a heart attack and with no indication of foul play. I later discovered this had happened recently in America when a nurse was able to become a serial killer with the aid of potassium chloride.

Gary's whole demeanour told us that his life was at imminent risk.

I rang Matthew Downie at the NAS. He could tell how panicked I was and immediately arranged for us to meet Professor Jeremy Turk at Gary's barrister's office in Doughty Street Chambers.

Gary didn't want to leave the house and was refusing to come with me but I knew he had to see someone urgently and I had no intention of leaving him alone. He trusted me and he trusted Lucy and Karen, so Lucy and I told him that Karen needed to speak to him urgently and we had to go. It was difficult to get Gary to even walk out of the door. His mind was in a dark place and it was becoming almost impossible to reach him. I knew I could lose him if we waited but we eventually got him into the car and into town.

Doughty Street Chambers is next to the Charles Dickens Museum, which used to be Dickens's London house. Sadly our judicial system was also beginning to feel Dickensian.

When we arrived at the chambers Professor Simon Baron-Cohen was there waiting to introduce Gary to Professor Turk. Both of them had just flown into Heathrow and came straight from the airport to Doughty Street.

We waited outside while Professor Turk spent time with Gary, who broke down and wept continuously. We were informed that Gary was most definitely suicidal and he was put on immediate medication. Gary hates taking medication but for the first time he didn't resist it: although the drugs made him feel zombie-like, his mind needed to be cocooned for now. It was a survival thing and we were all painfully aware of just how close we had come to tragedy.

We made arrangements for Professor Turk to oversee Gary's psychiatric care on a regular basis and to monitor his medication.

• • •

In November 2009, Home Secretary Alan Johnson announced that he would not block extradition.

Later that month I gave evidence to the cross-party Home Affairs Select Committee in Portcullis House. Gary's barrister told me that it was unprecedented for a lay person to be invited to give evidence under these circumstances. Committee chairman Keith Vaz obviously understood the importance of taking evidence from people directly affected by extradition.

I felt that I managed to get important points across and that the committee listened and took on board what I'd said.

Alan Johnson was called afterwards to give evidence and to be questioned by the committee. A lot of what he said was clearly wrong but as he gave evidence after me, I was unable to correct his errors.

Just after a break, before going back into the inquiry, Alan Johnson walked past me in the corridor outside the Thatcher Room, completely surrounded by a female contingent, apparently to ensure I couldn't speak to him. I held out my hand to shake his and he responded with an extremely brief brushing of the hand, while continuing to walk along the corridor, not stopping for a second. His female colleagues/advisers encircling him as he walked made for an incredibly odd scene.

The taste of salty tears on my lower lip made me annoyed at myself. It's just that I had stupidly expected more from him, and even from the female colleagues who encircled him. Alan Johnson was shown inordinate compassion from others after his mother died when he was a child. You foolishly assume that compassion begets compassion, but although Gordon Brown had felt compassion for Gary, it seems that Alan Johnson had not.

No politician in or out of power should be allowed to pronounce someone guilty when there has been no trial, as this flies in the face of the foundation of British justice. To publicly attack a British citizen, presumably in order to ingratiate yourself with another government, is to my mind an act beneath contempt.

• • •

As if things weren't bad enough, in December 2009 death threats were directed against Gary and me, and against almost every journalist who had reported the least bit favourably on our case. One such email said, 'We will start hurting British citizens every day that you continue your stance against US extradition … You will be contacted when this happens so you know we are for fucking real.'

Afua Hirsch from *The Guardian* wrote: 'The irony is that one of the arguments being put forward by McKinnon is that such is the intensity of hatred towards him in the US that he would not be treated fairly. Maybe death threats against journalists will end up forming part of his legal team's submissions.'

The journalists called the police in. The death threats Gary and I received from the same source were personal and more sinister, and frightening enough that we also had to call the police in. We started watching the cars behind us, wondering if we were being followed, and would turn off several times to lose any car we had concerns about. We would start to think people were looking sinister, like the man in sunglasses at the bus stop outside the house who looked out of place somehow, and like a cartoon image of a spy. We were suddenly thrust into living in a *Bourne Identity*-type scenario. Anyone approaching us suddenly or unexpectedly, or calling at our door, possibly wanting to read our meter or clean our windows, put us on our guard.

Death threats have to be taken seriously and we became vigilant to the point that we even started checking under our car for bombs. We were shocked when one day we found an object on the underside of our car. It looked like a small mobile phone inside a pouch fixed to our car with magnets. A friend who was with us told us it was a tracker and we stupidly pulled it off in a panic and smashed it into the ground. Had it been a bomb, we would most likely have been blown to smithereens.

We had no idea whether whoever was tracking our movements was the person or people who had sent us death threats, or the US government, or a journalist trying to find out where Gary was so they could photograph him. Of course, we imagined only the worst.

There had been a man running a website for American expats who claimed to have worked for the US embassy and professed to have been to funerals with American Presidents, and his rhetoric against Gary seemed similar to the style of writing that was used in the death threats. The police investigated and found that the threats came from a man in America. No prosecution was ever initiated by the UK or the US. We firmly believed that had the position been reversed the US would have extradited whoever was responsible for death threats against one of their countrymen.

It was a freezing cold day on 15 December when Gary's friend Dhiren and Lucy helped arrange a demo for Gary outside the Home Office. Mark from the Free Gary website publicised detailed directions and excellent advice on what to do and what not to do and what rights protesters have. Nick Clegg knew about the demo and his assistant rang asking me to meet Nick Clegg in his office for a chat. I had to say no as the demo was a priority, but I said that he was welcome to come along to the demo and to speak to me there.

Nick's assistant got back to me a few times to press me on coming to Nick's office for a chat but I was pleased when Nick decided to brave the cold and to stand by my side to demonstrate in support of Gary remaining in the UK. Gary's brilliant MP, David Burrowes, was also there, plus Keith Vaz, Danny Alexander, Kate Hoey, Alistair Carmichael, Chris Huhne and also Andrew MacKinlay, who had bravely resigned over Gary. A large contingent of Twitter friends came to the demo to add their support. I was proud of them, and of all of the politicians who braved the intense cold and took the time to come out onto the street outside the Home Office to support Gary and to hold 'Free Gary' banners in the air.

The thing is, at one time you would see a demo and interviews on TV and the next day they were gone and on to something new. But now if you record the footage and post it on Twitter and YouTube, you can extend its lifespan indefinitely – across the world. If people empathise or relate to a story or an interview, they will retweet it many times over and even a year or two later other people will pick up on it, making it a sort of permanent living historical record of things that people fought for or against at the time.

A young primary school boy from Belgium was asked by his parents what he wanted for his birthday, and he said that he wanted to go to London to join the demo to support Gary's fight against extradition – and, amazingly, his parents brought him. We were incredibly moved.

I had never used social media, including Twitter, which was fairly new at the time, until Wilson signed me up for it to help in my fight for Gary. It proved to be one of the best tools for campaigning that there is. There are some really good people on Twitter who care passionately about justice, including experienced campaigners and organisations only too eager to help if you are floundering.

Graham Linehan, writer of *Father Ted* and *The IT Crowd*, contacted me when I first went onto Twitter and, although we had never met, posted tweets to his followers asking them to follow me. There are also MPs and other celebrities on Twitter who leap forward to support you without being asked. Sally Bercow was also very supportive and as well as reposting my tweets she spoke up for Gary on Twitter and on TV many times, as did Terry Christian on *The Wright Stuff*. Sally and Speaker John Bercow have a son with autistic spectrum disorder, and supported Gary being tried in the UK.

Twitter friend Mike Garrick, who I've never met in reality, campaigned constantly for Gary and he and his friend Ed Johnson were responsible for helping over 5,000 people to put 'Free Gary' twibbons on their Twitter avatars.

We were thrilled when Stephen Fry and Jonathan Ross added the 'Free Gary' twibbon logo to their avatars and kept it on for months. This helped to bring even more supporters on board.

The power of Twitter is phenomenal: it is a place where people power thrives on an international level.

The demo outside the Home Office was the first time I had met many Twitter friends, including the amazing Kevin Healey from Staffordshire Adult Autistic Society (SAAS), who is the most astounding campaigner, and the inspirational and invaluable Claire Simmons. Claire had seen me on TV and decided I needed help, which became ongoing as she worked tirelessly, joining me in writing letters, comments and emails, making telephone calls, and lodging Freedom of Information requests.

Friends O and J came to virtually every single demo for Gary. Oliviea's voice is as loud as mine, so whenever I was being interviewed she was able to take over and lead the loud chant that the crowd followed.

The police supervising the December demo were friendly, but were much more alert than anyone could have realised, because suddenly in the blink of an eye the police tackled a smartly dressed man holding a package and walking towards the Home Office, pinning him to the ground in what seemed like a split second. This left us all wondering what mystery we had just witnessed.

I had brought flowers and a letter to hand in to the Queen, asking her to help to stop the extradition. The police told us that we weren't allowed to protest outside Buckingham Palace but lots of the protestors followed us as we made our way there. When we arrived at the gates of the palace several of the police behind the gates were armed with machine guns and looked very intimidating.

Standing there with my letter for the Queen in my hand, I thought about how virtually one hundred years earlier Emmeline Pankhurst was arrested at the gates of Buckingham Palace when she tried to present a petition to George V, and how in June 1913 suffragette Emily Wilding Davison died when she threw herself under the King's horse in her fight for women's rights.

If not for the bravery and sacrifice of women like these, how very different might the lives of women have been today?

I could see other policemen behind the gates of the palace, who were unarmed and friendly. They smiled and said they were expecting us and to leave the flowers with them, but suddenly one of the policemen received a phone call and said, 'Hold on. I've just been informed that Gary's mum, you,' he smiled, 'have been invited to take the flowers into the palace, but no one else can go in.'

The two friendly policemen who had been supervising the Home Office protest were still with us and they got really excited and announced to everyone: 'She's going in, they're taking her in.'

I walked into the palace on my own, holding my letter and trying to hold masses of bouquets that Lucy and the supporters had added to mine.

One of the policemen helped me to carry the flowers to the entrance of the palace but put them back on top of the bundle in my arms when I was going inside. My face and hair were buried in sweet-smelling roses, lilies, carnations and chrysanthemums, overwhelming the senses. I could hardly see where I was walking as I tried to stop the abundance of flowers falling from my arms.

The entrance to the first section of the palace I walked into was like an ancient castle and there was a large desk on the right-hand side.

I walked up a staircase that led to various rooms and the Queen's secretary was there, smiling as I peeked through the petals. He and a lady started gathering the bouquets from me to deliver to the Queen, as they chatted warmly and assured me that the Queen would personally read my letter and that Gary's case was very high profile.

When I came out, the policemen were all asking me what it was like and everyone was smiling. To be honest I can barely remember what it was like as I was smothered in flowers and all I could think of was that the Queen would now be well aware of Gary's plight. I hoped with all my heart that she might use her influence to help him.

With the highly controversial 2003 extradition treaty signed under Tony Blair's government using the Queen's prerogative, no British citizen was safe. Extradition could now happen even when you had never left your own country, had never fled from any other country and were not a fugitive – all without any evidence ever being presented against you.

It is an undisputable fact – as we discovered from Freedom of Information requests – that no American citizen has ever been extradited to the UK for any crime that took place while they were physically on American soil.

So if all men are equal, as they surely are, and if equal rights are to be adhered to, as they surely must, then our rights which were removed by Tony Blair's government must surely be returned to us.

Are we not equal to Americans?

Do we not deserve the same rights?

CHAPTER 16

MAY DAY

25 December 2009 marked yet another Christmas spent wondering when this nightmare would end. At least the courts being closed over Christmas and the New Year meant that no one could come and snatch my son away during this time.

I thought about how our government was sacrificing its own citizens to the US, regardless of the ludicrous sentences proposed, and of what might happen to them once they were extradited.

Cyberspace is a creation of science-fiction writers and has no more legal existence than never-never land. If they really want to start targeting computer geeks, then surely they should start by embracing some very basic technology and try them by video link.

Stanley Tollman, an American-born citizen who was fighting extradition from the UK, was given a one-day suspended sentence when he pled guilty by video link here in 2007. So why does this not happen with British citizens fighting extradition? Are foreign nationals being given preferential treatment?

Our crusade continued and Melanie Riley from Bell Yard Communications organised a text campaign. It really took off after I did interviews with Talk Radio Europe and with LBC.

Days later, after I did an interview with George Galloway on his radio show, we got over 1,000 texts in one night in support of Gary. They were automatically emailed to the Home Office with proof of the number of texts received.

• • •

On 13 January 2010 we got a landmark legal decision: the wonderful Justice Mitting ruled that we could judicially review Home Secretary Alan Johnson's decision to extradite.

I was ecstatic. I had long given up on Alan Johnson and because the court process tends to grind slowly, this gave me hope that a new government might be voted into power who would have the strength and wherewithal to bring in forum as they had promised and refuse to extradite Gary.

Forum meant that if the accused was physically in the UK during the alleged crime, as Gary was, a trial in the UK could take precedence over extradition.

We also had hopes that a new government would change the Extradition Act to bring in an automatic right to evidence that the accused could contest in a British court before any extradition could take place.

I was grateful to Justice Mitting for giving us the 'JR'. It was heartening to know that there were some courageous and fair-minded judges out there.

We kept thinking that it would all be over soon. But it just seemed to go on and on and our money was dwindling as we had no time to earn any.

We were working full-time on campaigning to save Gary and our financially precarious position meant I had to do something fast before we ended up losing our home.

I loved our house, which sat in a beautiful English village next to the village green, facing an eclectic mix of mainly independent shops. The village has a library and a post office, with good schools close by and beautiful woods and countryside on our doorstep. It also has the luxury of its own train station that takes you straight into King's Cross in just twenty minutes. This was intended to be our forever home.

I decided I had to go to the bank to arrange a loan. Normally Wilson would have been the one to deal with this, but Wilson had been so stressed lately that I was terrified he might have a heart attack or a stroke or something if he had to deal with this on top of everything else. The worry was eating away at us. Coping with financial worries and health worries on top of our all-consuming worries about Gary was difficult.

We had a fair amount of equity in our house so I thought borrowing money on it wouldn't be too difficult. The thing is, I'm quite shy and usually avoid doing things like that. I'd rather run a hundred miles than sit with the bank manager asking to borrow money. It's also a pride thing, feeling that you have to beg to borrow.

I dressed relatively smartly that day but without compromising my identity. I always have my longish hair hanging down and I wasn't going to wear it up or have it cut short, or try to portray a look I wasn't comfortable with. For better or worse I was me. Campaigning for our survival.

The bank manager called me in. 'Good morning, Mrs Sharp,' he said, shaking my hand, 'and how can we help you?'

'Well, I might as well get straight to the point. I would like a loan secured on our house, which has a fair bit of equity in it. We've had to stop work temporarily as working full time on campaigning for my son takes up every second of our time and I just need enough to tide us over for, say, a year? Until this is all over and we can get back on our feet again, which I'm confident wouldn't take very long.'

'I have to tell you, Mrs Sharp, things are very difficult at the moment. You know that we would love nothing more than to help but with this recession, and as you're not actually working at the moment, it ties my hands somewhat. But if you give me your paperwork and wait here, I'll check to see what I can do and I'll be back very shortly.'

Very shortly seemed to take forever and I thought I was just wasting my time but eventually he came back.

'Well, there are various options we can offer you for repayment, but I'm afraid that £15,000 is the maximum we could advance.'

'Fifteen thousand! But the equity in the house is worth much more than that.'

I thought about how our house in this prime location was unmodernised when we first bought it and how Wilson had fitted a new kitchen and bathroom, laid oak floors and put in a stunning fireplace. Even though Wilson did all the work himself, it still cost us significantly more than £15,000, and that amount of money wouldn't last long – not with the cost of fighting a campaign, train fares and just day-to-day survival.

Wilson and I have both always worked hard and managed to keep our heads above water and I told the bank manager that I had no doubt we could pull ourselves back up again once this ordeal was all over, but trying to convince someone in a bank that people in their sixties could do that was just not going to happen. They knew they couldn't lose with our house but £15,000 just wouldn't cut it for us so there was no point.

I wondered who had been clever enough to invent banks and encourage people to put their money there. I mean, what do we really need them for if they're only willing to give us money when we don't actually need it?

As I was leaving, the bank manager pointed to a side street. 'By the way, do you know whose car that is over there?'

I looked across to see Gary's bright yellow Triumph parked in a spot where there was no parking allowed.

'Yes, it's my son Gary's car,' I said, which the bank manager must have known, otherwise he wouldn't have asked me.

'Well, it's been parked there for some time.'

'Thank you,' I said to the bank manager, in the way that British people do even when they want to scream.

I came out of the bank and crossed the road to where Gary's car was parked. I couldn't believe how many parking tickets were stuck all over the windscreen. It looked grubby and abandoned, as though it had been sitting there for years. I had been so preoccupied that I had forgotten that Gary even had a car as he hadn't driven for so long.

I felt like crying as I went to meet Wilson at a coffee shop in town. I had so wanted to be able to tell him that financially, at least, everything was going to be OK and that we had a lifeline, but instead I was going to tell him that we'd have to sell our house.

I was also going to have to do something about Gary's car, as he owed a fortune in parking tickets.

I walked into the café and looked at Wilson sitting there. He looked up at me with crinkly smiling eyes, full of warmth and tenderness. He was so clever and talented and hardworking and loving; he was getting older and deserved so much more.

Wilson and Gary tended to think I was Goliath and that, thanks to my overly optimistic nature, I could always pull a rabbit out of the hat at the last minute. I tried to sound optimistic as I told Wilson that selling now and renting a place until house prices dropped was a really sensible thing to do, until after our fight for Gary was won.

I could hardly bear to look at the hurt in Wilson's eyes. He looked so defeated but tried to smile and agree so that I would feel OK. I wanted to hug him tight but knew if I did that I'd break down and cry.

There were lots of interviews over the next few weeks, including with Coast to Coast radio in America. I was worried about how American callers would react to Gary's story but I had no need, as everyone who rang in to speak to me was kind and compassionate and thought that Gary should remain in the UK.

When I told one caller that the alleged damage was around £400,000 ($700,000) he said, 'Jeez, is that all? The next advert coming up will cost more than that.'

That made me laugh but it was true. I was also interviewed by Jerry Pippin on his radio show. Jerry Pippin is an amazing American man who, when the police were making no headway finding the murderers of his mother, single-handedly tracked them down and had them arrested and eventually imprisoned.

Jerry supported Gary for years, devoting pages and pages on his website to our fight to save him. Many good Americans spoke out in support of Gary staying in the UK, including Dan Aykroyd, who has Asperger's, and Charlie Sheen.

• • •

10 February was Gary's birthday, and coincidentally Lucy's too. Gary was now forty-four years old. It seemed unbelievable that at the time of his arrest by the Hi-Tech Crime Unit in 2002, he had just turned thirty-six. Gary had essentially lost eight years of his life. All he wanted was peace of mind and freedom from fear and I couldn't give him that yet, but I was determined that I would, one day soon.

As Gary was no longer willing or able to do any interviews, Kerry Cassidy, who had interviewed him years before, flew over from America to interview me for Project Camelot, documenting the testimony of whistle-blowers, on the day after Gary's birth-day. It was a long, in-depth interview; the questions asked were different and interesting and it turned out well. The support Gary got from American people was just amazing and so appreciated.

Kerry's last question to me was, 'Do you know that lots of people in America believe that you work for British intelligence? Is there any truth in that?'

I started laughing. Now I had heard everything. If only I did work for British intelligence; Gary would have been safe long ago. But nothing could be further from the truth. Kerry laughed too.

I imagine I was pretty unpopular with the intelligence services, who I believe regarded me as a thorn in their sides. On several occasions I had heard comments from official people on both sides of the pond, saying things such as, 'They should extradite his mother and leave him here.'

What is it with those people? Do they ever listen to music? Or dance? Or run in the woods, or swim in the sea? Are they human? Or are they some kind of new species that feeds on fear? The world seemed crazy to me at that point in time. People who thought that Gary was an alien and that I worked for British intelligence definitely seemed to be from another planet.

Gary's legal team and I had to submit our up-to-date evidence by the middle of February. Gary's barrister, Ben Cooper, like Karen, held onto Gary tightly and refused to let go. Karen, Ben and Edward Fitzgerald submitted medical and legal evidence and I wrote the best statement I possibly could and included every potential piece of evidence I believed could help us.

I'm lucky I'm able to write a reasonably good letter, thanks to my parents instilling in me the importance of letter writing. This helped me to somehow get through to influential people from all walks of life. So many people already viewed what was happening to Gary as unjust, and that gave me an opening, as they were at least prepared to read what I had written.

On 3 March we saw the Home Office evidence and were shocked. The Home Office had appointed a doctor who had no expertise whatsoever in Asperger's to provide an *in absentia* medical report on Gary. The report was damning and it was crystal clear that its author had no knowledge whatsoever of ASD – something which the said doctor at least had the decency to admit to at the end of his report.

Now, why on earth would the Home Office decide, when appointing an expert witness for the prosecution, to appoint a doctor with no expertise in the condition he was to give evidence on?

The Home Office-appointed doctor also referred to Gary having a girlfriend, as though this is unheard of in people with Asperger's. Yet as all the experts in the field know, Asperger's is thought to be hereditary. Having a girlfriend or a wife would therefore have to be pretty common for this to be the case.

I was despondent, as any hopes for an independent medical report from the Home Office were fading.

• • •

It was our wedding anniversary, but any celebration was the furthest thing from our minds.

Zena, who worked closely with Nick Clegg, was constantly in touch with me, as were several of his right-hand people. The Lib Dems were very supportive of Gary at that time. Nick Clegg gave endless interviews to the newspapers to say that Gary should not be extradited and could be tried here in the UK, as did David Cameron, David Burrowes, David Davis, Keith Vaz, Kate Hoey, Boris Johnson and many others.

The support for Gary from around the world seemed never-ending. There is no doubt that the internet has created a platform for people to unite for a just cause. The strength of international people power should never be underestimated.

Many songs were written about Gary, including one in the form of a letter to Alan Johnson by Dan Bull, a well-known musician and songwriter who has Asperger's.

Young American Nathan Pitt, who has Asperger's, went to Senator Dianne Feinstein's state director Jim Molinari and begged him to allow Gary to remain in the UK. A video of this was posted on YouTube and everyone I spoke to about it said it had brought tears to their eyes.

A Swedish film on Gary was posted on YouTube and cited him as a hero.

I was starting to think that we might not need our hard-won judicial review of Home Secretary Alan Johnson's decision. There was an election looming, and the key players in the Conservative and Liberal Democrat parties had taken up Gary's cause, so we were naturally desperate for them to win as they were our best hope.

The minority of real socialists left in the Labour Party – people like Tony Benn – supported Gary, but real socialists are now almost never given Cabinet positions in the New Labour government.

Zena and Nick Clegg asked me to write a piece for the Lib Dem book *Why Vote Liberal Democrat?*, which I did. However, I didn't say who I would vote for, as actions speak louder than words and I needed action from principled politicians who would live up to their promises.

• • •

I was angry that prior to Labour being elected Jack Straw had said that the Queen's prerogative was undemocratic and should never be used – yet once elected, the Queen's prerogative was exactly what Labour used to bring in this horrendous extradition treaty.

Although it was the safest Labour seat ever, I decided to stand against Jack Straw in the general election, with no hope or wish to become an MP, but purely to highlight the betrayal of our civil liberties and to keep Gary's case in the public eye at this crucial point in time.

Paul Stevenson, whom I encountered on Twitter but had never met, travelled 200 miles to help me get nominations as he had lived in the area and knew people there. Paul is an incredible man. He has Tourette's and campaigns to dispel the ignorance that exists about this condition. He is also a prize-winning photographer for, among others, the National Trust. Paul's wife is a schoolteacher and following unforeseen circumstances they adopted Paul's two young grandchildren.

I travelled up to Blackburn on the train to present my nomination papers. The ultimate destination of the train we were travelling on was Glasgow Central station. I hadn't been to Glasgow since my mum died in 1980 but it was as though a bolt of lightning hit me. A well of tears suddenly flooded from the depths of my soul when I saw the destination of the train. I suddenly remembered arriving in London with Gary when he was just six years old. I wanted to be able to somehow go back in time to change everything that had happened. I had a desperate urge to just grab Gary and take him back to Glasgow to safety.

Logically I know that Gary would be no safer in Glasgow than in London but our birth town instinctively felt like safety to me and a depth of emotion was unleashed that totally overwhelmed me.

Because of a volcanic dust cloud from Iceland all UK flights were cancelled, so the train was jam-packed, with no available seats. When the train was about to leave we sat in someone else's reserved seats rather than standing but Virgin decided to delay the train departure by fifteen minutes, so the holder of the reserved tickets arrived late and apologetically claimed his seats back.

I thought we'd have to stand all the way to Blackburn, but the lady serving tea told us we could sit in the first-class dining carriage. It was a good journey for us after all and tea and sandwiches were served, which was totally unexpected and so appreciated.

We arrived in Blackburn and went straight to the Town Hall, handed in my papers and paid the £500 deposit. When we came out I talked to some people in Blackburn and asked what changes really mattered to them which they believed a good politician could help them to achieve. Among the things that bothered people most were potholes in the road, being free from the debt of student loans, and the lack of work and money. A woman who was a carer for a Down's syndrome child put civil liberties high on the agenda. Her other priority was more help for people with mental health issues and their carers. When I asked a student about civil liberties she said that she wasn't really political and never thought about that.

Many people I spoke to had no intention of voting as they no longer had faith in any politicians. However, undecided voters were waiting to listen to the first ever UK televised leaders' debates before deciding who to vote for.

We then headed off for Radio Lancashire, where I'd been asked to do a short interview. The interviewer basically asked me only one question several times over and seemed to want me to say that I was standing merely to gain more publicity for Gary and that I wasn't really interested in civil liberties. He was wrong:

I've always cared deeply about civil liberties. I believe that we all have to stand up and speak out in order to stop our civil liberties being eroded faster than we could ever have thought possible. It reminded me of Orwell's *1984* and how the majority of people are compliant until it's too late.

After a hectic day we eventually headed back to the railway station to go home. We changed at Preston and found that our train was over an hour late. There were a lot of photographers and newsmen on the platform; one of them recognised me and we started chatting. It turned out that they were permanently travelling around with Gordon Brown during his election campaign.

As Brown had been rehearsing for the leader's debate, to prevent the press from becoming bored the Labour Party had arranged for them to spend the day with Peter Mandelson, who had put on a dance show in the Winter Gardens in Blackpool. The journalists said that Peter Mandelson was a pretty good dancer and that they were all kept well entertained and were even given ice cream.

The journalist we were chatting to was just as concerned as us about the erosion of civil liberties – we spent almost an hour talking and before we knew it the train had arrived. We got into Euston station well over an hour late but got back home just in time to see the televised leaders' debate with David Cameron, Nick Clegg and Gordon Brown.

I constantly needed new ways to keep Gary's case as high profile as possible and arranged to release ninety-nine balloons from Westminster Bridge on the river Thames, facing the Houses of Parliament, on May Day.

May Day has lots of connotations, both historically and politically. It is to mark Labour Day, which advocates eight hours for work, eight hours for recreation and eight hours for rest.

One of my favourite photos of Gary as a child. I love his smile and his tousled auburn hair.

Gary on his first computer (an Atari).

Gary in Studio Three at Abbey Road Studios, known as The Beatles' studio, where the Fab Four recorded their albums with George Martin and used the same piano as Gary is playing. The man in the background is Peter Vince, a senior figure at Abbey Road who engineered on The Beatles' sessions and produced many artists, including us.

LEFT Peter Howson is an internationally famous Scottish artist whose paintings have been bought by David Bowie, Mick Jagger and Madonna. This dramatic painting of Gary was one of several Peter painted that he auctioned to raise money for autism charities, including Research Autism. Peter also suffers from Asperger's syndrome.

RIGHT I was angry, emotional and upset during interviews outside the Royal Courts of Justice after the court upheld a decision to extradite and refused to allow an appeal.

BELOW Some of the excellent politicians from all parties who joined our demo outside the Home Office in December 2009 to protest against the decision to extradite.

A photo of me standing outside Westminster with Baron Maginnis of Drumglass, a champion of autistic rights and a staunch supporter of Gary remaining in the UK.

An excellent portrait of Gary by Michael Frith, who kindly presented it to us with his own personal dedication.

Alongside Gary's MP David Burrowes outside the Palace of Westminster with a Christmas card for Gary, newly signed by many MPs and Peers inside Parliament.

Here I am outside the Home Office with Chris Huhne, Michael Meacher and David Davis after they had a meeting with Alan Johnson asking him to keep Gary in the UK.

LEFT My very supportive MP Grant Shapps at a garden party at his home that residents of the village attended.

RIGHT With Jane Asher at an autism event which my husband Wilson filmed, including an appeal by Jane Asher for donations for the charity Research Autism.

This was the day that PM David Cameron and President Barack Obama raised Gary's case at a worldwide press conference held in Washington, resulting in our house and garden being filled with camera crews from across the world.

Shami Chakrabarti and her team from human rights organisation Liberty joined us outside the US embassy with Liberty's Extradition Watch, launching a spectacular and artistic campaign for Gary to remain in the UK.

Feeling overwhelmed and honoured when receiving my Liberty Human Rights award on stage inside the Queen Elizabeth Hall on the Southbank Centre at Liberty's annual award ceremony.

ABOVE This photo was taken at a debate on extradition in Westminster Hall when I was addressing some of the issues with politicians and peers in attendance.

LEFT With Benedict Cumberbatch during the Liberty awards ceremony, where I was presenting a Human Rights award – as was Benedict, who presented an award to Gary's barrister Ben Cooper.

LEFT AND RIGHT With Gary immediately after the announcement of Theresa May's decision not to extradite. The photos say it all.

ABOVE AND MIDDLE The press conference in Doughty Street Chambers in London after Theresa May's decision that Gary was to remain in the UK. This was my chance to thank everyone, including the media, for all they had done to highlight Gary's case and to help achieve this momentous decision that saved Gary's life. With me are Gary's legal team, his MP David Burrowes and Shami Chakrabarti.

LEFT With Trudie Styler, a woman of substance, at a party held at Trudie and Sting's house on Thanksgiving Day to celebrate Gary's freedom from a decade of fear.

My husband Wilson and Gary's solicitor Karen Todner with Gary and me at Trudie and Sting's house in London. The beer in Wilson's hand belonged to Mark Lever from the National Autistic Society, who took the picture for me.

With Gary at home at Christmas after the CPS decided not to prosecute Gary. This was our first worry-free Christmas in eleven years and is one I will never forget.

'Mayday' is also the word used as an emergency distress call: this was an emergency, Gary was in distress, and we were desperately calling for help. May also featured in my mum's Christian name, Mary Mae, and coincidentally also in the surname of Theresa May, who within weeks was Home Secretary when a Conservative-led coalition became our new government.

The reason for us releasing ninety-nine balloons was based on the German band Nena's song '99 Red Balloons', which was a story about the military mistaking ninety-nine red balloons for an invasion by UFOs, triggering a nuclear response that resulted in the destruction of our world, leaving only an apocalyptic aftermath.

Ninety-nine balloons seemed appropriate because of Gary's obsession with UFOs and his search for information on them via NASA and Pentagon computers that led to US misinterpretation and overreaction.

I persuaded Gary to come along that day. Lots of our friends from Twitter also joined us for the release of the balloons.

Young tourists walking past us on the bridge inhaled some of the helium to make their voices sound high like a child's, which made everyone laugh.

Sally Williams of ITV's *London Tonight*, who had highlighted Gary's case for years, filmed the event. It was sunny but windy by the Thames and the balloons flew over Parliament and soared higher and higher in the sky.

We used environmentally friendly balloons and tiers that would not land in the sea or kill birds or animals as ordinary balloons can and often do.

The sun continued to shine; it became warmer and we all walked on to Trafalgar Square. By chance, Lib Dem candidate Paul Burstow was there campaigning for election. Lots of people interviewed us and everyone was supportive of Gary but he wouldn't speak. Our friend Oliviea stood in the sun on the steps of Trafalgar Square and campaigned loudly for Gary with a megaphone she had borrowed from the Lib Dems, which led to journalists from all over the world wanting interviews with Gary and me. Gary still wouldn't speak.

In Trafalgar Square we met a young woman from Australia who had been told she was seriously ill, with a poor prognosis, so she had decided to travel around the world on her own, to the surprise of her husband and children. She wanted to know all about Gary and went to an Australian pub afterwards with Lucy and Free Gary supporters and they all had an amazing day. It was a stark reminder that we weren't the only ones with a fight for life on our hands.

The balloon release was televised and as well as looking beautiful, it helped to keep Gary's case to the fore during the election campaign. I carried on doing interviews. Russian, Australian and French TV stations covered Gary's case and Dutch TV did a lengthy feature on it, as did *The One Show* on BBC1, with Karen and me participating.

• • •

The general election was held on 6 May and we travelled up to Blackburn as a matter of courtesy to hear the results.

Jack Straw won the election in Blackburn as everyone knew he would, but when we all stood on stage for it to be announced, I shouted out 'Free Gary McKinnon!' knowing that it would be transmitted on TV stations all around the world.

All the candidates then had to take it in turn to give a little speech. I spoke about how the 2003 extradition treaty was the biggest betrayal of British citizens by their own government, and the audience applauded loudly.

This May election was going to be by far the most important election ever for us: we needed a government that had the guts to say no to the US and refuse to extradite Gary.

CHAPTER 17

ALL CHANGE

On 7 May 2010 the Conservatives 'won' the election but failed to gain an overall majority. This made it a hung parliament. It was clear that a coalition would have to be formed but it wasn't clear which political party the Lib Dems and the smaller parties would attach to. Over the next three days talks continued, until the Conservative–Lib Dem coalition government emerged.

On 11 May Gordon Brown left Downing Street with his wife Sarah and their two beautiful children, who had never really been seen in the limelight before. The family looked lovely together and people warmed to them as they made their dignified exit.

Journalists of all political persuasions felt that had Gordon Brown been filmed with his children during the election, he would have had attracted significantly more support from the masses.

We were overjoyed when David Cameron became Prime Minister, as we firmly believed that Gary was now safe and that forum would finally be introduced as promised, to protect others against extradition. David Cameron had raised Gary's case during the election campaign:

I simply see no compassion in sending him away to serve a

lengthy prison sentence, thousands of miles away from his home, his family and his friends.

If he has questions to answer, there is a clear argument to be made that he should answer them in a British court.

The Extradition Act was put in place to ensure terrorists didn't escape justice. It was never intended to deal with a case like Gary's.

It should still mean something to be a British citizen – with the full protection of the British Parliament, rather than a British government trying to send you off to a foreign court.

This case raises serious questions about the workings of the Extradition Act, which should be reviewed.

On 13 May I was told during an interview with Three Counties Radio that the BBC had rung Gary's solicitor, Karen Todner, but that Karen's husband, a barrister, had answered and had told them that the extradition treaty and Gary's case had formed part of the coalition discussions. We were bowled over by this news.

When we heard that Dominic Grieve was being made Attorney General we were ecstatic. He had not only spoken up for Gary many times, including at the Conservative Party conference, he had also fought hard for forum to be introduced, to end the gross inequality of the 2003 extradition treaty:

The Gary McKinnon case throws into sharp relief the crude and clumsy extradition procedures Britain now has in place.

The Extradition Act was introduced after 9/11 so that we could fast-track terrorist suspects to face trial abroad. The intention was reasonable. But it was never intended to operate in cases like this, diluting the safeguards protecting such a vulnerable man – and a British citizen at that.

Ministers must make every effort to see justice done for Gary McKinnon.

David Cameron was the new Prime Minister. Theresa May was Home Secretary, the most powerful woman in British politics. And Nick Clegg was Deputy PM, and had said of Gary during the election campaign:

> It is wrong. It is simply wrong for our government to have signed a treaty in secret which sells our rights down the river while protecting the rights of American citizens. It is certainly wrong to send a vulnerable young man to his fate in the United States when he could and should be tried here instead. It is simply a matter of doing the right thing.

Our happiness was boundless when Theresa May adjourned the upcoming judicial review and put a halt on extradition to allow her to personally consider all of Gary's medical evidence, including the very newest medical evidence that no one had yet seen.

We were the happiest we had been for years and wept with joy as we felt our nightmare was finally, at long last, coming to an end.

More and more primetime interviews took place and were being repeated on the hour on News 24. Support for Gary was at an all-time high. The journalists and interviewers said they had never seen me look so happy, and I was.

• • •

On 22 May, Wilson and I were attending the wedding of our friends Pauline, who was Scottish, and Steve Ballam, from

Enfield, who was the drummer in our band many years ago.
They were both in the midst of adopting Christopher, their little
autistic boy they had fostered since shortly after his birth.

Thanks to all the interviews I'd been doing, I'd had no time to
buy anything to wear. On the morning of the wedding I went
into Chez, a French clothes shop in Enfield Town, and bought
a beautiful off-white three-quarter-length flowing silky open
jacket that had delicate black and clear rhinestones and sequins
sewn onto the sleeves and on part of the front.

We had five minutes to get to the wedding, which was being
held just around the corner in Gentleman's Row, in the historic
heart of west Enfield. It has a river running through it that had
families of ducks and swans swimming under the little bridges
on this bright sunny day. The open space is surrounded by beautiful old buildings, one of which is the register office that Steve
and Pauline were getting married in.

We got to the door of the hall where the marriage was to take
place, just in time. When we walked in I saw a familiar-looking
dark-haired young woman on the stage, ready to conduct the
ceremony. I couldn't believe it.

'Look, Wilson! It's Rebecca! How can Rebecca be marrying
Pauline and Steve? She's an actress.'

'Are you sure it's Rebecca?'

'Yes, look! She hasn't changed. It's Rebecca from *Lunar Girl*.'

I walked over to Rebecca to say hello before the ceremony got
underway.

'Janis!' she exclaimed.

'Hi, Rebecca, I can't believe seeing you here, and that you are
marrying our friends! It's surreal. How can you be conducting a
wedding ceremony when you're an actress?'

Rebecca laughed as she said, 'I was between acting jobs and
I saw an ad looking for people to train to marry people and I

thought, that sounds interesting, and I was able to do it at the weekends, so it was perfect and helps pay the bills.'

I looked around as I could hear Wilson calling my name in a half-spoken, half-whispery voice. He was staring at me, pointing and signalling to tell me to look at my jacket and to take it off but although it was a beautiful day, I wasn't too hot, so I couldn't think why he was saying this, unless he really hated my jacket.

When I walked back to my seat Wilson whispered to me urgently, 'There's a huge skull on the back of your jacket.'

'What do you mean a skull?'

'A skull! ... A huge black skull on the back of your jacket. Look!'

I took my jacket off and looked, and there it was: a huge skull made of sequins and rhinestones, with the words 'Challenge Everything' written below.

I started laughing and put it back on as it was too late to do anything about it. In spite of it being a skull, I still thought it was beautiful, although maybe not really what anyone would expect to see worn at a wedding. And the words 'Challenge Everything' kind of suited where my head was at the moment.

I looked up and saw Pauline staring at Rebecca with a puzzled expression.

Just before the ceremony Pauline and Rebecca had gone into the back of the register office to sign papers and Pauline had said, 'I know you from somewhere, how do I know you?'

After much confusion they both pointed at each other and said in unison, 'Janis and Wilson!' and they both laughed.

Pauline had seen Rebecca in our *Lunar Girl* film and now, knowing who was going to marry her and Steve, she got a fit of the giggles. Pauline has the kind of laugh that infects everyone around. The wedding was beginning to seem more like *Four*

Weddings and a Funeral but you know what, the atmosphere was just so good that I wanted to laugh and cry at the same time.

Christopher, the little autistic boy who Steve and Pauline were adopting, had been chosen to give his mummy away. However, after he did, Christopher decided that he wanted to stand and to be married along with them. He was upset when he was taken back to sit on his aunt's knee, so he started calling out to them.

Rebecca was beaming during the ceremony as she pronounced Steve and Pauline man and wife, and everyone in the room was smiling and laughing. The music was interesting and included The Corrs' 'Toss the Feathers', a rock version of a traditional Irish jig, and the atmosphere was as warm as the sunshine. We all poured out of the French windows to have photos taken in the gardens and it was truly a day to remember.

Two women were surprised to see that they were wearing identical bright red frilly dresses and the photographer literally took hours to take the photos, but everyone was happy and smiled continuously throughout.

The wedding reception was held at Pauline's brother's house. Her sister-in-law Lorraine, with her art students, had pasted huge photos of Steve and Pauline onto the outside and inside doors of the house and onto all the cupboard doors.

The photos were from each of their childhoods, up to the present day, and displayed a photographic history of their youth and of their lives together. It was beautiful.

This had been a good day.

• • •

We were still struggling financially, and the time had come to sell our house. We had found a buyer who wanted to exchange

ALL CHANGE 193

quickly and was anxious to complete, but we still hadn't found a house to rent and having two dogs didn't make it any easier.

It was hard, having to leave our home. I loved the garden and the whole feel of the house. I loved sitting in the kitchen in the morning and watching the birds outside. I wondered if we would ever be able to afford to buy a house of our own again.

I wondered if whoever moved in would cut down the trees or the blue butterfly bushes that the bees loved, and whether they would feed the wild birds that we put food out for on cold winter and dry summer days when the ground was hard. It just seemed odd to think of strangers walking around our house and sleeping in our room.

However, leaving our home paled in comparison to my worry about what was happening to Gary.

We managed to rent a place nearby at the last minute and the landlord didn't mind us having dogs. The house was a bit run-down but the garden was really lovely and there was a pond full of fish that no one knew was there. Tony the landlord had bought the house intending to convert it into flats at some point and hadn't noticed the fish, which we were happy to look after.

On 25 May I was shocked when Nick Clegg said in an interview on BBC 5 Live that he might not have the power to halt an earlier court decision to allow extradition. This totally contrasted with comments made while in opposition. However, I had to believe that after so much pre-election support for Gary, this government would not let him down.

On 8 June Keith Vaz, who is Lucy's parents' MP in Leicester, raised a question about Gary's case in the House of Commons. A few days later Mr Vaz invited me to return to give evidence on extradition to the cross-party Home Affairs Select Committee for the second time.

Good politicians are seldom given the credit for the good work they do, but there are many first-class MPs out there.

Gary's Member of Parliament, David Burrowes, met with Home Secretary Theresa May and gave her a letter I had written, and Karen submitted new medical evidence. I was really pleased that David Burrowes had actually spoken to Theresa May, as I knew that David would have made her fully aware of the medical evidence and of the personal and emotional cost and the deterioration of Gary's mental state. Sending letters and emails you never know if the Home Secretary ever actually gets to see them, or if they're just answered by one of her team or even just by a general Home Office employee. I'll be forever grateful that David Burrowes was Gary's MP, as he fought fearlessly with every ounce of his being for Gary to remain in the UK.

On 11 June I got an email from Damian Green telling me that Theresa May was working to try to find a solution for Gary.

On the same day, Lord Tebbit spoke out in support of Gary in his *Telegraph* blog. Lord Tebbit's wife was a nurse who was paralysed in the bombing by the IRA at the Brighton hotel they had been staying in during the Conservative Party conference many years before. Lord Tebbit said that America had refused to extradite alleged IRA terrorists to the UK on the grounds that they would not get a fair trial here.

There was no doubt that Gary's plight was being taken up by people in high places across the political spectrum and that this in turn highlighted the controversial extradition treaty.

We were incredibly lucky that so many people from all walks of life and political persuasions supported Gary. Whenever I said that we were lucky, people thought I was mad because our circumstances were so dire, but I did feel fortunate that such an eclectic mixture of individuals were brewing a kind of people-powered force for good.

An investigative journalist named Mark Ballard won a British Telecom Journalism Award for a lengthy piece he had written showing exactly what Gary had done – and showing that Alan Johnson had exaggerated Gary's crime and had publicly accused Gary of things that even the US had not.

I followed this up by emailing the evidence to our great supporters Lord Maginnis and Baroness Browning and to various other peers. I emailed MPs from every political party, with the facts as opposed to the allegations, and appealed for them to help to have Gary tried in the UK.

The trouble is that so many people have no real understanding of computers or of what hacking – as opposed to phishing – really entails.

A judge had already ruled in a London court that companies with poor security having to pay to upgrade their computer equipment to make it secure does not constitute damage, as the equipment would have had to be upgraded in any case.

When you expose misinformation or lies, it allows the truth to shine through. But exposing the truth can be a long and difficult process, especially when so many in the judicial process have scant understanding of computers and, as George Orwell said, 'In a time of universal deceit, telling the truth is an act of rebellion.'

• • •

I woke up and the sun was shining. It was the kind of day that in spite of the constant worry made you feel that anything was possible. On days like this I had no doubt that I could win Gary's freedom.

Michael Seamark from the *Daily Mail* came over to take us out for lunch, as he often did. It was always a huge treat for us – a change of scene, good food, diverse conversation – and leaving the computer behind gave us much-needed respite. Michael is easy to talk to and, like us, has an opinion on just about everything.

We went to visit our friends Sue and Kooi later that day and Sue said, 'Come into the garden, Janis, I've found something that I think you'll like.'

Sue took me to the shed at the bottom of her garden and six tiny kittens emerged from under it. They were so beautiful. The mother cat was a gentle stray who appeared shortly afterwards and was clearly starving, so we fed her and encouraged the kittens to eat a little food, which they were just about old enough to do.

I love animals and knew we'd have to find them all a home but I was worried about how our hound dogs would react to having a cat around.

We took one of the kittens back to our house for a few days until he could be taken to his new home in Leicester, but when we were packing in anticipation of moving house, I let one of our dogs into the same room as the kitten by mistake. Too late I realised what I had done. I ran into the room and was almost afraid to look but was then amazed to see our dog Jackson lying quietly beside the kitten as though to protect it. Lucy took the kitten to her friend's house in Leicester a few days later, where he still lives happily with his new owner.

We took two more of the kittens home. Gary and Lucy kept the little tabby one and we kept the white one, so we now have a much-loved cat, Pinksy: named because of her pink paws, pink nose and pink ears – and as a shout-out to the wonderful David Gilmour, whose band was Pink Floyd.

Homes were found for all of the kittens, and also for their mother.

On 8 July the European Court of Human Rights halted the extradition of Babar Ahmad, Talha Ahsan and Abu Hamza, as the ECHR was taking on their cases for review, and this would be likely to take several years to complete.

Unbelievably the ECHR refused to even consider taking on Gary's case for review, despite his mental health issues and possible sixty-year sentence. I couldn't understand this. We felt crushed. I was worried about Gary and asked him if he was OK, which was a silly question but I asked it anyway and Gary said:

> You know, I'm walking down the road and suddenly I find I can't control my own legs, and I'm sitting up all night thinking about maniacs wanting to have me dragged and locked up in some godforsaken American prison, where I'd be attacked and raped and disconnected from my home and family, and I think about the cruelty in the world, mostly for monetary gain, and I think … I don't belong in this world.

I looked at Gary as he looked past me with a faraway gaze and I thought, 'Neither do I, Gary, neither do I.'

• • •

Despite having stopped fostering children for a time as campaigning for Gary was all-consuming, I was beginning to feel extremely tired – really earth-shatteringly, head-hung-down, not-wanting-to-get-up kind of tired. I was putting it down to the weeks of hot weather and the fact that I was constantly sitting at the computer.

I got up from my chair and looked at myself in the mirror and saw a face I didn't recognise looking back at me. Who was this tired-looking woman in the mirror? I felt sorry for her. She looked sad and broken. Her hair needed a wash, her clothes were shabby and she looked run into the ground.

I thought I had looked OK for my age not that long ago, but suddenly I realised that was years ago. I had been sitting at this damn computer ever since Gary was arrested! But where had the old Janis gone? The roots of my hair were grey, I had put on weight and I looked awful.

What was wrong with me? I was strong, what was I doing feeling sorry for myself? I was angry at this pathetic person who was me, who should be thinking only about her son and what he was facing rather than giving way to such self-pitying thoughts. What was wrong with me? Can anyone tell me if I'm even a person anymore?

I had become an extension of a computer. I hadn't sung or written any songs for years, or even touched a musical instrument. I hadn't bought any nice clothes, or done anything fun or frivolous. I had also become the most boring person ever, as the only thing I wanted to talk about was Gary. I didn't want to do small talk about meaningless moments or this shop or that shop, or texting or phoning.

I just wanted to see Gary home and dry.

I sat down and cried in a way I hadn't done in years. 'God, I need to get myself together, I think I'm cracking up,' I thought, as I ran my fingers through my hair, knowing I needed to get back on top of things. 'I need to look after myself.'

I took time to weigh myself the following day, which I hadn't done in a long time, and was shocked to see that my weight had increased by a massive two stone. I now weighed 11st 6lbs. 11st 6lbs!

Wilson had put on weight too and I knew we were both going to have to lose weight or we might end up becoming ill or having heart attacks and then what would happen to Gary?

We changed to eating low-carb, but not no-carb, and started losing weight without going to a gym or doing any strenuous

exercise. We just walked our dogs regularly as we always have …
and walking in the woods soothed my soul.

I wanted Gary to walk, run, swim or cycle as he used to, as
he desperately needed respite, but he wouldn't, he couldn't. He
rarely left the house and just hid away from the world.

This was sad and an absolute waste of life as Gary is so
talented. He has the most beautiful singing voice and writes
really good and unusual songs, but all that had fallen by the
wayside because of his naivety and foolishness seemingly being
deliberately misinterpreted by overzealous prosecutors hunting down and trying to extradite computer geeks as terrorists,
simply because they can.

Wilson had a dream about asking President Obama to help
Gary. Obama asked what Gary had done. Wilson couldn't
remember and said, 'Oh, something silly.' And the President
said, 'I'll see what I can do.'

I laughed when Wilson told me. I loved hearing Wilson's
dreams as they always made me feel optimistic for some reason.

Weeks later I discovered that David Cameron was going to
America on 19 July to meet with President Obama, so I wrote
to MPs asking for this golden opportunity to please be used to
raise Gary's case. However, what followed surpassed any hope or
expectation I had.

On 20 July Wilson and I had our coats on and were going
out the door and for some unknown reason I turned around and
put the TV on. There looking out at us were the Prime Minister
and President Obama.

David Cameron looked over at ITN journalist Tom Bradby
and said, 'I think we have a question from Tom Bradby.'

Mr President, Tom Bradby, ITV News. Quite a lot of people
in the UK feel that your determination as a country to

continue to push for the extradition of computer hacker and
Asperger's sufferer Gary McKinnon is disproportionate
and somewhat harsh. Do you think it is time now to consider
some leniency in this case?

Wilson and I were sitting on the edge of our seats, transfixed
at what was taking place. We almost fell off our chairs and I
screamed. I couldn't believe it and I listened with my heart in
my mouth as Tom Bradby continued talking about Gary:

> And, Prime Minister, you've expressed very strong views on this
> matter, suggesting that Mr McKinnon shouldn't be extradited.
> Your Deputy Prime Minister has expressed even stronger views.
> Did you discuss that with the President today? And if not, would
> now be a good moment to share your views with us once again?
>
> *David Cameron*: Shall I go?
>
> *President Obama*: Please, go ahead.
>
> *David Cameron*: It is something that we discussed in our
> meeting. I mean, clearly there's a discussion going on between
> the British and the Americans about this, and I don't want
> to prejudice those discussions. We completely understand
> that Gary McKinnon stands accused of a very important and
> significant crime in terms of hacking into vital databases.
> And nobody denies that that is an important crime that has
> to be considered. But I have had conversations with the US
> ambassador, as well as raising it today with the President,
> about this issue, and I hope a way through can be found.

It was as though some kind of magic had happened, a once-
in-a-lifetime moment. The President of America and our Prime
Minister, during their first ever joint worldwide press conference, were talking about how to help my son.

President Obama: Well, one of the things that David and I discussed was the increasing challenge that we're going to face as a consequence of the internet, and the need for us to co-operate extensively on issues of cyber-security.

We had a brief discussion about the fact that although there may still be efforts to send in spies and try to obtain state secrets through traditional Cold War methods, the truth of the matter is these days, where we're going to see enormous vulnerability when it comes to information is going to be through these kind of breaches in our information systems. So we take this very seriously. And I know that the British government does as well.

Beyond that, one of the traditions we have is the President doesn't get involved in decisions around prosecutions, extradition matters. So what I expect is that my team will follow the law, but they will also co-ordinate closely with what we've just stated is an ally that is unparalleled in terms of our co-operative relationship. And I trust that this will get resolved in a way that underscores the seriousness of the issue, but also underscores the fact that we work together and we can find an appropriate solution. All right? Thank you very much, everybody.

This had to be the beginning of the end. Happy tears rolled down my face as I picked up the phone to tell Gary and when he answered I was so shaken that the only words that came out were a scream of 'David Cameron! President Obama! On TV! All about you! It's going to be OK!!! You're going to be OK!!!'

We were laughing and crying and feeling that a miracle had just taken place and Tom Bradby was amazing. I mean, here were our Prime Minister and the President of America talking about Iraq, Afghanistan, the global economy and little Gary McKinnon!

In the past, Home Secretaries had refused to extradite
General Pinochet to Chile and had refused to extradite terrorists; publicly raising Gary's case with the US President was
something I doubt any other leaders would have done and huge
respect to David Cameron for that. It's something we will never
forget and will be eternally grateful to him for.

The phone started ringing and didn't stop, and another round
of non-stop TV interviews took place over the next few days.

The following day in Washington, Tom Bradby interviewed
David Cameron:

> *Tom Bradby*: President Obama said yesterday that cybercrime
> is an enormous threat to America, which it surely is, you
> know that, I know that. We also know that it's about govern-
> ment agencies, it's about the Mafia. It's not about some lone
> guy with Asperger's sitting in a room in north London. That
> is not what it's about. So surely, if this great friendship you
> seem to be developing with Obama means anything it's got
> to produce a result on something like this. Hasn't it? And if it
> doesn't you're going to look very silly.
>
> *David Cameron*: Well, that's why we're having these
> discussions.

People on Twitter and in the street and in shops were congratulating us, as they all firmly believed that Gary would be OK
now. We kept waiting and hoping and expecting an announcement but Parliament went into recess on 27 July and wasn't due
to return until 6 September, so despite David Cameron's brave
stance, it seemed that our wait wasn't over yet.

I felt as though we were trapped in a maze. Every route I took
consisted of twists and turns that led to a dead end and I was
desperate to find the exit. We needed to get Gary out.

• • •

We had only just moved into our rented accommodation when the local authority got in touch to ask if a group of three siblings we used to care for could come back to spend one weekend a month with us. We immediately said yes. It transpired that the local authority had removed the children from an abusive foster carer and, although their newest foster carer was a good and kind woman, she didn't normally look after so many children and wanted some respite.

It was lovely having the children back with us, but it was also heartbreaking that they had been abused after leaving our care because we hadn't been able to keep them with us due to our uncertain future.

That's the thing about fighting extradition: it affects not just one person but everyone involved in your life.

I did an interview for ITN about pensioner Christopher Tappin, whom the US was trying to extradite despite him being the carer of his seriously ill wife Elaine.

People in this country are supposed to be innocent until proven guilty and that premise has always been an essential part of British justice. If the US really wanted to have someone convicted, they could quite easily provide the CPS with the evidence and, as MP David Davis said about Gary, 'I do not know why the Americans should think it better for Gary McKinnon to spend two years in an American prison than for two American witnesses to spend two weeks in a hotel in Britain while the case is tried.'

It is also rare for any trial to take place in the US – 96 per cent of cases are settled by plea bargain, and many innocent people will accept a guilty plea as they're so afraid of the disproportionate sentences they're usually threatened with.

If the UK insisted on equality with the US, a UK trial could be ordered under these circumstances.

• • •

I went to our friends Jim and Helen's house to have my hair cut as I knew I had to start looking after myself. Their friend Dave is a great hairdresser who used to cut the hair of many rock stars and regularly came to their house to cut Helen's hair. A simple trip to catch up with friends felt like respite to us.

Dave the hairdresser told us about a customer who had been perfectly healthy but started having a few headaches. He was due to cut her hair later that day but had had a telephone call from his customer's friend to tell him that she had just died of a stroke. It was shocking how, in a heartbeat, a life was gone.

On 21 September we had to go to a course in Luton and Rosemarie, the supervising social worker, was there. Rosemarie always smiled and laughed and made everyone feel happy. She was so gentle and lovely but was quieter than usual that day and wasn't her happy smiling self. I spoke to her and she told me she had a bad headache which she'd had for a day or two. I had also had a bad headache for a day or two but I felt worried about Rosemarie after what Dave had told us about his customer dying suddenly. Five days later, Rosemarie died in her sleep from a stroke. We were so upset. Rosemarie had just come through a difficult divorce and she had two teenage daughters who must have been devastated by their mum's death. She had just acquired a little puppy and had been so happy.

On 28 September my friend Claire's dad died suddenly from a brain tumour. I had met Claire Simmons via Twitter and apart from Wilson she was my right-hand person in my daily fight to save Gary. She was devastated by her dad's death and desperately worried about her mum. It was all so sad.

These three sudden deaths all in a row, all preceded by headaches, brought home to me just how quickly life can be snatched away when we least expect it.

I started to worry about what would happen to Gary if anything happened to me. Who could fight for him as well as I could?

That evening I walked over to Wilson, who was sitting in his swivel chair in front of the computer. He spun round and looked up at me.

'Wilson, I need to ask you something.'

'Yes?'

'I need to know that if anything happens to me you'll look after Gary and make sure that you'll do whatever it takes to make sure he stays here.'

'Of course I will, Janis, you know that.'

'But I need you to promise me, that you won't under any circumstances allow Gary to be extradited. I need to hear you saying that. I have to know that you'll keep him safe.'

'Nothing is going to happen to you, Janis!'

'You have to promise me, Wilson,' I said anxiously.

'I promise, Janis. I will never allow Gary to be extradited to America. I would die before I would allow that to happen.'

We held each other tight and I felt able to breathe again.

• • •

It seemed to be taking forever for the government to refuse to extradite, which I was sure they were going to do. But on 5 October, David Cameron said in an interview with Tom Bradby from ITN that there would be a decision on Gary in weeks rather than months. This was a huge relief but I knew I still had to do everything possible to help to make sure that the decision would be the right one.

A senior police official who regularly works in Iraq and Afghanistan was an ex-neighbour. He's Britain's main expert on lie detectors and I asked him if he would put Gary on a lie detector to prove to our government that Gary did not cause the damage alleged and also that the risk of suicide was a stark reality and not an idle threat.

D. and his wife were really nice people and during a conversation we'd had years before he'd made us laugh when he was talking about vetting his daughter's new boyfriend with the use of a lie detector. The scenario he painted sounded a lot like the film *Meet the Parents*, the parents in the film being the 'Fockers'.

We pitied their daughter's boyfriend but couldn't stop laughing at the idea of what he must have been put through, and we totally understood how in his specialised job Mr D. would have been likely to have seen the very worst of people, and would be overly anxious to protect his daughter.

I spoke to Gary to get his agreement for me to approach our ex-neighbour. Gary was absolutely unfit to be extradited to America and I felt that a lie detector would prove that.

The questions I had prepared included:

1. Did you knowingly cause any damage to any US computer systems?
2. Do you believe you caused any damage to any US computer systems?
3. Do you believe that suicide is a preferable option to extradition to the US?
4. Do you believe in aliens?
5. Do you believe that you have an alien implant in your foot?

6. Do you believe aliens work with the American government?

7. Do you believe aliens work against the American government?

8. Do you believe there is an American space fleet in space?

The reason I asked about the implant is because Gary firmly believes that an alien implant was inserted in his foot during the night many years ago and is still there.

D. was extremely kind, but broke the deeply disappointing news that lie detectors don't work on people with Asperger's.

He also told me that Gary had walked aimlessly in front of his car recently and that he nearly ran him down. The problem was that Gary was living in a twilight world and no longer cared if he died.

After considering Gary's case for six months, the government asked for Gary's mental health to be reassessed by two Home Office-appointed medical experts. This was despite Gary having been assessed several times over by five world experts in autistic spectrum disorders and depression.

It was a huge blow to us as this meant yet more delay. David Cameron had said only a week before that there would be a decision on Gary soon, so it was difficult for me to tell Gary that they wanted even more assessments of his mental health, as it meant he'd be locked in limbo for many more months to come. He could barely cope as it was. The expectation that the end was close and that the government would refuse extradition was what had kept him going.

• • •

On 13 October 2010 thirty-three miners were rescued in Chile after being trapped deep underground for months. The rescue was incredible and was being watched around the world twenty-four hours a day. To see the miners finally free was an extremely moving and truly uplifting experience.

Watching the rescue of Chile's miners reminded me of how, at the time when Jack Straw was the Justice Secretary, the British government had refused to extradite Chile's notorious dictator General Pinochet, said to be responsible for the disappearance of thousands of Chileans.

Now some of the same Home Office advisers who had kept General Pinochet's medical evidence secret from the CPS and from Spain – thus preventing Pinochet from being extradited or from being tried in the UK – appeared to be doing the opposite in Gary's case. They actually listed all of the American allegations against Gary at the start of their instructions to the psychiatrists appointed by the Home Office to assess Gary's mental health. I found this shocking, as the damning and unfounded allegations might well negatively influence the psychiatrists.

Gary had already effectively served a British life sentence of mental torture for an eccentric crime that in 2002 the CPS said would have been likely to attract a six-month community service sentence.

CHAPTER 18

HOME AFFAIRS

November 2010.

When Justice Mitting granted Gary a judicial review of the Home Secretary's decision in January 2010, the criteria he gave for being able to refuse extradition were:

'Did the opinion of Gary's psychiatrist amount to a fundamental change in circumstances? Did the evidence show that suicide would be an almost certain inevitability should he experience extradition?'

If the answer is yes, the Home Secretary can refuse to extradite.

The answer was yes. And in addition to that, there was still further evidence that no court had yet seen, including evidence from psychiatrists in Glasgow of a history of mental illness existing in three generations of Gary's family, the evidence of Gary's mental health issues in his NHS records, the newest assessments of Gary's mental health by top psychiatrists and the fact that the Home Office psychiatrists had now stated in evidence that they could offer no assurance that Gary would not commit suicide... Surely this was more than enough medical evidence for extradition to be refused?

The courts had very recently refused to extradite a convicted

American paedophile who was married to a British Ministry of Justice policy manager, as apparently extradition to his own country would be against his human rights. Yet everyone wanted to see this man locked up. He was described by America as a 'most wanted' criminal, but is now free to wander the streets of London despite being a danger to children.

It puzzles me that Alan Johnson didn't choose to complain about the refusal to extradite to the US this convicted American paedophile. Nor did he complain about the refusal to extradite US-born Mr and Mrs Tollman, or an alleged IRA bomber.

It seems that only Gary, a vulnerable British computer geek with Asperger's syndrome, arrested and indicted prior to the US–UK extradition treaty even being written, incurred Mr Johnson's outrage, despite the CPS confirming that no evidence of the alleged damage has ever been presented to them. I'm glad, however, that Mr and Mrs Tollman were not extradited to the US.

• • •

We were listening to the Jeremy Vine radio show and he was having a phone-in on Gary. The first caller turned out to be Rachel Glastonbury, Gary's very first girlfriend, who he had met at a school camp. Rachel was now a doctor and spoke about how Gary had always been obsessed by space and UFOs, how even as a child she could see how vulnerable he was, and how heartbroken she was over what was happening to Gary now.

Rachel also spoke about how her similarly vulnerable brother Dan, a gentle and talented musician, had taken his own life when he was still in his teens.

We hadn't seen or heard from Rachel in more than twenty years and were really moved by her call and by her kindness and willingness to help Gary.

During this time the National Autistic Society launched a petition for Gary, receiving thousands of signatures within a week in support of him staying in the UK.

On 30 November I was due to give evidence to the Home Affairs Select Committee for a second time. Shami Chakrabarti from Liberty and Jago Russell from Fair Trials were also giving evidence, as was David Blunkett, who had actually signed the extradition treaty but later agreed that he had given too much away.

Just before I was about to appear I got a text from Duncan Campbell of *The Guardian*, saying that the paper was about to publish extracts from WikiLeaks detailing how our previous Prime Minister, Gordon Brown, had personally gone to both the American ambassador and Hillary Clinton asking for Gary to be allowed to serve any sentence in the UK. Gordon Brown had done this without informing anyone, including his own Home Secretary, Alan Johnson.

I was pleased to hear this, as I had no idea that Gordon Brown had raised his head above the parapet and lobbied the Americans to try to help Gary.

Keith Vaz was smiling broadly when he read out the WikiLeaks information that had come through at such an opportune moment. WikiLeaks was the new buzzword and was transforming political perceptions throughout the world.

In the committee hearing, Shami Chakrabarti and Jago Russell put forward an extremely strong case for fairness and forum to be introduced in extradition cases.

I gave evidence last. The Home Affairs Select Committee asked pertinent questions and I was confident in my answers. That they were taking account of such a cross-section of evidence gave me hope that the 2003 extradition treaty really would be changed.

I thanked Duncan Campbell for letting me know about Gordon Brown and WikiLeaks, and Duncan said, 'Julie said you can use her name as a supporter.'

'Julie?'

'Julie, my wife.'

'Julie Campbell?' I said.

'Julie Christie,' said Duncan.

'Julie Christie! I had no idea you were married to *the* Julie Christie.'

I smiled and thanked Duncan and asked him to thank Julie.

It made such perfect sense that Julie and Duncan were married to each other. They were both good people, both creative and both voices for justice.

When we first met Duncan in court, he initially reminded me of Terence Stamp, the actor, but Duncan was younger and nicer-looking and had a gentler and kinder persona. Our friend Joe Winnington (David Gilmour's brother-in-law) told us that the song 'Waterloo Sunset' by the Kinks was about Julie Christie and Terence Stamp. I don't know if this is true, but I do know that Julie Christie and Duncan Campbell just seem so right together, in harmony politically as well as emotionally.

Duncan was so open to listening to what Gary had to say: he always reported the facts, but with compassion and understanding and his take on the effect of world politics on individuals.

On 14 December, my birthday, Gary's MP, David Burrowes, booked a room in Portcullis House for a few hours and we asked MPs to attend to sign a huge Christmas card and to write a message for Gary. The card was made by Gary's barrister's artistic mother, who did a beautiful drawing of the Houses of Parliament on it. Melanie Riley and Liberty were present, and the event gave us a chance to talk to the cross-party MPs who took the time to come.

A man with blond hair entered the room, with style and panache. He stood out from the crowd and we all wondered who he was. It turned out that he was Desmond Swayne, David Cameron's parliamentary private secretary. Everyone thought this was a good sign, believing that he would not have signed Gary's card without David Cameron's blessing.

Dennis Skinner, my sister's MP, also came in to sign Gary's card and I was able to speak to him. Dennis also stands out from the crowd, a charismatic character who never minces his words. I was impressed that such diverse politicians from all political parties, including Angus MacNeil from the Scottish Nationalist Party, took the trouble to sign the card and wish Gary luck.

Theresa May was giving evidence to the Home Affairs Select Committee in Parliament that afternoon. My brother Ian was visiting us from Scotland and he came in with us to listen to her. Ian was fascinated by the workings of Parliament and the grandeur and history of the building. True to form, Keith Vaz again raised Gary's case with the Home Secretary and asked how soon a decision was expected.

There was press outside Parliament, asking me to risk life and limb by standing in the busy road in the freezing cold to have photographs taken of me holding the very large card, so of course I did. Somehow you feel as though Christmas can conjure up a miracle. The story duly appeared in the press, ensuring that Gary's plight wouldn't be forgotten over the Christmas period.

• • •

One of the doctors the Home Office had chosen to assess Gary for suicide risk did not have the required expertise in autistic spectrum disorder, and the other doctor was one of Gary's expert witnesses. Surely using Gary's doctor as theirs was highly unethical and a conflict of interest? The Home Office initially said that they would not wish to use the same doctor, but then changed their mind and insisted on doing just that.

When we strongly objected to this, the Treasury solicitor informed us that they could appoint Gary's psychiatrist if they wanted to and there was nothing we could do about it.

We informed the Home Office that we would be happy for Gary to be assessed by any psychiatrist recommended by the National Autistic Society. However, the Home Office were not prepared to do this: the acting Chief Medical Officer insisted that a psychiatrist with no expertise in the field was perfectly capable of assessing depression, and specifically suicide risk, in someone with ASD. This was a claim we and the National Autistic Society strongly disputed, but the Home Office refused to consider the NAS's offer to forward them a list of experts in the field.

As Gary's life depended on the assessments, we refused a doctor who did not have the expertise required and we objected to Gary's expert witness becoming an expert witness for the Home Office – which would have meant that he could no longer be Gary's expert witness.

Gary had been individually assessed, face to face, by Dr Thomas Berney, Professor Simon Baron-Cohen, Professor Jeremy Turk and Professor Murphy, all of whom were leading experts in the field and all of whom agreed on the diagnosis.

To try to appease the Home Office we arranged for Gary to be assessed by Dr Vermeulen, a Home Office-approved consultant forensic psychiatrist recommended by the NAS. We first invited the Home Office to solely appoint Dr Vermeulen, or any consultant forensic psychiatrist recommended by the NAS, but they refused.

This all seemed to fly in the face of logic and I was feeling deeply uneasy. So I did what everyone regarded as the unthinkable and flatly refused for Gary to be assessed by either of the Home Office's choices.

Gary's legal team hastily arranged a conference and concluded that although it was far from ideal, we had no choice but to do as the Home Office said. We had a very heated discussion in conference as they felt I was making their position difficult and that the Home Secretary might well just decide to extradite Gary if we did not agree to comply.

I've always believed in fairness and transparency, and I firmly believed that what was being forced on us was wrong.

It seems to be well known in legal circles that even the barristers and lawyers refer to certain doctors as hitmen. I'm certainly not saying that was the case with either of the doctors concerned, but I was determined to ensure that absolute fairness was applied.

I was not going to fail in my duty as a parent.

• • •

On 16 December 2010 Lord Maginnis raised Gary's case in the House of Lords.

Extradition: Gary McKinnon
    Question
    Asked By Lord Maginnis of Drumglass
    To ask Her Majesty's government what is their current position regarding the request for the extradition of Gary McKinnon.
    The Minister of State, Home Office (Baroness Neville-Jones): My Lords, a judicial review of a decision by the previous Home Secretary to uphold an order for Mr McKinnon's extradition stands adjourned. My Right Honourable Friend the Home Secretary is reviewing the case against the sole legal test, which is whether, given Mr McKinnon's medical condition,

extradition would breach his human rights. My Right Honourable Friend has sought Mr McKinnon's consent to a psychiatric assessment by clinicians recommended by the Chief Medical Officer. A response is awaited from his solicitors.

Lord Maginnis of Drumglass: I declare an interest in so far as I chaired the independent review of autism services in Northern Ireland and currently chair the Northern Ireland autism regional reference group. I am grateful to the Minister for her Answer, but does she accept that inadequate recognition and the total lack of appropriate interventions for those with an autistic condition, which was first identified and defined by Kanner in 1943, have deprived someone in Gary McKinnon's age group of his human rights and that to extradite him would exacerbate the social neglect that he has suffered? Do we not have a more compelling moral responsibility in this instance than a legal one?

Lord Dholakia: My Lords, many of the judicial avenues open to Mr McKinnon have now been exhausted. The sad part about it is the particular state of disablement that he suffers. A conversation was recorded between the Prime Minister and President Obama in July this year where they said that they were looking for agreeable solutions. Has such a solution been found? Will the Minister confirm that the Extradition Act 2003 does not require contestable evidence? Does it not work to the detriment of British citizens, and should it not be reviewed?

Baroness Neville-Jones: On the first point, as my Right Honourable Friend the Home Secretary has made clear, we have a legal framework within which Mr McKinnon's case is being considered. On the second point, my Right Honourable Friend has asked for a review of extradition provisions, including the US–UK treaty as well as the European extradition warrant. Sir Scott Baker will be considering some of the issues to which she has made reference.

Baroness Browning: My Lords, having been actively involved in the other place in the Gary McKinnon case, I have read his psychiatric reports that were made available to the Home Secretary before the general election. I understand that the Minister is seeking further medical reports. Does she agree that the evidence already before the Home Office shows overwhelmingly that the threat of self-harm is not an idle threat but is very real? Does she also agree, in the light of the damage that has been caused to the American government by WikiLeaks, that, rather than trying to imprison an autistic savant, the Pentagon would do well to employ Gary McKinnon to sort out the weaknesses in its computer system?

(Much laughter even from Baroness Neville-Jones)

Shortly after this the Home Office instructed their doctors to assess Gary *in absentia* i.e. without seeing him. Once again, I was shocked.

In the meantime Karen, Gary's solicitor, asked Dr Vermeulen for an assessment. He was a Home Office-approved expert who had worked in Broadmoor Hospital for many years and had also performed hundreds of assessments on behalf of the Home Office, including being an expert witness in murder cases. We concluded that the Home Office could not ignore Dr Vermeulen's evidence from his face-to-face assessments of Gary.

Karen Todner had stuck by Gary for years and always appointed the very best QCs, barristers and medical experts. She had saved Gary's life on countless occasions by never giving up; even when we had supposedly come to the end, Karen, Ben and Edward, Gary's legal team, always found another way to keep Gary here.

I knew we were firmly on the same side but as Gary's mother I also had to follow my instincts.

Gary's barrister, Ben Cooper, also fought long and hard for Gary and refused to give up on him and was determined to win.

Gary's QC, Edward Fitzgerald, is gentle and kind. Whenever Edward's wife rang him, he would always stop what he was doing and take the time to speak to her. The character played by Colin Firth in the film *Bridget Jones's Diary* is reputed to be based on him.

He also studied all the evidence and paperwork beforehand and didn't just look at the paperwork at the very last minute and then walk into the court and wing it.

Edward would also argue with me, sometimes heatedly, but we didn't fall out and Edward didn't storm off the case in a huff as many QCs could have done. Edward listened and discussed everything, as did Karen and Ben.

No QC or lawyer is infallible, no matter how revered they are. It's important to make sure you fully understand what's happening, trust your instincts and fight your corner if need be.

Edward said to me one day, 'They think I can tell you what to do and they don't understand that I can't.'

I assumed Edward meant the judges and I wondered why anyone was trying to persuade Edward to tell me what to do. Of course, it could have been the DPP or even the prosecutor, but I suppose I'll never know for sure.

Christmas and New Year was the saddest time: arguing with Gary's legal team had made us really fed up. It's always more upsetting to fight with people you like. We were all on the same side, but we each thought we were right, so the atmosphere was tense and highly charged.

I was working on Gary's case on New Year's Eve and I emailed Lord Carlile, not expecting an answer at two minutes past midnight, but he emailed me straight back with a very kind message that made me feel better. Gary's barrister, Ben Cooper, was also working on Gary's case as the bells of Big Ben chimed to bring in the New Year.

When you're feeling scared and vulnerable and are fighting against the odds, simple acts of kindness mean a lot.

Professor Turk was talking about Gary possibly having to be sectioned. The thought of my son being confined to a mental institution like his great-grandma terrified me. What was happening to Gary was wrong on every level. He had never hurt anyone and was gentle to the core. He was also very talented and seeing him imprisoned in fear for so many years was such a waste. He hadn't touched a computer or a musical instrument since 2005.

Gary's psychiatric treatment was expensive and the NHS trust had refused to pay for the care Gary was receiving from Professor Turk at the Maudsley Hospital. They said that Gary would have to see the local mental health services, but when we contacted the local mental health services they told us they had no one there with any expertise in ASD and to contact the National Autistic Society. But it was the NAS who had recommended Professor Turk, who the trust was refusing to pay for. It was a catch-22 situation.

We were incredibly lucky as David Gilmour and Alex Paterson from The Orb had donated royalties to pay for Gary's lifelong psychiatric care. What happens to those who need expert care who can't get it on the NHS and can't afford to pay for it privately?

We were feeling stressed and once again Michael Seamark of the *Daily Mail* came to our rescue by taking us out for lunch. It was such a relief sitting there having pear tart, toffee sauce and ice cream, real comfort food. Just being in another environment to discuss our views and options was often extremely helpful, and Michael always managed to make us smile.

One late night the police brought a two-year-old boy and his baby sister to us as an emergency. When Michael Seamark arrived the following day to take us out for lunch and saw the babies, he just smiled. I said, 'We can all go for lunch together, or we can't go.'

Michael said, 'Of course we will all go out to lunch.'

It was quite an upmarket restaurant and the baby slept peacefully in her carrycot by my side and the two-year-old sat happily in his high chair, smiling and eating.

It had now been eight months since the Home Secretary, Theresa May, had put a halt on extradition, and Gary's anxiety was at an all-time high. 'How long can this go on?' I thought. It felt as though we were trapped in some sort of time warp that we couldn't seem to get out of.

Julian Assange was in court on 7 February and I'd heard that he had chosen to come to the UK because Gary had managed to fight extradition for so many years, and Julian thought he would be safer in the UK. I wondered then if he had made the right decision.

• • •

We were still fostering the three young siblings for one weekend out of every month. Taking them swimming and on outings gave us respite from the relentless routine of working from dawn to dusk, and it was good to see them laughing and having fun.

After each enjoyable weekend the children went home and at the start of a new week I got back to working as hard as possible on the campaign. I wrote to Lord Maginnis and Baroness Browning to thank them for raising Gary's case in the House of Lords.

Lord Maginnis quickly responded and told me about his extensive background in autism and that he was determined to do all he could to help Gary remain in the UK. Ken Maginnis was a fighter with a wealth of experience in politics and in all things to do with autism.

Angela Browning wrote back with an invitation for me to meet her in the Palace of Westminster to discuss ways that she could help. We met there with Angela and with Gary's MP, David Burrowes, the following week.

Baroness Browning is the vice-president of the National Autistic Society and has a first-class understanding of the condition. She talked to me about her son who also has Asperger's and the challenges he faced. She also mentioned the time she had a meeting with adults with Asperger's syndrome who were accompanied by their parents, who did all the talking. Eventually Angela asked one of their sons what he did for a living and he told her he was an astrophysicist.

Angela smiled and said that only in the Asperger's community would you find adults who are astrophysicists and the like, all sitting silently around a table while their parents did all the talking for them.

David Burrowes and Baroness Browning suggested we cancel Gary's appointment with Dr Vermeulen to give the Home Office an opportunity to agree to appoint him to assess Gary. Unfortunately, even with their input, the Home Office still wouldn't budge on its insistence that Gary be assessed by a forensic psychiatrist with no expertise in ASD.

Lord Maginnis has a strong background in autism and always answered my emails, rang me, did TV interviews and stood by my side at 10 Downing Street. He raised Gary's case in the Lords time and time again; he is a fighter who made his voice heard.

Lord Maginnis was a teacher and joined the army and left with the rank of major. He entered politics and was an Ulster

Unionist spokesman on internal security and defence. There were a number of attempts on his life, both as a soldier and as a politician. He described his relationship with religion as saying that 'if my neighbour needed help, I'd help him and he would do the same for me. It didn't matter where you went to Church on Sunday.' He described his passion for rugby as being a good way of building relations between the north and south of Ireland.

Lord Maginnis raised Gary's case in the Lords again on 23 March 2011 and the other lords came on board thick and fast.

Asked By Lord Maginnis of Drumglass

To ask Her Majesty's government what recent discussions they have had with the government of the United States about the extradition of Gary McKinnon.

Lord Maginnis of Drumglass: My Lords, I am grateful to the Minister for that Answer, but it tells me little more than I already know. Is it not ironic that a Parliament which has voted against the lengthy detention of criminals should keep a young man suffering from the condition known as Asperger's syndrome in psychological torture for more than 3,300 days? Is it not time for the Home Office to liaise with those who have expertise in autism? Perhaps the department should go to the National Autistic Society and ask for a list of people with expertise in the area rather than relying on the normal line of, 'Let's see what the Chief Medical Officer says.'

Baroness Browning: My Lords, when I met Mr McKinnon's mother last week, she informed me that his state of health is deteriorating all the time. I hope that my noble friend will be concerned to learn that Mr McKinnon spends every day behind closed curtains and does not participate in life as he used to.

When the Chief Medical Officer chooses an appropriate

psychiatrist or a panel, it is essential that the psychiatrist is someone who specialises in adults with an autistic spectrum disorder. That is because to date, the doctors who have seen Mr McKinnon at the behest of the government have not been specialists, and at the end of their investigations have openly admitted that this is not their specialist area.

Baroness Wilkins: My Lords, does the Minister accept that Gary McKinnon had a history of mental health issues prior to any of these legal issues? Indeed, there is a history of mental illness on both sides of the family going back three generations. It is not just a matter of him having been diagnosed with Asperger's syndrome.

Lord Tebbit: My Lords, is the noble Lord aware that we are all sympathetic to him personally, for he is the victim of a very unfair, unbalanced extradition treaty? If he has any trouble with the American authorities, will he tell them that he has no more confidence that Mr McKinnon would get a fair trial there than some Americans had that IRA suspects would get a fair trial here when the extradition of IRA terrorists was refused by the United States on the basis that they could not get a fair trial in this country?

Lord Tebbit served with the Royal Air Force, during which he flew Meteor and Vampire jets and once had to break open the cockpit canopy of a burning Meteor aircraft to escape from it.

Lord Morris of Aberavon: My Lords, are the government giving any consideration to the fairness of the extradition treaty and will they revisit it?

Lord Marks of Henley-on-Thames: My Lords, accepting the requirements of the extradition treaty and given that the

Home Office already has reports on Gary McKinnon's case from two of the best-known experts on Asperger's and autism – Professor Jeremy Turk and Professor Declan Murphy, both of the Institute of Psychiatry and both of whom are regularly relied upon by Her Majesty's government in relation to these conditions – why has it concluded that it needs a further medical report, and why was it originally looking for a non-specialist report rather than specialist reports, which we now understand the Chief Medical Officer is hoping to provide?

Many politicians want to get rid of the House of Lords but I personally think they frequently act as a safety valve that can prevent unwise or hastily thought-out ideas being pushed through because of government knee-jerk reactions. Although some are political appointees, the lords often tend to act together as a counterbalance that can rein back the government with a tempering voice.

Shortly after the Lords debate we got a letter from the Treasury solicitor giving us seven days to agree to Gary being assessed for suicide risk by the same non-expert doctor we had consistently refused. I had no intention of allowing this.

Gary was assessed by Dr Vermeulen, for the first time on 1 April 2011, April Fool's Day. We hoped this wasn't a bad omen. Gary was incredibly nervous on the way into town and couldn't understand why he had to keep having assessments as he had been assessed multiple times already and was seeing Professor Turk on a regular basis. We sat in the waiting room, which was also the waiting room for Icelandic Airways, and flipped through books with fascinating photos of Iceland.

The harsh-looking way of life was like stepping into the past. It looked cold and bleak and the people were very self-reliant, much as they were in the crofts in the Highlands of Scotland where my dad came from.

We all liked Dr Vermeulen the moment we met him. You knew you were in the presence of a gentle genius whose modesty attempted to disguise that fact. After talking with Gary, Dr Vermeulen interviewed Wilson and me at length and then spent several hours assessing Gary. It was a sunny day and we walked around London and sat in Fitzroy Square until Gary's assessment was complete. Lucy arrived later and while she was being interviewed, Nadine Stavonina came in with a painting to help raise funds for Richard Mills's Research Autism charity. Nadine and Bernard, who works for Research Autism, told us that at their last charity auction a painting of Gary by the Scottish artist Peter Howson had sold for a fair amount of money.

Dr Vermeulen visited Gary at home the following week to further assess him – and to do a safety check to ensure that Gary had limited opportunity to harm himself. Dr Vermeulen was a Home Office-approved forensic psychiatrist who had acted as an expert witness for the Home Office for many years. He was an expert through and through. He knew that Gary was an extreme suicide risk and was doing everything he could to prevent a tragedy from occurring.

US Attorney General Eric Holder came to London on Friday 13 May. Another ominous day – Black Friday.

It proved to be just that when Eric Holder pronounced Gary guilty on British television. This was pretty shocking to everyone, as 'innocent until proven guilty' has always been the bedrock of British justice. This confirmed that Gary would have scant chance of a fair trial in the US when its Attorney General had just publicly pronounced him guilty before any trial had taken place.

Gary had always denied the alleged damage that is said to be required before extradition can be sanctioned, but despite the CPS confirming that no evidence of damage had ever been provided to them, our judges had approved extradition.

Eric Holder's remark naturally added to Gary's anxiety and to my upset and anger.

President Obama arrived in London later that month, officially beginning his state visit on 24 May. The President gave a speech in Parliament and the Queen hosted a banquet in Buckingham Palace in his honour. I'd had such high hopes when Barack Obama was first elected but was becoming increasingly unsure that the US President had the power to lead in the way he might want to.

On 25 May we were watching TV, half-hoping but not expecting anything this time around. However, once again the wonderful Tom Bradby of ITN raised Gary's case with David Cameron and President Obama, and once again we could barely believe it and were jumping up and down, laughing, screaming and crying as we felt that this had to have been pre-planned and that a deal really must have been done this time around to keep Gary in the UK.

Tom Bradby: Mr President, you've talked about the need for robust action on your country's deficit and debt positions. Do you agree with the Prime Minister's supporters that he led the way on the issue or do you feel that, in fact, he has travelled too far and too fast?

And can I just ask you both as a side bar, this time last year we talked about the case of computer hacker Gary McKinnon, on which the Prime Minister expressed very clear views. You said you would work together to find a solution. So, have you found one?

President Obama: On your second question, Mr McKinnon, we have proceeded through all the processes required under our extradition agreements. It is now in the hands of the British legal system. We have confidence in the British legal system coming to a just conclusion. And so, we await resolution, and we'll be respectful of that process.

David Cameron: Thank you. First of all, in the case of Gary McKinnon, I mean, I understand the widespread concern about this case, and it's not so much about the alleged offence, which everyone knows is a very serious offence, it's about the issue of the individual and the way they're treated and the operation of the legal system. And, as the President said, making sure that legal system operates properly and carefully.

The case is currently in front of the Home Secretary, who has to consider reports about Gary's health and his well-being, and it's right that she does that in a proper and effectively quasi-judicial way.

I totally understand the anguish of his mother and his family about this issue. We must follow the proper processes and make sure this case is dealt with in the proper way. And I'm sure that that is the case.

I thought it was wonderful that David Cameron spoke with such compassion about Gary, and when President Obama said that Gary's fate was a British decision that America would be respectful of, everyone in the country thought that Gary was at last home and dry.

The phone didn't stop ringing, interviews were endless and people in the street and in supermarkets and even in the bank were coming up to congratulate us. Many of them had tears in their eyes – everyone was so happy for Gary.

President Obama hosted a dinner for the Queen at the US ambassador's residence in London and we were wondering if the Queen, the Prime Minister and the President might be going to create one of those fairy-tale moments that everyone dreams of and that are seen in so many American films, where the President, the Queen and the PM jointly announce that the little person is pardoned, and the friendship of both countries is reinforced and celebrated by a royal banquet.

Our world desperately needed some fairy-tale endings, and we hoped that Gary's story was going to become one.

CHAPTER 19

STAND UP

The human rights bar to prevent extradition is set so high that it seems to be designed to ensure that virtually no one can reach it. However, prior to the coalition coming to power, extraditions had been refused in several cases under the 2003 treaty, despite most of these people having significantly less reason than Gary for extradition to be refused.

When Gary's case was being heard in the Lords in 2008, when referring to the passage of time that could prevent extradition, one of the Law Lords had said, 'It's not as though it's been ten years.'

Well, it was now ten years so extradition should surely be refused.

I was feeling tired again; totally exhausted in fact. We had so much on our plate I had forgotten all about our low-carb diet and had been comfort eating instead, so I was going to have to start all over again to make sure I stayed healthy. I weighed 11st 3lbs. (I still tend to think in stones and pounds instead of metric as it was so ingrained in me as a child.)

I bought Quorn burgers that were just seven carbs each, and as eggs and cheese have no carbs, omelettes were another good choice. On a low-carb diet I was even able to have strawberries and cream, and also home-made asparagus and celery soup, with or without cream, so I thought I should be able to stick to this and reach a healthy weight again.

What I also needed was to get out and away from the computer and into the little sunshine we tend to get. I'm sure London used to have much longer periods of good weather than it does now.

Julian Assange was in court again for three days in July, and Twitter was full of tweets from people either supporting or condemning him. Twitter becomes like an interactive soap, with everyone as judge and jury, speculating on the real-life dramas of people currently in the news.

It always made us feel nervous when any extradition case came up, as extradition is such a terrifying thing for anyone to face.

Wilson and I desperately needed a break and later that day I saw a post on Twitter from Groupon, who were offering tickets at a really cheap price for an Elton John concert at Hatfield House.

Hatfield House is close to where we live and hosts various events in the grounds of the estate. I decided that this would get us out into the open air and we'd be surrounded by music, so I bought tickets for ourselves and our friends.

Cliff Sullivan had a daughter named Sophie who was very ill when she was born premature. When little Sophie was fighting for her life Cliff and his wife used to listen to a song I wrote called 'I Believe in Miracles'. Fortunately a miracle happened and Sophie pulled through. This was before I met Cliff via Twitter. He and Mike Garrick and the Free Gary followers fought tirelessly for Gary and had regular tweet-storms which loads of people supported. Cliff often included a link to a song called 'I Wish I Knew How It Would Feel to Be Free' by the

Lighthouse Family, relating this to Gary's wish to be free from ten years of mental torment.

I hadn't heard of the Lighthouse Family for years and didn't even know if they were still going but we thought of this as Gary's song.

On 17 July we went along with our friends to the Elton John concert and trudged across the fields to get to the section of the grounds where the concert was being held.

Although it was initially sunny, by the time the main act was about to come on the heavens had opened, and we all stood under umbrellas to create a very English scene – standing in the pouring rain listening to music. There were lots of acts performing that day and shortly before Elton John took to the stage it was announced that the Lighthouse Family was the next act to play. When their first song was 'I Wish I Knew How It Would Feel to Be Free' it was an emotive moment for us. This was Gary's song and tears flowed like the rain as we wished with all our hearts that Gary would soon be free.

Elton John came on afterwards and was amazing. I had forgotten just how good he and his band are and what an amazing pianist Elton is. Raining or not, we had a great time.

• • •

The Rupert Murdoch phone-hacking scandal was taking hold of the country and the Twitter jury were out in force. It was mainly celebrities who were affected, and only when it was found that murdered schoolgirl Milly Dowler's phone had been hacked did all hell break loose, as it was thought that hackers had deleted her voicemail messages. The definitive truth about how the messages were deleted is unlikely ever to emerge. However, recent newspaper stories say it was later established that the messages had probably been deleted automatically by the phone company.

It was now October and we still had no decision on Gary; I couldn't understand why it was taking so long, especially after President Obama had said it was a British decision that America would respect. It was difficult having your hopes raised to the heavens and then crashed to the ground so many times over. It was a cruel game that fate was playing with our lives. Living through extreme ranges of emotions that you never knew you possessed wears you down.

The three siblings we looked after every fourth weekend were finally being placed with a permanent family, who seemed really nice. The children were lovely and anyone would be lucky to have them as part of their family, so we were optimistic that they would all bond.

Trudie Styler invited me to her and Sting's house in London, as she was guest-editing the *Big Issue* and doing a double-page spread on Gary.

When we walked into the living room the first thing I noticed were the cushions on the sofa, which I loved as each cushion had pictures of Trudie and Sting's children imprinted on them. The room is beautiful but, more importantly, it feels like a warm and comfortable home.

Anita Sumner, Sting's sister, was there with Trudie, as she usually is. Although Anita keeps a low profile, she is a warm and caring human being and she and Trudie seem to work closely together on various projects.

We had tea and cakes and Trudie chatted so naturally that it didn't feel like an interview.

The *Big Issue* has come a long way since it was first launched and is now up there with the best of the glossy magazines. Importantly the money paid goes straight to the homeless sellers to give them a hand up and to help them get their lives back on track. So please don't underestimate the professionalism involved in the *Big Issue*'s production or the hard work of the sellers, who bear the brunt of the coldest of weather and deserve to be treated with the same respect as any other working person.

David Gilmour and his wife Polly care passionately about homelessness and gave over £3 million to Crisis, the homeless charity, from the sale of their London home, in an effort to help people suffering from the damaging and debilitating effect of homelessness.

Apparently, after it became public David and Polly tried to persuade some other celebs they knew to do what they had done, but most tended to look away nervously and to change the subject while wandering towards the other side of the room.

Shami Chakrabarti from human rights organisation Liberty also fights constantly for justice. Liberty contacted me to say that I had been shortlisted for a Human Rights Award because of my campaign for Gary and against extradition. I felt honoured as Liberty are such a fantastic organisation that fights constantly against torture and injustice. I didn't think I had a hope of winning and thought it was amazing just to be nominated.

I tweeted to let my friends know, and Liberty emailed me to say that I wasn't supposed to be telling anyone just yet. It was too late – the news was out there.

I had to get something to wear for the Liberty award ceremony but I'd had no time to buy any clothes and money was tight. However, Wilson and I had now lost so much weight that all of my very old clothes fitted me again. At 9st 8lbs I had effectively gained a new wardrobe of all the clothes that I hadn't worn for years.

After trying them all on, I chose a dress that was twenty years old and that I had only worn once. It felt good to be able to fit into it again and since becoming thinner I didn't look or feel so tired anymore.

Wilson, Lucy and I went together to the Liberty award ceremony, which was being held in the Purcell Room at the Queen Elizabeth Hall in the Southbank Centre. I tried hard to persuade Gary to come along as I was worried about him never leaving the house, but he just didn't feel he could face people. Gary has such a distinctive look that everyone recognises him immediately.

When we walked in everyone was so welcoming and Shami and the Liberty staff were all chatting and having drinks. We later went into the main hall and sat near the front row. Sir Patrick Stewart (Jean-Luc Picard of the starship *Enterprise*) was seated in front of us and I thought Gary would have liked that.

Attorney General Dominic Grieve, Kenneth Clarke, and the Norwegian ambassador were there. Norway had suffered a horrific tragedy only a few months earlier when seventy-seven of their young people were gunned down by an extremist.

Simon Hughes MP and Justine Roberts from Mumsnet came onto the stage and announced that the winner for the Liberty Close to Home Human Rights Award was Janis Sharp.

I was overwhelmed. When Simon and Justine presented me with the award I felt shy but gave the following off-the-cuff speech:

> I'd just like to say thank you so much: it's an incredible honour to get this award. People died for our civil liberties and human rights and no government of whatever political persuasion has the right to give them away, because they are not theirs to give and we have to protect them, stop them being eroded.
>
> This government has said that it's going to change the extradition treaty and I believe it will, and they're going to reintroduce the right to have evidence before the horrendous

punishment of extradition can be carried out – and it is a punishment, a horrendous one.

This year, this Christmas will be Gary's tenth since he was arrested; it's the longest time anyone has ever been on bail in this country. He hasn't murdered anyone. He hasn't raped anyone. He was on a computer in his bedroom, and of course what he did was wrong, but if it was so serious he would not have been left on the internet by the authorities for three and a half years after the event.

We really have to protect civil liberties and hold politicians to their pre-election promises and what they say they'll introduce has to be the case, and I believe they will do it and when they do change this treaty – not if, but when – at least Gary will know that ten years of what is mental torture will have achieved something.

And Gary said this to me: knowing that no one else will ever have to go through this again will make what he has gone through worthwhile, and that's the kind of person Gary is.

Gary has Asperger's. He's no ordinary man, he's an extraordinary man and he cares about everyone on this planet and I'm proud to be his mother.

And I would like to thank Karen Todner, his solicitor, and his barrister, Ben Cooper, and Edward Fitzgerald, his QC, and Edmund Lawson, his QC who sadly died.

I'd like to thank my husband Wilson, and Lucy, who's seen Gary through everything, and I also want to thank David Gilmour, who has paid for Gary's psychiatric fees and more. David Gilmour also puts millions into Crisis, the homeless centres, and into mental health. Thank you also to Trudie Styler and to Alex from The Orb, who has helped Gary so much, and Gary's amazing MP, David Burrowes, and to all the politicians, peers and people who have stood by Gary and stood by us, and we will change this extradition treaty, we have to and everybody must stand up and demand it. Because British citizens deserve equal rights to every other nation and no other nation has signed its citizens' rights away, and please, this government ... put them back again. Thank you.

It felt good to have the backing of Shami and Liberty, who stood by us and helped us so much and had done the most incredible Extradition Watch campaign. They made lots of large two-tone paper aeroplanes with 'Don't Let Gary Go' printed on them. Anyone could download the aeroplanes and print them on paper or card, and people all over the world photographed themselves and their families flying the planes in parks, gardens and simulations of space and uploaded them to the Liberty website. It was such an innovative and artistic campaign and seeing people of all ages, abilities and nationalities doing this for Gary was so moving.

This human rights award was for Gary, as I believed it was largely because of his case that forum seemed more likely to be introduced to the extradition process.

On 24 November the Conservative MP Dominic Raab obtained a debate on extradition in Parliament. This was due to Babar Ahmad getting 141,000 votes on a government e-petition asking for him to be put on trial in the UK. Babar Ahmad was fighting extradition for operating a website that allegedly provided material support to terrorism.

Gary's MP, David Burrowes, told us he was going to raise Gary's case in the debate.

Oscar-winning actress Julie Christie wrote:

The debate offers a wonderful opportunity for MPs to strike a blow for decency and fairness in the extradition process and to stand up to bullying and vengeful tactics. It is also important that the case of Gary McKinnon is remembered in this debate so that finally the ordeal of this vulnerable man can be ended and his case can be dealt with in Britain, as should always have been the case.

That evening, Wilson and I were intently watching the extradition debate live online when our mobile phones started ringing constantly. We didn't answer. Then our landline started ringing constantly. We recognised the number and knew it must be a social worker, but still didn't answer.

We periodically fostered children for respite and on an emergency basis during this time, but we were at a crucial point in Gary's case and this debate could be momentous.

However, one of the social workers clearly wasn't giving up, as finding foster carers, especially for siblings, is not easy. So our phones continued to ring.

We were transfixed listening to Gary's MP, David Burrowes, giving a riveting speech that deserved an Oscar.

We usually describe debates of this sort as timely, but, although this evening's debate is timely in the context of the government's current consideration of the Baker review, it would be hard for my constituent Gary McKinnon, who has been living a nightmare and who now faces his tenth Christmas awaiting extradition, to see it in those terms, especially given that the outcome for him will be determined not retrospectively through the reform of extradition laws, which I support, but by medical evidence that is before the Home Secretary as we speak.

Parliament has given time to debate the issue of Gary McKinnon and extradition. We had a vote on forum in 2006 during the passage of the Bill that became the Police and Justice

Act 2006. We have also had urgent questions, Opposition day debates, the report from the Joint Committee on Human Rights, and Westminster Hall debates – and here we are having this debate today. What has not been in short supply is parliamentary attention. What has been in short supply is responsibility – responsibility for the plight of constituents such as Gary McKinnon, and for the injustice that has been done to them. The motion, which is welcome, seeks the restoration, at long last, of responsibility where it should lie.

I want to tell the House about an individual who was blamed for causing the biggest computer hack to hit the United States with an electronic attack on America's biggest port, Houston, in 2001. He was a young British man with Asperger's syndrome. He was not Gary McKinnon, but Aaron Caffrey. He was not extradited to the United States, but was tried in this country and found not guilty.

Then there was the man who was said to be doing 'more harm than the KGB' and to be the 'no. 1 threat to US security'.

He had UFO posters on his wall. He broke into the United States defence and missile systems. He too could have been, but was not, Gary McKinnon. He was prosecuted in this country, and was fined £1,200. And there was the computer virus that inflicted an estimated $5.5 billion worth of damage and controlled 50,000 machines, hijacking sites run by a United States department. Again, that was not Gary McKinnon. It was Andrew Harvey and Jordan Bradley. They were prosecuted here and received six and three months' imprisonment respectively.

Why then is Gary McKinnon being pursued remorselessly by the United States authorities? I believe that one of the motivations is instructive to the debate. The US ambassador on a number of occasions has made his position clear on behalf of the US government. Indeed, several years ago, I asked him directly why the US authorities were doing that. When he replied, he recounted the alleged damage to US naval systems – he went through that in some detail – but then his voice and emotions rose, the severity of his tone increased and he said, referring to the comments left by Gary McKinnon on various websites, 'He mocked us.'

Many of us would think that Gary McKinnon should be praised for exposing flaws in US systems by typing in passwords and getting through systems, as a terrorist could have got through their systems, but that comment, 'he mocked us', shows that, whether we like it or not, politics plays a part in extradition.

Look at WikiLeaks. Just before President Obama came to speak to us, the US Attorney General demanded that Gary McKinnon be extradited. Today, the Right Hon. Member for Sheffield Brightside and Hillsborough [David Blunkett], a former Home Secretary, talked about how he tried to arrange a TV link for Gary McKinnon's trial. I understand that that had no legs because video conferencing is illegal under US law. It requires live cross-examination of witnesses.

… The Baker review, then, has done nothing to give that proper safeguard. Tonight we can do something important. We can make Parliament's views abundantly clear. The reform of extradition law is needed to stop more cases like that of Gary McKinnon. The US ambassador felt mocked by Gary McKinnon's words that were left on US systems, but what about these words and the medical evidence that is before the Home Secretary from Professor Jeremy Turk? He said that 'suicide is now a real probability and will be an almost certain inevitability should he experience extradition'.

Does not this disproportionate extradition of a suicidal and sectionable person, Gary McKinnon, make a mockery of our extradition laws? Are not the life-threatening effects of extradition avoidable by prosecuting him in this country? As I said in 2009, how ill and vulnerable does Gary McKinnon need to be in order not to be extradited to the United States? Tonight, Parliament can say that it will not be mocked, and that it continues to demand proper judicial safeguards. I support the motion.

As David Burrowes was ending his speech we felt proud of him. It was moving and uplifting, one of the best speeches we had ever heard.

We were still transfixed on the screen when our doorbell rang and I jokingly said to Wilson, 'That will be the social workers with children.'

We answered the door and there stood two young social workers with a baby and a toddler who had been taken into care.

'It's completely impractical, Janis, we can't do it right now,' said Wilson worriedly.

'Look at them, Wilson, we have to take them.'

'We can't.'

'We have to, Wilson, look at them. We're not going to let those two little things be carted around or split up and they'll most likely be split up, you know they will. Of course we'll look after them,' I said.

The social workers smiled with relief and brought the children inside. Wilson's look of concern disappeared as little Tommy ran around the living room exploring every corner while baby Chloe lay fast asleep in her crib.

'Tea, anyone? And what would you like, Tommy?' said Wilson with a smile as his familiar kindness shone from his eyes.

Now we were at the height of our fight for Gary but with two little ones to look after. Crazy maybe, but children and animals always fit right in with us.

After putting the kids to bed I wrote to David Burrowes to thank him and to congratulate him on his amazing speech. I then sat writing to politicians and to newspapers about the extradition debate, then fed the baby again and crawled into bed at 1 a.m. I fell asleep instantly until I was awoken at about 4 a.m. by baby Chloe crying. Sleepily peering into her cot I thought how tiny she was.

Walking downstairs to make the baby's bottle I thought there was something comforting about having a baby in the house. Tiring but comforting. Although waking up every three hours to feed and change her took some getting used to as we hadn't done this in a while.

Apart from that Chloe slept most of the time but little Tommy was a bundle of energy from 7 a.m. to 7 p.m.

What Wilson and I found the most wearing was having to drive a forty-mile round trip to take the children to see their parents five days a week. While totally understanding that any parent would want to see their children as often as possible, it makes you realise why local authorities might be finding it difficult to find foster carers and why younger carers aren't prepared to do this. It leaves little room in your life for anything else and we had endless other things to deal with.

• • •

There was another, even bigger, debate on extradition due to take place in the House of Commons, and Trudie Styler's two-page spread on Gary and on extradition was in the *Big Issue* on the same day.

When we saw the piece in the *Big Issue* we were impressed – the interview really highlighted what Gary had been going through for almost a quarter of his life. The article was very professionally presented and the photographs of Gary were artistic and powerful.

In another section of the magazine they had interviewed the *Big Issue* sellers themselves, and this was an inspirational piece accompanied by the most amazing photographs.

On 14 December, someone sent me a large, beautiful bouquet of flowers. The colours were amazing and the scent filled the house. I looked at the card and it was from Michael Seamark and James Slack of the *Daily Mail*. I couldn't believe that they had remembered my birthday.

Pinksy, our little white cat, rubbed herself against the flowers, covering her face in yellow pollen. She looked incredibly cute, but I found out later that lilies are highly toxic to cats, so it was extremely lucky that there were no lilies in the bouquet.

The bell rang again and it was a large hamper from Trudie and Sting. It included organic oil and honey and wine made on their estate in Tuscany. To know that you are in people's thoughts when you are going through a difficult time is just so nice and so appreciated. To complete the day Wilson made a fantastic meal – and I had a great birthday.

In February 2012 we arranged to go to 10 Downing Street to mark Gary's tenth year of being on bail. It was also Gary's birthday on 10 February and we were handing a letter in to the PM to remind him that Gary was still waiting while his life was passing him by … and to remind the politicians that we weren't going away.

David Cameron had arranged for me to meet with Damian Green in the House of Commons later that day, as he was one of the ministers dealing with extradition for the Home Office. I believe that my MP, Grant Shapps, and Gary's MP, David Burrowes, were partly responsible for this meeting. The importance of having a good MP on your side when your back is against the wall cannot be overestimated. Gary and I were fortunate to have two MPs who fought with all their might to keep him in his own country.

We left the children with our good friends Pauline and Steve, award-winning foster carers who had recently adopted their son Christopher. Tommy and baby Chloe had been in their home lots of times so we didn't have to worry about them while we were in town for a few hours.

When Trudie Styler discovered that I was going to No. 10 she dropped everything and flew in from New York to offer her support, as she had done so often before.

We took a huge number ten to Downing Street with a signed letter from lots of eminent people, but we weren't allowed to take the number ten through the gates. Lord Maginnis and our MPs, David Burrowes and Grant Shapps, negotiated with the police until they eventually allowed us in with our huge number ten.

I handed in the letter to the Prime Minister.

It was a freezing cold day and after leaving No. 10 Trudie drove several of us back to her house in the centre of London, where we were treated to warm home-made soup and hot drinks. I'd been there several times before and Sting's sister Anita Sumner was there too.

I chatted to Trudie about Gary and told her about the two little ones we were fostering. Trudie said that she could do that but probably wouldn't be allowed to foster because she travelled a lot.

'Do the newspapers know you do this?' she said.

I told her they didn't as my fight was for Gary and that I hadn't spoken about other aspects of my life.

I explained how children were often underweight when they arrived and that Tommy didn't talk and didn't know or answer to his own name when he arrived. But in the space of just weeks he was answering to his name, and within months had learned lots of words and even a few very short sentences. He had also started experimenting on a grand piano belonging to friends of ours, and seemed naturally very musical. Both he and baby Chloe had put on weight and were happy.

Trudie smiled, a really warm, I-can-empathise-with-that kind of smile.

Trudie genuinely cares about people, is serious enough to be interesting but has a sense of humour that had us falling around laughing when she put on a convincing Irish travellers' accent in the car when she was taking off the character that Brad Pitt had played in the film *Snatch*. Trudie was executive producer of Guy Ritchie's film *Lock, Stock and Two Smoking Barrels* and the follow-up *Snatch*.

I was meeting immigration minister Damian Green and his advisers later that day. Trudie's car took us to the Palace of Westminster and we both attended the meeting, where I felt I was literally fighting for Gary's life.

Damian listened as I put Gary's case across. Trudie asked why Downing Street was now blocked off from the public when years ago we could walk right up to the door.

When the meeting ended Damian said I'd put Gary's case across passionately and he was going to think about what I'd said and discuss it with Theresa May and her advisers. A senior Home Office adviser who was present shook my hand warmly, but no one knows what's really in another's mind. It later transpired that some government advisers wanted Gary extradited, so I fear a warm handshake can sometimes mean little in the corridors of power.

When we came out of the meeting Trudie, Wilson, Claire Simmons and I met up with Zac Goldsmith, who wanted to treat us to lunch on the terrace of the House of Commons. Unfortunately I had two TV interviews lined up so had to leave.

• • •

Wilson then told me that Rebecca, our supervising social worker, had been phoning us constantly, wanting to know who was caring for the children while we were in town. She said that our friend Pauline, who was babysitting for us, didn't have an up-to-date CRB (Criminal Record Bureau) check. Rebecca had informed social services of this and said that social services were placing the children with other carers.

I informed Rebecca that Pauline actually did have a current CRB check which was still valid, as it had been required by the local authority when Pauline and Steve were adopting their foster child. Rebecca responded that they had to have a CRB check from the agency – a local authority CRB check wasn't good enough.

I pointed out that Pauline and her husband had worked for and were award-winning foster carers for the same fostering agency for years and that the local authority's own rules on their own website stated that friends who you would trust to look after your own children could be used to babysit your foster children, and that if you felt your friends needed to be CRB checked then you shouldn't be using them in the first place.

It was clear that the children, who knew our friends well, were happy and being well cared for during these few hours.

We walked into the TV studios and Alastair Campbell was there. I had never met him before and we talked briefly, but I felt too upset to say much.

I was feeling tearful as I was worried about Gary and I was

worried about the children. During the interview I was fighting to hold back tears as I'd had to do many times before and I managed it, but only just. Everything that was happening seemed so cruel and unnecessary.

I cancelled the next interview as Wilson and I had to get back home to say goodbye to the children. I had also lost a prime-time BBC slot that would have helped Gary's case.

Rebecca rang us again when we were on the train to tell us that the local authority might be collecting the children directly from our friend's house. Not only might we lose our chance to say goodbye to the children, but Pauline and Steve would be upset about social workers possibly barging into their house when their autistic son was there.

When we got home after collecting the children from our friends, the social workers were waiting in a car outside our house.

I was dreading telling little Tommy that he was going to another house, as he was so settled with us and had been coming on in leaps and bounds. The young local authority social workers were nice, and sensitive to everyone's feelings. They were uncomfortable about the unplanned removal of the children and didn't seem to understand themselves why our friends, who had just adopted their autistic foster child and had a local authority CRB check, were deemed unsuitable as babysitters because their CRB check had not been commissioned by the very fostering agency they had worked for for years. Nothing was making sense to me any more. The unnecessary removal of the children from a very happy home resonated with the unbearable fear of Gary, our own son, being forcibly removed from his home and family to be locked up in a horrendous foreign prison thousands of miles away from everyone and everything he had ever known.

It was odd as, although we had never had a lot of money, we used to live a kind of charmed life – but suddenly, in a heartbeat, our lives were embroiled in a nightmarish reality.

Watching a usually happy and energetic three-year-old, who rarely cried, sitting quietly and completely still on the sofa while his lip trembled until he was physically sick was the saddest thing. I sat him on my lap to try and comfort him.

This totally unplanned removal of the children at their bedtime was difficult for everyone but our concern was the effect on the children, who everyone agreed had settled so well with us. They didn't understand what was happening. Had the move been planned so that we could have introduced little Tommy and his baby sister to the new carers, it would have been so much easier on them. A sudden removal from a happy home usually has a detrimental effect on a child, and who really knows how deeply felt or how long-lasting this will be.

The local authority social worker called the agency social worker the following day to say she had not been happy about how the placement had ended the previous night.

No complaint was ever made against us.

Rebecca the social worker turned up at our home the next morning with her manager, and both appeared to be in superiority mode. I was sad and tired so was going to let it go, but when they came into our house, seeming to pull rank and attempting to treat us like wayward children, I decided I'd had enough. Whether it was US officials or agency social workers, I felt I had to fight this injustice. I didn't want what had just happened to happen to other children and to carers less able to stand up for themselves.

I pointed out that current government guidelines said that using trusted friends to babysit was the preferred choice. They then responded by saying that the agency's rules were of a higher standard than either the local authority's or the government's. Hearing someone try to justify the wrong that had happened by saying something that to me sounded so silly would have been embarrassing and laughable if it hadn't been so desperately sad.

On the local authority's own website it quotes regulations stating that only trusted friends should be used to babysit and if a foster carer or local authority feels that a babysitter has to have a CRB check undertaken then that person should not be babysitting.

Rebecca later said that the reason for the unplanned removal of the children was because we left them with a carer who did not have a CRB check. Yet when Rebecca and her manager came to discuss the matter after the event, one of them suggested that it was acceptable to leave foster children with a neighbour for a few hours, which was in direct contradiction to everything they had said and is something I would never do.

The agency and local authorities had signed up to the government guidelines. Tim Loughton, under-secretary of state for children, said: 'I would like your help in promoting the clear default position that children should as far as possible be allowed the same opportunities to take part in normal everyday activities as would reasonably be granted by parents to their own birth children. We also need to challenge the myths around CRB – and tackle excessive administration that may have arisen around the day to day parenting decisions of foster carers.'

To undermine such a sensible policy from a government minister, brought in to prevent foster children from being marginalised and made to feel different from their peers, undermines both the carers and the very children who were intended to benefit from that policy. Foster children need to feel that they are part of a family, and that includes the carers' extended family and trusted friends who are an essential part of their lives.

I decided to lodge a complaint. The agency acted swiftly and professionally and a highly competent senior manager sorted it out, put us back on the vacancy list and everyone agreed that the removal of the children should never have happened.

We were asked to foster again soon afterwards but we declined and weren't sure whether we should ever foster again.

However, I have to say that the agency we work for is one of the very best and fully supports their carers. We have also worked with some fine social workers, who work extremely hard to protect vulnerable children and families.

CHAPTER 20

HUMAN RIGHTS AND HUMAN WRONGS

Pensioner Christopher Tappin was extradited on 24 February 2012 and he and his family were devastated. Seeing Christopher saying goodbye to his wife Elaine at Heathrow airport was heartrending.

Gary was hugely upset by this and said, in a matter-of-fact kind of way, that they should have taken their own lives to avoid Christopher being extradited. To Gary this was the logical answer to escape the terror.

Mrs Tappin was in tears as her husband, who was also her carer, was extradited to the US to face however many years' imprisonment. Mrs Tappin has a rare illness and her prognosis is not good, and for Mr Tappin, aged sixty-five, the stress of extradition could easily lead to a heart attack or a stroke, meaning they might never see each other again.

Elaine Tappin was bravely giving evidence to the Home Affairs Select Committee and I was in the audience, as were David Bermingham and Melanie Riley. We were very moved listening to Elaine eloquently delivering her evidence while struggling emotionally.

When Elaine had completed her account, Attorney General

Dominic Grieve and Director of Public Prosecutions Keir Starmer gave their evidence.

They had not been present to listen to Mrs Tappin's emotive evidence and to see how much she hurt, as she bravely fought back tears, some of which escaped and rolled down her cheeks, tugging at everyone's heartstrings.

When the Director of Public Prosecutions and the Attorney General started talking they began to appear more like a couple of wayward schoolboys doing a gig, acting smart and smiling inappropriately when answering questions from the Home Affairs Select Committee. They seemed totally lacking in empathy and their demeanour and answers made them sound foolishly insensitive but I don't believe they had any conception of this, or of the lives being ruined by the extradition treaty.

Journalist Quentin Letts was annoyed at their behaviour and said loudly at the end of the session, 'Bad show, boys, very bad show.'

I couldn't understand it. Keir Starmer had written six books on human rights. I had such faith and expected so much more of him as DPP, but when I made a point of speaking to him after the session there was no trace of understanding.

'I'm feeling very uncomfortable,' said Mr Starmer. 'Speaking to you is making me feel very uncomfortable.'

Did he have any idea how that sounded to me, when he was supporting the extradition of my son to some foreign hellhole?

When I told the DPP of the mental torment Gary had been living in for a decade, he responded with the same stock phrases that officialdom used: that it had been through many courts and they had all agreed that extradition should take place. Yet officialdom knew full well that no evidence was required to extradite anyone from the UK anymore, that allegations could no longer be contested in extradition cases, and that 'having been through all of the courts' meant nothing, as the judges' hands were basically tied because of the iniquitous one-sided treaty that the DPP was now apparently trying to defend.

Writing about human rights is one thing, but actually upholding human rights is another. It requires action and the courage to acknowledge that even countries such as the UK and the US are capable of abusing human rights.

Would our Director of Public Prosecutions and our Attorney General really feel able to look a man in the eye who had been locked up in solitary confinement for an inordinate number of years, and say to that man that it made them feel uncomfortable?

If not radically changed, the effects of this treaty will be a damning legacy left to the children and grandchildren of those who defend it, as well as of those who fought to change it, and of those who did nothing.

One of the things that shocked me during my ten-year fight was the discovery that some senior unelected government officials seem to believe that it is they who are running our country rather than our elected politicians.

The same advisers are often there through successive governments and some have worked under – or should I say 'over' – six or seven different Home Secretaries and seem to think that politicians are merely front-men for their policies.

Our elected leaders are constantly sent out to do 'appearances' which keep them so busy that without working 24/7 they can end up rubber-stamping crucial decisions that are being made by the same old unelected officials. Is this democracy?

Programmes like *Yes, Minister* and *The Thick of It* are uncomfortably closer to the truth than most people realise and without leaders who have the guts to make their own decisions, democracy could be all but lost.

I was up against UK government advisers as well as the might of the US government. I knew they were capable of crushing even the most powerful – but the power of love is an awesome force, and I had that.

Some politicians can forget that the reason they are there is because they work for us and were elected to protect our interests.

Whenever judges and the government talk about a case being 'in the public interest' I'm at a loss to know just who they believe the public are.

However, there are some incredible politicians out there on all sides of the political spectrum, who really do dedicate their lives to helping their constituents and strive to make the UK a better place to live in.

• • •

David Cameron was going to America on 12 March. Two people rang from the House of Commons to tell me that, among other things, he was going to raise the extradition treaty with President Obama.

Gary and I were afraid to get our hopes up again, as Prime Minister Cameron and President Obama had spoken about Gary at both their joint worldwide press conferences and here we were, still waiting and still worrying.

I was glad that Samantha Cameron was going to the US with her husband. David Cameron had been fighting hard for Gary and for a fairer extradition treaty and I didn't want that to change. When he flew on Air Force One without his wife, I was afraid that he might be compromised or 'got at' in some way.

So many leaders become almost unrecognisable once in power that I sometimes wonder if they've been cloned. Obviously I don't really believe that, but what the heck causes some people to change so much once elected that their personalities can become so different?

I did more interviews as TV and radio also got wind of the fact that David Cameron might be raising Gary's case again with President Obama.

We were also waiting to receive copies of the *in absentia* medical reports from the Home Office-instructed doctors. When they finally arrived they were worse than we expected.

One doctor, without seeing Gary, had totally altered his opinion from his original – and only face-to-face – assessment. His new report bore virtually no resemblance to the original, yet the original had been based on even stronger face-to-face assessments by eminent psychiatrists.

Channel 4 News was shocked at the glaring discrepancies between the assessments and Cathy Newman did a big piece that evening, pointing out, line by line, the stark differences in the doctor's medical opinion on Gary once he had been instructed by the Home Office.

Shami from Liberty appeared on the news and made it clear exactly what she thought of this incomprehensible change of opinion.

The BBC started running a ticker along the bottom of their screen saying words to the effect that Gary was no longer a suicide risk and was likely to be extradited.

Gary was distraught. I was angry. Friends were ringing up, shocked and upset, thinking that we'd lost and that Gary would take his own life.

I didn't believe that what had just happened was anything to do with the government; however, unelected senior officials in government were another story.

The Home Office had given us a very short time to respond to their *in absentia* medical reports and we decided that the best form of response was for Gary to have three new face-to-face medical assessments from Professor Simon Baron-Cohen and Professor Jeremy Turk, both leaders in the field, and Dr Jan Vermeulen. The NAS, among others, recommended Dr Vermeulen, a Home Office-approved consultant forensic psychiatrist who had conducted countless assessments on behalf of the Home Office and was their expert witness in numerous court cases.

Why on earth the woman who was standing in as the Chief Medical Officer chose not to appoint any of the experts recommended by the National Autistic Society remained beyond my comprehension.

I spoke to Karen and she instructed all three doctors to do separate, urgent, up-to-date assessments of Gary's mental health and suicide risk.

I also wrote out my witness statement for Karen to submit to the Home Office.

Sky News and ITV wanted me to do interviews again and ITN sent a car to collect us. The driver who arrived to take us home afterwards was a Jamaican man with a really cool accent, as opposed to the Ja-fake'an accent which a lot of younger people who have never left London tend to use when trying to impersonate the real McCoy.

I love a real Jamaican accent where Jaguar is pronounced 'Jagwwa'. In fact I love accents and I hate it when some people say, 'Oh! You've still got a Scottish accent,' as though it's something I should have lost the second I set foot in London. I usually respond by saying, 'If you went to live in Scotland do you think you would acquire a Scottish accent?' And almost without fail they say 'No!'

The taxi's sat-nav wasn't working, the driver had no idea where he was going, and he looked tired, really hangdog, dead-in-the-water-type tired. He could barely keep his head up and was struggling, the way you do when you've been working all day and night and can't think properly.

He got a call from his office telling him that his next stop after he dropped us off was Cornwall, to pick up CDs from a well-known band and bring them straight back to London.

'Cornwall!' I exclaimed. 'We're in London; do you know how far away Cornwall is?'

'Half an hour away?' said the driver hopefully.

'No! It's about 300 miles away and will take you about four or five hours to get there and another five hours to get back and I can see you're already almost falling asleep.'

'Three hundred miles away? Are you sure?'

'I'm sure.'

We stopped and showed him where Cornwall was on the map. With the sat-nav not working, finding his way in the dark was going to be even harder.

He laughed, a cool resignation kind of laugh. 'I have to go,' he said. 'I'm working off a debt to the man who runs the taxi firm and that man is a hard taskmaster.'

'Well, isn't there someone you can take with you to share the driving? You'll never make it otherwise.'

I felt sure he would have an accident if he drove all that way and I eventually persuaded him to phone one of his friends, who as it turned out was happy to go to Cornwall. We stopped off at his friend's house to pick him up and much to my relief his friend was alert, wide awake and in good humour.

They dropped us off at home and we wished them well but I was annoyed at the exploitation of people that still goes on today. Whatever the driver owed the man who owned the taxi firm, I bet he had paid back his debt a hundred times over.

When we got in the door we were hungry, but had to take the dogs out before we could eat. When we got back I was too tired to even hold a cup in my hand and fell fast asleep, head on table, in front of the computer, which I had switched on in the vain attempt to write a letter. Wilson woke me up with tea and biscuits and we watched some TV and then went to bed.

· · ·

Dr Vermeulen rang to arrange to see Gary on 1 April to do another assessment. It was so odd, as the first time we had taken Gary to see him a year ago it had also been April Fool's Day. I think fate has a weird sense of humour.

Days later we took Gary to Cambridge by train to have a new assessment with Professor Simon Baron-Cohen. Just leaving the house had been incredibly hard for Gary. His entire future would be based on these assessments and he was in a desperate state of mind. I wanted to comfort him but there was nothing I could say to pull him back from the brink. It was agonising to see him like this and at that moment I could understand why he thought death would be an escape.

We took Gary to Trinity College, with its cobbled pathways and castellated exterior, with arched entrances, mullioned windows and medieval oak-panelled doors. Wilson and I left Gary with Professor Baron-Cohen for his assessment while we wandered around Cambridge. The narrow, cobbled streets and little cafés and street markets are lovely to walk around, and a bicycle being the most popular mode of transport adds to the university town atmosphere.

When we went back to collect Gary, Simon asked us to come back later as he needed more time. Gary had been crying, a release he desperately needed. For so long he had seemed almost frozen and stiff, with clenched teeth and hands and a rigidity of mind and body, which were ill equipped to contain the turmoil, tension and terror he was experiencing.

After the up-to-date assessment of Gary's mental state was over, for some reason I felt a huge wave of relief as we headed back to the train station. It turned out that the next train wasn't due for another hour, so we went for tea in a Turkish café close to the station. Gary and I had green peppermint tea with real peppermint leaves, Wilson had Turkish coffee and we had the best-tasting cakes, some with fresh strawberries. It was just so nice sitting there. No one knew where we were so we felt safe. We asked for the bill and the woman told us it was £80.

'Eighty pounds!' exclaimed Wilson. 'How can it be £80?'

After a lot of discussion with the owner, it transpired that it was eighteen pounds, and the confusion was in the accent.

As we took Gary back on the train I looked at this intelligent, gentle and hugely talented person sitting opposite me who had so much to offer and I wondered when the powers that be had become so cold and unforgiving and lacking in humanity or perspective. I loved Gary so much and would have liked and admired him even if he wasn't my child. He is an extraordinary human being.

Karen was going on holiday to New York for her birthday, which was on 10 April. We had to have the evidence from Dr Vermeulen, Professor Turk and Professor Baron-Cohen and all our witness statements served on the Home Office in good time.

• • •

On Karen's birthday, the European Court of Human Rights ruled against Babar Ahmad and Talha Ahsan and ruled that they could be extradited to America. This was devastating news for them and their families. Babar Ahmad had been imprisoned in the UK for eight years and Talha Ahsan for six years, so to my mind it seemed that they had already served their sentences, even if the website they were accused of running had been illegal.

Talha Ahsan is by all accounts a gentle man, a poet with Asperger's syndrome. He was twenty-six years old when he was arrested in July 2006 and accused of jointly running a website with Babar Ahmad, although the website had apparently been shut down by the authorities four years earlier.

In the days before the court's final decision, Talha's brother Hamja said he listened to one of Gary's songs, 'Something in Silence', on repeat late into the night. Since the decision on his brother, Hamja has been recognised for his art and for his campaign work and Talha has been recognised for his poetry.

I met Talha's brother and parents in the Houses of Parliament and they were kind, gentle and warm, as was Babar Ahmad's family. These were not radical Muslims who refused to shake hands with a woman: Babar's sister was a doctor. It was heartbreaking that both sets of pensioner parents might never see their sons again if they were extradited.

How on earth can it not be against someone's human rights to be locked up in a maximum security prison, in solitary confinement, in an alien country, when the United Nations and the American human rights organisation ACLU have branded similar cases as torture?

At least one man has been held in solitary confinement in the US for forty years.

How one human being can do this to another is beyond my comprehension.

The entrepreneur Karl Watkin was prepared to personally finance a private prosecution of Babar Ahmad and Talha Ahsan in a bid to have them tried in the UK, but this was rejected by the Director of Public Prosecutions.

Talha Ahsan and Babar Ahmad were subsequently extradited and are being held in solitary confinement at Connecticut's supermax prison, which is the subject of a recent documentary by Yale Law School entitled The Worst of the Worst.

CHAPTER 21

JUBILEE FOR JUSTICE

had written a letter to the Queen on 20 April and by chance I discovered that it was the Queen's birthday the following day. I was hoping that the Queen might be able to issue a pardon, or have a quiet word in President Obama's ear asking him to agree to Gary being tried in the UK.

Gary's nightmare had begun during the Queen's Golden Jubilee. Ten years later the Queen was now celebrating her Diamond Jubilee, so it seemed an appropriate time to ask for a pardon.

I sent a copy of my letter to the Queen to Gary's MP, David Burrowes, and he wrote about the original meaning of the Jubilee and how it applied to Gary:

The last time this country celebrated a Diamond Jubilee was in the reign of Queen Victoria. In 1897 it had a deeper meaning, with a celebration of dignity and freedom – the principle that no one had the right to take advantage and enslave anyone.

Gary McKinnon is a slave of the unfair extradition process which has sold away his rights as a British citizen to a foreign land.

This week Gary's mother Janis Sharp drew upon the Queen's prerogative power of mercy, which has only really been used to save someone from execution at the scaffold or for a sentence miscalculation. It is not far off where we have got to with Gary.

I told Parliament earlier this year that the extradition of Gary would be tantamount to his execution and Damian Green, now the minister responsible for extradition, agreed in 2009 when he described him facing 'an explicit death sentence'.

The Jubilee originates from biblical times and a Jubilee year (normally fifty years) would result in slaves and prisoners being freed.

Gary's call is a Jubilee call for freedom and justice, not impunity; for a trial here – the country of his citizenship, the country where the offences were committed and the country where a domestic police investigation took place ten years ago.

As we celebrate the Jubilee I hope that we will witness an end to the 'cruel' prospect of extradition for Gary McKinnon and see the 'compassion' spoken by the Deputy Prime Minister and Prime Minister.

It would be worthy of a toast bigger than in 1897 and would be led by Gary's mother Janis Sharp, who wrote: 'This compassion for a vulnerable man from the monarch of our nation would surprise and touch the hearts of everyone and would make all parents, including those of disabled and mentally challenged children, feel that they mattered.'

David Burrowes is a man in a million and the most amazing MP to have on your side.

• • •

I woke up one day with the song 'The Edge of Glory' in my head and for whatever reason it made me feel really optimistic. I grabbed some tea and honey on toast and switched on my computer. There was an email from Nick Clegg's office, asking us to remove their email address from our website as they could not cope with the volume of emails in support of Gary.

This made me laugh. I was incredibly happy about the level of support Gary was receiving and I had no intention of removing their email address from our website as that would defeat the purpose.

I got a letter from the Queen thanking me for my letter and saying she understood my distress and concern as a mother, but that as a constitutional sovereign she acts only on the advice of her ministers and remains strictly non-political at all times. The Queen instructed that my letter be forwarded to Home Secretary Theresa May, and the Palace sent good wishes for Gary and me for the future.

That the Queen had responded was great, but I had been hoping that, as the Queen's prerogative was used by Tony Blair's government to bring in the extradition treaty, the Queen could use her prerogative of mercy in her Diamond Jubilee year to pardon Gary.

• • •

It was now July. We were informed that a directions hearing was to take place in the High Court on 5 July and that, in addition, two further court dates had been set aside for 24 and 25 July. Directions hearings are usually very short affairs, so I was baffled as to why the extra days might be needed. And with the Home Secretary in her quasi-judicial role about to make a decision on Gary, surely his case no longer had anything to do with the court?

I was suspicious of the prosecution's motives.

At the last minute I decided to submit a statement to the

court as I wanted to make sure the judges were fully aware of all the facts, including the extent of the new medical evidence that had been submitted.

Gary's QC was working abroad so his barrister, Ben Cooper, was dealing with the hearing. Ben made sure that the judges were given my statement in court that very morning before the court was in session.

Wilson and I walked into the court, which was filled with journalists keen to find out why these court dates had been arranged. We sat behind Gary's barrister and the judges came into the room and addressed the court.

Prosecuting QC Hugo Keith claimed that the Home Office had received one medical report with regard to Gary. One of the judges – Sir John Thomas, President of the Queen's Bench – looked surprised and said, 'Have you read this?', referring to my statement.

Mr Keith muttered something about 'another one of Mrs Sharp's statements'.

The judge repeated to Mr Keith, 'Have you read this?'

Sir John Thomas knew from my statement that Gary had undergone multiple medical assessments by some of the foremost experts in the field. He said to Mr Keith, in what seemed like a stern voice, 'I suggest you sit down and read this', which Mr Keith duly did.

Extract from my statement to the court dated 4 July 2012:
In May 2010 the Home Secretary halted the proposed extradition of my son Gary McKinnon in order to review and to consider the medical evidence.

In October 2010 David Cameron announced that a decision on my son Gary would be given in a matter of weeks not months.

In November 2010 the Home Office suddenly decided to

request further medical reports, which we provided and which included new medical evidence from face-to-face reports.

Gary provided the Home Office with multiple assessments, including three separate 2012 face-to-face assessments: one by Home Office-approved consultant forensic psychiatrist the esteemed Dr Jan Vermeulen, another by Professor Baron-Cohen, one of the most internationally respected experts in his field, and another by psychiatrist Professor Turk, an internationally renowned expert in Asperger's syndrome who has overseen Gary's care on a regular basis.

Professor Baron-Cohen and Professor Turk's 2012 evidence also qualified and reinforced Professor Murphy's original face-to-face evidence.

As the National Autistic Society twice wrote to the Home Office to say that only a consultant forensic psychiatrist who was an expert in autism should be used to assess Gary, we were understandably unable to agree to the involvement of any doctor without the required expertise in ASD.

Professor Simon Baron-Cohen stated in his August 2008 report on his assessment of Gary,

'With such a low EQ, it is important to recognise that his [Mr McKinnon's] emotional age or social intelligence is at the level of a child, even if his intelligence in systemizing is at an advanced level.'

Dr Vermeulen in April 2012 deemed my son, Gary McKinnon, Unfit for Trial and at Extreme Suicide Risk.

Gary rarely ever leaves his home as he is traumatised to the core. A boy who cycled, swam, composed music and sang, now sits in the dark with his cats and never wants to see or speak to anyone. He has no life, and is broken, like a wounded animal with no outlet and no hope, seeing only the dark side and the cruelty that exists in the world.

My only child has lost ten years of his youth and has aged and died before my eyes.

The National Autistic Society recommended several consultant forensic psychiatrists including Dr Vermeulen, and both NAS and Gary's solicitors invited the Home Office to appoint 'any one' of the said psychiatrists to assess Gary.

Gary's solicitor had Gary assessed by Dr Vermeulen, one of the consultant forensic psychiatrists recommended by NAS.

Dr Vermeulen, a consultant forensic psychiatrist and Home Office-approved expert in assessing risk, in his April 2012 report defined Gary as being UNFIT FOR TRIAL and at EXTREME SUICIDE RISK.

There is no disagreement between Dr Vermeulen, Professor Baron-Cohen and Professor Turk's opinion.

The judges were also surprised that the acting Chief Medical Officer for the Home Office had appointed a doctor who was not an expert in the condition to assess Gary. They said that they could not tell the Home Office which expert to choose but felt that an expert in the field should have been appointed.

The judges had assumed that the court dates set for 24 and 25 July were for them to hear Gary's case. They seemed annoyed at Mr Keith for not having informed them that 24 July was only a contingency court date, but they decided to go along with it anyway, to give us further time to choose whether or not to agree to Gary seeing the doctor who lacked the required expertise.

We were happy to rely on the existing very new medical reports, but decided to accept the additional time offered in order to provide further explanation from Dr Vermeulen, which the judges thought would be helpful.

The point of that day's hearing appeared to be to force Gary to have yet more medical assessments. These would then supersede the brand-new assessments which were all in his favour. We wondered why the prosecutor was bothering do this, given that he appeared totally confident that the Home Secretary would rule against Gary.

We were getting close to the end and I was so worried about the *in absentia* medical reports from the Home Office doctors that I felt I needed to get some independent advice as to what action I could take.

On 9 July I visited an important doctor who knew his stuff and had a reputation that carried weight. Dr C. read the 'before' report by the doctor who had conducted a face-to-face examination of Gary and then written the contrasting 'after' report without seeing Gary, once the said doctor was appointed by the Home Office. Dr C. said that I had a strong case, as there was no basis to explain the doctor's radically altered opinion after he was engaged by the Home Office.

The next morning I was searching through the online newspapers and couldn't believe my eyes when I saw the headline 'Gary McKinnon hacking prosecution called "ridiculous" by US defence expert'.

'Hackers like McKinnon should be recruited, not prosecuted, if the US wants to dominate cyber-warfare,' said Professor John Arquilla.

This was the best news I had heard in a long time. John Arquilla was an expert in naval warfare and in 'cyber-warfare' – in fact, he was the one who had coined this phrase. His opinion carried real weight, and I was so proud of him for bravely standing up for a vulnerable British man he had never met.

It was also good to see the compassionate face of the US: there had been so many anti-American comments in various publications because of the perception that we were being bullied and abused by overzealous US prosecutors.

Professor John Arquilla was an intellectual who worked with and understood hackers – he described them as being like shy woodland creatures. Up until now I hadn't encountered any intellectuals in this field who were involved in prosecutions of cybercrime.

• • •

Dr Vermeulen saw Gary again on 22 July and attended court on 24 July in order to give evidence if the judges needed it.

I submitted another statement to the court:

> Being locked in a permanent state of fear has not only destroyed my son Gary's life, but is destroying my husband's health and our family's lives.
>
> It seems one of the very few people still intent on extradition in Gary's case is the same Home Office adviser who advised Alan Johnson on Gary's case.
>
> To say that refusing to extradite in Gary's case would set a precedent seems something of a red herring when reviewing the cases below.
>
> 1. The extradition to America of American-born Mrs Beatrice Tollman was refused on medical grounds by Britain in 2006, despite her medical evidence being unchallenged by the Home Office. (A friend of Mrs Thatcher.)
> 2. The extradition to America of American-born Mr Stanley Tollman was refused by Britain in 2007 and he was allowed to plead guilty 'via video link' and was given one day's suspended sentence. (A friend of Mrs Thatcher.)
> 3. The extradition of accused bomber/alleged IRA terrorist was refused by Britain in 2006. (A friend of Gerry Adams.)
> 4. American/Irish convicted paedophile Shawn Sullivan, who

is a fugitive from America and is officially listed as one of the 'most wanted' criminals by America, had his extradition to the US refused by Britain in 2012. (Married to MOJ policy manager.)

5. Sarah Ferguson, the Duchess of York, whose trial is under-way *in absentia* in Turkey, had her extradition refused by Britain. (A member of the royal family.)

However, I fully agree with the Duchess of York's actions as her motives were the protection of vulnerable children. None of the above can be tried in Britain for their alleged crimes.

6. Hacker Ryan Cleary was allegedly part of an interna-tional hacking group, and has admitted hacking into the Pentagon, NASA and the US Air Force. Ryan Cleary was tried in the UK and given a short sentence.

7. Aaron Caffrey, arrested in 2002 for allegedly breaching US security systems and bringing Port Houston to a halt immediately after 9/11, was tried in the UK and acquitted.

In 2002 the CPS intended to and were keen to try Gary in the UK as it was an open-and-shut case as Gary had naively admitted to computer misuse without having a lawyer. The British police informed Gary when he was questioned in 2002 that he could expect a sentence of six months' commu-nity service. However, the CPS was 'ordered' later in 2002 to hand Gary's case to the US for them to deal with it.

Is There an Appetite to Extradite?
According to Keith Vaz, chairman of the HASC, America no longer has an appetite to extradite in Gary's case. Mr Vaz learned this during the HASC's recent visit to America.

President Obama announced on TV during a May 2011 joint worldwide press conference with David Cameron that Gary's case was a British decision that America would respect and accept.

John Arquilla, an expert in cyber-warfare who is an American defence adviser to the US government, came out publicly in July 2012 to say that prosecuting Gary McKinnon would be ridiculous.

Mr Arquilla's colleague, also in the military, said in July 2012 that Gary should not be jailed.

During the 2009 'JR' against the CPS it was agreed in court that Gary had committed significantly less serious offences than other British hackers who had been given no sentence, or a very low sentence, in the UK, and the CPS stated that the US had provided only 'hearsay' in Gary's case.

As the Home Secretary has not yet made her decision on my son Gary, I don't understand why Gary's legal team expects that on 24 July 2012 that the judges will give direction for service of evidence and skeleton arguments and fix a court date.

This seems premature, as to do so would, I feel, set up a clear expectation in the minds of the public and the media of an adverse decision being given by the Home Secretary.

I believe to create this expectation of defeat before the Home Secretary has even made her decision would be in the interests of only the prosecution.

Compassion has always been an essential part of natural British justice and I weep at the unrelenting cruelty being imposed on Gary and on our family.

Gary hasn't murdered, raped or hurt anyone and cannot understand why this is happening to him.

We desperately need a just, speedy and compassionate end to this seemingly never-ending mental torture.

I have faith that the Home Secretary will rule in Gary's favour and will keep Gary here in the UK where he belongs.

We wait with bated breath for a good and compassionate end to my son Gary's ten-year nightmare.

Yours sincerely,

Janis Sharp (Gary McKinnon's mum)

CHAPTER 22

THE SPEECH, THE LETTER AND THE LAW

The Olympic Games opened on 27 July and the ceremony was truly spectacular. It was much more impressive than I could ever have imagined and had such a positive atmosphere, bringing people inside and outside of the country together, and drew towards its finale with the uplifting and emotive music of 'Eclipse' from *Dark Side of the Moon* by Pink Floyd.

As David Gilmour and his family had helped Gary so much this was a meaningful moment for us.

Theresa May said that she would be giving her decision on Gary after the Olympics and for some reason the opening ceremony made us feel more optimistic about the future.

Wilson had recently had an operation and had to rest. I was relieved that he had managed to get his operation performed on 22 May, as opposed to the initial suggestion of 1 August, a date nicknamed Black Wednesday, as the death rate apparently goes up hugely as all the new, inexperienced hospital doctors start work on that same day.

Our dog Jackson suddenly became ill after a long walk in the woods. He couldn't lift or turn his head, refused to eat and just lay on the floor as though he was dying. We took him to the vet, who, after doing blood tests, listening to his heart and checking him over, suggested he should have an MRI scan that would cost a minimum of £1,500.

I couldn't believe the amount of money being charged for an MRI. It wasn't as though he was an Olympic athlete; he was our dog.

I got in touch with our friend John Davis, who used to work as a vet for the Blue Cross animal hospital in Victoria and went on to have his own practice. He was the one who'd passed on my letter to his neighbour, David Gilmour of Pink Floyd. Here I was asking John for help again, even though I hadn't seen him for years, but that's the thing about real friends: it doesn't matter how long it's been since you've seen them, you know that you would always help each other no matter what.

Coincidentally, John had recently had the same experience with his own dog and told me to ask the vet for anti-inflammatories, as, combined with a lot of rest, they had sorted his dog out. So I did, and by the last day of the Olympics Jackson was well again and could run like the wind.

I discovered later that there's a mysterious illness which dogs in certain areas of the UK were contracting immediately after a walk in the woods. Many of them died from it so I'm extremely grateful to John.

• • •

I had to work harder than ever on Gary's case as we were perilously close to the end. I couldn't afford take my eye off the finish line for a second, as the life-saving marathon I'd been running had yet to be won.

The Paralympics was next and London was buzzing with excitement and anticipation.

Julian Assange had taken refuge in the Ecuadorian embassy on 19 June after he lost his bid to reopen his appeal.

On 15 August the UK had apparently threatened to storm the Ecuadorian embassy and some of Julian Assange's supporters who were protesting outside the embassy were arrested. This shocked people, as asylum is a right that has historically been respected by civilised nations.

On 4 September there was a Cabinet reshuffle and my MP, Grant Shapps, was made co-chairman of the Conservative Party and minister without portfolio in the Cabinet Office. While many ministers and MPs were in Westminster, awaiting that all-important call, Grant was here in Hertfordshire, working for his constituents with no expectation of promotion.

Grant Shapps has had his fair share of misfortune. He was in a car crash in the US which left him in a coma; he recovered but later developed cancer and was diagnosed with Hodgkin's lymphoma. His family shed tears but again he recovered, and after receiving chemotherapy his children were conceived by IVF.

Grant clearly adores his family, not to mention his cat and dogs, one of which was difficult to manage and was left with him by a friend. I think that people who have gone through personal tragedy often have more empathy for others whose backs are against the wall. Grant is a bit different from other MPs. His cousin is Mick Jones, a former member of punk rock bands The Clash and Big Audio Dynamite. Apparently Grant does a good rendition of 'Rapper's Delight', with the odd punk rock song thrown in, at karaoke sessions held in the Houses of Parliament.

Shame there aren't any tickets on sale to the public, as that would be an event worth seeing. I wonder which other MPs are included in the line-up.

• • •

I decided to write to David Cameron and Theresa May, but I didn't know how to make sure that my letter would be seen and read by them. For inspiration I watched Gary's favourite video, 'The Most Astounding Fact in the Universe', on YouTube. It always helps me put things in perspective. The music is wonderful and the entirety of this film fills my soul; especially the knowledge that the atoms in the human body came from the stars.

I sat at my computer to write the following letter from my heart:

Dear Theresa and David,

As you are aware, my son Gary McKinnon, who has Asperger's syndrome, a form of autism, was arrested in London in March 2002 for computer misuse and has now been under virtual house arrest for over ten years while fighting extradition to the US.

People find it hard to believe that this can be happening in Britain in the year 2012 but happening it is.

Gary was arrested more than ten years ago for allegedly hacking into NASA and Pentagon computers from his bedroom in London while searching for evidence of UFOs and Free Energy that Gary believed was being suppressed by the American government. It's true that Gary left cheeky cyber-notes telling the US that their security was virtually non-existent and that he'd continue disrupting by leaving cyber-notes until someone at the top listened to him and installed passwords and firewalls that should have been there in the first place to protect their systems but weren't.

To his detriment Gary also left a cyber-note saying that American foreign policy was akin to state-sponsored terrorism.

Had this been scrawled on a wall few would have noticed and to a young man with Asperger's syndrome, telling the truth as he saw it was as natural as getting out of bed in the morning. However, Gary had now not only embarrassed the US by highlighting their lack of any basic security, but he had angered them.

No one, but especially someone with Asperger's, could ever have realised the horrendous consequences that would arise from a country whose first amendment is one of free speech, or that an extradition treaty with America, yet to be written, could allow him (without any evidence being presented to a British court) to be forcibly removed from his home, his family and all that he has ever known, to be taken to a foreign land where he could be incarcerated in a foreign prison for up to sixty years of his life, for a crime that, according to the British Hi-Tech Crime Unit in 2002, would have been likely to attract a sentence of six months' community service in Britain.

My son has now been under arrest for longer than any British citizen ever has. He hasn't raped anyone, he hasn't murdered anyone, so can't understand how this can be happening to him, as no matter how much anyone may choose to exaggerate his crime, the fact is that his crime was tapping on a keyboard in his bedroom in north London in search of information on Free Energy, Anti-Gravity and reversed technology from Alien spaceships from outer space.

Ten years of being in a constant state of fear while fighting to stop my son Gary being taken from his home and family has made the days, months and years indistinguishable from each other, as hopes raised to the heavens come crashing down to earth on a regular basis.

We were elated when, in a bid to have Gary tried in the UK, you, our Prime Minister, raised Gary's case with President Obama during your first televised joint worldwide press conference in America in 2010, and when President Obama said an appropriate solution would be found, we were moved to tears. We waited and waited and waited, but the months passed and nothing happened.

We were again ecstatic when you raised Gary's case with President Obama for a second time during your second joint worldwide press conference in London in 2011, but in spite of President Obama stating that it was a British decision that America would respect and despite great expectations from all who heard, and constantly being congratulated by strangers in the street, nothing happened.

When Gary's MP David Burrowes asked the American ambassador why the US was still pursuing Gary, he ended his answer with: 'He mocked us.' (http://www.londontv.net/ exradition-debate-2011.html)

I wrote to the Queen during her Diamond Jubilee to ask her to bestow the gift of mercy on my son, who was arrested before even her Golden Jubilee began ten years prior, but in a response from Buckingham Palace it seems only our government are privy to the Queen's powers, which she herself is unable to use, as she can only act on the advice of her government.

I constantly write letters in the hope that the pen really is mightier than the sword and that I can reach souls of courage and compassion in the heart of our government, who can put an end to this decade of mental torture.

Whether the rain falls or the sun shines means little anymore, as we live in this unreal world where Gary sits in the dark and I spend each day and night until the early hours of the morning working on trying to save my son from virtual death. I no longer have any other conversation as I'm unable to escape from this mental imprisonment grounded in fear.

I am hoping with all my heart that Theresa May, our Home

Secretary, who I believe is a strong woman, will have in her heart the courage and compassion that will allow her to do what is right and to give my son his life back.

Gary has lost more than ten years of his life and as his case draws closer to the end, the deterioration in his mental health is marked, as the mental torture becomes increasingly intolerable.

Gary does not deserve to be driven to suicide, or to suffer irreversible damage to his mental health, or to face the prospect of ending his life in a foreign prison or being confined to a mental institution for fifty years and dying there as my grandmother did.

Gary does not deserve either a real or a virtual death sentence. I do not deserve to lose my only child.

I pray that one day I will see the light return to my son's eyes and that this seemingly never-ending torture will soon come to an end.

As Aung San Suu Kyi made her historic return to Britain and spoke to both our Houses of Parliament, seeing the strength she portrayed in her struggle for the freedom of her country, and the sacrifices she made while standing up to an oppressive government, will hopefully have inspired our government to once again become leaders of a proud and sovereign nation who is prepared to stand up, speak out and fight for the values that our forefathers fought and died for, including the rights and the protection of the most vulnerable in our society.

If our government is afraid to make a right and just decision for fear of upsetting our friends then something is wrong with that friendship which must be put right, or we as a nation are allowing our people to be enslaved, making us unable to command respect that by its very nature has to be earned.

Aung San Suu Kyi has earned the respect of the world and will go down in history as a woman of courage who was not afraid to stand up for the rights, freedoms and civil liberties of the Burmese people.

I pray that one day her country will attain the freedom and democracy she craves, and that our country will remember who they are and will strive to regain and retain the rights and freedoms we have sacrificed in order to appease another nation.

We are now at the final hurdle and it takes strength and courage to make that final jump, but jump it we must, if we are to emerge with dignity and self-respect.

Our government's first duty is to protect British citizens, including our most vulnerable. Please have the strength to do what is right and to give my son his life back.

With deepest respect,

Janis Sharp (Gary McKinnon's mum)

After I'd written my letter I was racking my brains trying to think of how I could get it into the hands of the Prime Minister and the Home Secretary. Knowing how busy they were, I didn't know if they would even be able to take the time to read it, especially as the Paralympics was ongoing and the grand closing ceremony was almost upon us.

I then thought that if it was an open letter printed in the newspaper that the PM and the Home Secretary would hear about it and would be more inclined to read it.

I emailed my letter to Duncan Campbell of *The Guardian* and the paper published it in its 'Comment is Free' section on 7 September.

The Guardian got more than 400 positive responses to my letter so I was hopeful that David Cameron and Theresa May would read it.

The Paralympics ended two days later and everyone agreed that it was the best Paralympics ever. People in the UK were so proud, and new stars and role models were produced who did endless TV interviews. It was heartening to see disabled athletes at last being valued in the same way that able-bodied athletes were. There was new hope that the world really was changing.

I was getting nervous again, as now that the Olympics and the Paralympics were both over, Theresa May would be making her decision. We were informed that it would be given on or before 16 October, but that meant it could be announced virtually any time.

Gary's MP, David Burrowes, took the opportunity to spectacularly raise Gary's case yet again on 18 September, the day Parliament went into recess for a month.

Mr David Burrowes (Enfield, Southgate) (Con): Following the theme of relying on assurances and promises given, I want to talk about my constituent Gary McKinnon. I welcome the Deputy Leader of the House, who will respond to the debate. He is in a good position to do so, having been on the picket line, in effect, to protest about the treatment of Gary McKinnon. Earlier this year he tweeted: 'DC must intervene on medical grounds to stop extradition proceedings.'

I could not put it better myself, and I hope that his response will echo that statement. In making it, he is in good company. The Prime Minister, the Deputy Prime Minister, the Justice Secretary, the Attorney General and the Minister for Policing and Criminal Justice have all stood shoulder to shoulder with others in the House, and others who have not been able to come here today, who stand alongside Gary McKinnon and the many campaigners on his behalf.

This could be, and I hope that it is, the last debate that we need to have on Gary McKinnon before a decision is finally made. The Prime Minister has said: 'Gary McKinnon is a vulnerable young man and I see no compassion in sending him thousands of miles away from his home and loved ones to face trial.'

In 2009, the Deputy Prime Minister said: 'It is certainly wrong to send a vulnerable young man to his fate in the United States when he could and should be tried here instead. It is simply a matter of doing the right thing.'

He went on to say: 'Government ministers have let this sorry saga drag on for seven years, heaping misery on Mr McKinnon, his family and his supporters.'

We are now ten years into the sorry saga, with misery still heaped on Mr McKinnon, his family and his supporters. The Deputy Prime Minister also said in 2009: 'It would be fair and it would be right to try Mr McKinnon in Britain. But the clock is ticking. The Prime Minister just needs to pick up the phone to make this prosecution happen. I urge him to do so, before it is too late.'

The Attorney General asked the Conservative Party Conference: 'Can someone tell me how counter-terrorism will be served by extraditing Gary McKinnon to the United States for hacking into government computers in search of UFOs?'

The new Justice Secretary has said: 'I hope the House of Commons will send a message to the government that really this is not what the extradition system is supposed to do. These new rules were set up for very serious offences, for terror offences. I don't believe Parliament ever intended them to be used to extradite somebody with autism issues to face a charge like this.'

Kate Hoey (Vauxhall) (Lab): I pay tribute to the hon. Gentleman's dedication over a long period in sticking up for his constituent, and I join him in what he is saying. Does he agree that it beggars belief that this has taken so long and we still do not have a decision? Does he agree that millions of people – the vast majority throughout the United Kingdom – want this case to end in justice for Gary McKinnon and his family and to put an end, once and for all, to the ridiculous idea that he should be sent to the United States?

Mr Burrowes: I pay tribute to the hon. Lady, who has been very much an hon. Friend in the campaign over many years. Indeed, ten years is an extraordinary time for someone to have his life hanging by a thread. Countless people are alongside my constituent and this must end – it must happen.

I wanted to bring the debate to the House because after today we are not sitting for a while and this is the time when we must reflect on why a decision has not been made, promises have not yet been kept and justice has not yet been delivered for Gary McKinnon.

New evidence has been submitted to the Home Office from Professor Murphy ... and from Dr Vermeulen, Professor Jeremy Turk and Professor Baron-Cohen. All have concluded that Gary McKinnon is an extreme suicide risk. In April this year, Dr Vermeulen said that Gary McKinnon was unfit for trial and an extreme suicide risk.

Extradition 'is suicide'.

The position is that we have had three 2012 face-to-face assessments. We therefore need to bear in mind the words of Professor Jeremy Turk, who has overseen the care of Gary McKinnon pretty much throughout. Professor Turk is an expert in Asperger's and he said: 'I am happy to go on record as believing that Gary has had an incredible number of most scholarly and expert opinions which are striking in their agreement and consensus ... I see no indications, nor any utility, in exposing him to further evaluations, his single major need now being clarity regarding his status in relation to the spectre of extradition that continues to hang over him like a sword of Damocles.'

Perhaps people will say that a decision to keep Gary

McKinnon here would set a precedent. Perhaps the Home Office says that it would set a precedent for terrorists facing extradition. Let us consider other cases. Hacker Ryan Cleary admitted hacking into the Pentagon, NASA and the US Air Force. Aaron Caffrey [was charged with hacking] into US security systems and bringing the port of Houston to a halt immediately after 9/11. Like Gary McKinnon, both were accused of hacking; like him, both have autism and Asperger's syndrome; but unlike him, both have been tried in the United Kingdom.

Let us consider the cases of Róisín McAliskey and Shawn Sullivan. Like Gary McKinnon, they faced extradition; unlike him, they faced extremely serious charges of terrorism and paedophilia and unlike him, they have had extradition requests refused. The only precedent being set by Gary McKinnon is that of facing the threat of extradition for ten years, living in conditions not far short of house arrest. It is more like what would happen to someone living in Burma than Britain. It would be unprecedented to extradite him in the face of such compelling medical evidence. It would be totally dispro-portionate when he could be tried in this country.

Can the Deputy Leader of the House assure us that the time-scale for a decision is not affected by the parliamentary or party conference timetable, bearing in mind that Gary McKinnon's life is hanging by a thread? Now is the time to decide. There is compelling medical evidence that provides a basis for a deci-sion not to extradite Gary McKinnon, and to deliver justice and keep our promises to him. The final word goes to his mother, and I agree with what she says: 'Our government's first duty is to protect British citizens, including our most vulnerable.'

There follow words to the Home Secretary: 'Please have the strength to do what is right and to give my son' – and my constituent – 'his life back.'

David Burrowes sacrificed his time and energy to fight valiantly for Gary for many years. He was so spectacularly selfless that he was even willing to sacrifice his job, threatening to resign if extradition took place. David Burrowes knew that he was literally fighting to save Gary's life.

• • •

On 26 September, when Parliament was still in recess, we at last received the medical report from the Home Office psychiatrists. After studying the compelling new medical evidence, the Home Office psychiatrists agreed with the opinions of Gary's doctors, and especially with the opinion of the esteemed Dr Vermeulen.

At last! Years of ups and downs, of elation and devastation, were finally coming to an end.

No more fate playing games with us, feeding off our fear. Gary was staying, as even the Home Office psychiatrists were now in agreement with Dr Vermeulen.

Although Parliament was closed until 15 October, the requests for interviews never ceased, as the decision on Gary was drawing ever closer. I was in ITV's Gray's Inn Road studio, sitting on the sofa feeling quite composed, when without warning Gary's face appeared on the monitor. That always got to me.

They were showing an interview Gary had done years before and tears started surging from that dark place inside that I needed to avoid. I couldn't cry; I wouldn't. I had to stay in fight mode.

I looked at Gary on the monitor and it pierced my heart as he was on TV for all the wrong reasons. He looked so vulnerable as he answered honestly in his softly spoken voice. He was so talented and it seemed wrong that he wasn't there for those reasons.

How did we ever end up in this totally surreal scenario? It reminded me of all those 'enemy of the state'-type films but we were just an ordinary family and Gary had the furthest thing from a criminal mentality that you could get. How could this be happening to us – and for ten long, excruciating years? We desperately needed a good ending.

There were more interviews over the next few days. I suddenly started to panic as I could feel it wasn't over and knew that I had to fight harder. Wilson sensed this too. The medical evidence in Gary's case was now overwhelming but from what I'd heard, it seemed that some government advisers were still doing all they could to have Gary extradited.

I widely distributed full details of the new Home Office medical reports to ensure that the decision makers actually got to see the evidence in full, as apparently only a brief is given to ministers by their advisers, and if some advisers happened to have a different agenda I worried about just how brief that brief might be.

I had also noticed that there was one very short sentence in the corner of the Home Office psychiatrist's report that did not make any sense and I feared this might be designed to be the only sentence forwarded to the Home Secretary.

I learned later that Theresa May makes sure she has the full facts to hand and is usually better informed and more up on matters than her civil servants are.

I also noted examples of other cases where extradition had been refused, with substantially less reason than in Gary's case, and I included every piece of evidence that I believed met the bar for extradition to be refused.

I sent evidence to local constituency offices as well as to the Commons and the Lords: getting the truth out there was crucial.

Unknown to us, presumably because they had received the

psychiatrist's new report at such a very late stage, the government was still discussing the medical evidence and Theresa May was continuing to read it in depth and to take last-minute legal advice before finally announcing her decision.

CHAPTER 23

I BELIEVE IN MIRACLES

On 15 October 2012 we were informed that Theresa May would announce her decision on Gary on the following day at around 12 noon.

A young woman from Sky News came to our house to interview me. Her name was Victoria. She was pregnant and brimming with emotion, the way women are when carrying new life.

When the latest round of interviews was over, I was looking through my emails and got this lovely message from Trudie Styler:

I am thinking about you and Gary, Janis.

I am so sorry I cannot be with you when the news comes but I'm stuck in NY awaiting my green card and am also on stage each evening next week but I am with you in prayer and spirit.

My feeling is and has always been that Gary will stay.

You are the best mom in the world, Janis.

I send you my love and prayers in this agonizing time. Kisses to G.

We'd had such huge support that I felt Kate Hoey was right when she said in her Commons speech that virtually the whole of the UK was behind Gary.

In the meantime I had arranged for Gary to be a hundred miles away with Lucy and friends and family, as I wanted to be sure that he would not hear the news until we heard it first and made whatever arrangements were necessary.

I looked through the papers; it was being reported in the *Telegraph* that the government was thought to have reached a compromise to have Gary tried in the US but to serve any sentence here in the UK.

Was this what we had fought so hard and waited so long for? No! This would be a death sentence, whether physical death or death of the mind. Gary would be likely to suffer irreversible damage to his mental health even if he did not succeed in taking his own life.

I just didn't believe it. I believe in good and I believe in miracles and I believed that even at this late stage Theresa May would do the right thing and would save my son.

Melanie Riley rang me and asked me if I would give her two quotes for the newspapers in preparation for Theresa May's decision on Gary. One quote saying how happy I was, providing the decision was a good one, and another quote saying how upset I was, if the decision went against Gary.

I refused to give Melanie two quotes and agreed to give her only one, to be used in event of a refusal to extradite. I felt that as long as I continued to believe, the best would happen.

Karen said that we would be informed of the decision about an hour beforehand. Every minute felt like an hour. People were emailing and ringing to wish us well but I was trying to keep the landline and the mobile clear for Karen to get through to us with the decision.

She rang at around 11.30 a.m. but I missed her call as the phone never stopped ringing.

Karen rang again later and Wilson answered. Suddenly he looked at me and was in tears.

'Tell me, Wilson, tell me!'

Wilson was crying and tightly holding the phone with Karen on the other end.

'Wilson, tell me!' I screamed.

'I can't speak,' Wilson was trying to say, but his voice was cracking and then I heard what I thought was 'he's OK'. But I still wasn't sure as Wilson's voice wasn't clear.

'It's OK, Janis. It's over,' Wilson cried as he handed me the phone.

Karen was crying and could barely speak and I was crying with absolute relief. It was the happiest day of my life. My son was safe, he was going to live, he was going to survive, he was staying here with his family, on the island he was born on, right here where he belonged. Wilson and I hugged and laughed and cried and held hands.

Karen said that Theresa May would officially be announcing her refusal to extradite and we weren't allowed to go public until after the announcement.

The night before, I had dreamed that Wilson and I were holding hands and jumping up and down on the bed and laughing.

I rang Lucy's friends and asked to speak to Lucy. I knew that even though it was the most amazing news ever, it would still be a huge shock to the system. Even absolute relief can take its toll.

Lucy and Gary both put the phone to their ears and Gary sounded like a wounded animal as he covered his face and moaned with relief.

Lucy cried and cuddled and comforted Gary. I know exactly what happened and how it looked at the very moment that I gave Gary and Lucy the news, as the friends they were with

filmed their reaction on two mobile phones and later gave us an
SD card with the video on it.

Although it was the happiest moment of our lives, it was also
hugely painful to witness Gary's reaction and was much too
personal to share visually, so I didn't.

I spoke to Michael Seamark from the *Daily Mail*, who had
somehow got wind of the decision. They wanted to photograph
Gary and I explained that he wasn't here, he was with Lucy.
Michael said, 'Don't worry, we'll send a car to pick them up and
bring them to your house.' I explained that they were actually
more than a hundred miles away.

'What! Let me ring you back in five minutes.'

Michael rang back. 'Janis. I've just spoken to my colleague
Christian Gysin who works here and Christian is going to drive
up to your house, pick you up and take you to wherever Gary is
and the photographer will meet us there and get some photos of
you all together. Is that OK?'

'Yes, but as I'm supposed to be at the press conference in
London by 2.30 p.m., what I could do is ring Lucy and get her
to start driving Gary towards London and we could meet them
halfway?'

'Right, let's do that.'

I rang Lucy and Gary and explained how important it was
for us to do this, as the *Daily Mail* had supported us and had
run their 'Affront to British Justice' campaign for Gary for years.
This was such a tiny thing to do in return.

Gary and Lucy spent a short time with her parents, just crying
together, and Lucy then started to drive Gary towards London.

Christian Gysin of the *Daily Mail* arrived at our house
and crowds of new young journalists hoping for a break were
standing outside our door wanting to know the decision. I
couldn't risk the news being published before Theresa May had

announced it, as that would get Gary's lawyers into trouble. On the way out to the car, young journalists and photographers were all crowding around asking for news and I felt bad that I couldn't tell them, as they were all just doing their jobs. But all the journalists I knew were on their way to the press conference and confidentiality was crucial.

Christian's sports car was suited to fast travel and he was a really good driver. I couldn't wait to see Gary. Lucy and I kept in touch during the journey via a hands-free car phone to make sure we all stopped off at the same service station, which ended up being Watford Gap.

We got out of the car and the wind was howling. Nick Clegg rang me on the mobile but I couldn't hear him properly because of the wind, so he was going to ring back in a few minutes.

When we started to walk over the footbridge to get to the motorway restaurant on the southbound side the wind almost blew us off our feet.

The phone rang again. It was Nick Clegg ringing back to congratulate us on the outcome and to say that he hoped I understood why he couldn't meet with me when I'd asked him to. I told him how proud I was of the government and of Theresa May for her tremendous decision and I thanked him and David Cameron for giving her their full backing. But the wind was blowing so hard it was impossible to have a conversation while I was on the footbridge.

David Davis rang several times to congratulate us, though regrettably I kept missing his call.

We walked into the Road Chef motorway restaurant and Christian and I sat down to wait for Gary, Lucy and the photographer. Wilson was holding the video camera waiting to capture the moment when Gary walked in. The memory of seeing Lucy and Gary arrive in the car park, knowing that Gary was a free man, will be ingrained on my soul forever. Tears are flowing again at the memory of that feeling of release.

Gary walked into the large restaurant and I could see that he was still in a daze. He was tall but he looked little to me and just seeing him outside in the world again, smiling through tears, was a sight to behold.

We stood in the middle of the floor and just hugged and cried and hugged and cried. A decade of stress released in a sea of tears, like a river bursting through a dam and flowing free again. This was our once-in-a-lifetime moment.

All eyes were fixed on us. People who recognised Gary had tears in their eyes and others were watching curiously, no doubt wondering who we were and what was going on. The photographer arrived and Lucy and Gary and Wilson and I all went out to the grassy part of the car park and hugged and jumped for joy as the camera lens captured these magical moments of freedom.

Wilson insisted on staying behind the camera but I wish he had been in the photos too, as he has been my rock, my support, my solace, my love.

We then hugged Gary and Lucy goodbye as I had to go to the press conference, where everyone was waiting, and Gary and Lucy headed for home, as Gary needed to rest and to let the day's momentous events sink in.

• • •

Christian was an excellent driver and his sports car just flew down the motorway, but I was worried about just how late I was going to be, as the traffic once we reached London was bound to be a problem. But I told myself that as Karen Todner, David Burrowes, Shami Chakrabarti, Edward Fitzgerald, Ben Cooper and Mark Lever were all there the press conference would go ahead without me.

Melanie rang in a panic to find out where I was and I told her I was almost there, which wasn't quite true. When I eventually arrived at Doughty Street Chambers, I couldn't believe the number of journalists and photographers waiting outside. The atmosphere was fantastic and the press were all smiling and laughing and many had tears in their eyes. Alex Magill, a film maker who highlights injustice, was the first one to greet us and gave me a big hug.

When I went inside the chambers I felt guilty, as instead of finding everyone sitting at a large table giving a press conference, as I expected, Melanie ushered me into a little room that Karen, Shami and the others on the panel were squeezed into, waiting for me to arrive.

I said hello and apologised to everyone and told them how nice they looked, as everyone apart from me was all dressed up. We went into the main area, where the very large room was packed wall to wall with journalists and camera crews. We sat down at a long table and the press conference began at around four o'clock; everyone had been hanging around for about an hour and a half and, unbelievably, they had not only waited for me, they didn't seem annoyed at having to do so.

I always think the press are so patient and generally really good humoured.

Karen spoke first, which I was grateful for, as the events of this day were overwhelming and I couldn't speak. Mountains of emotions were rushing through my mind and body, making me want to laugh and cry and to hug everyone. I had no sense of logic or thought, just pure emotion.

Karen was so eloquent and thanked the people who had helped us. After everyone on the panel had spoken, it was my turn. When I stared out at the crowd of journalists I was smiling and felt myself starting to cry. I couldn't speak and thought I wasn't going to be able to. I looked ahead and there right in front of me was Victoria Wade, the young pregnant journalist from Sky News who had interviewed me the day before. Victoria was smiling and her eyes were filled with empathy and tears as she silently told me that I could do it.

It's a mother thing, a female thing, a human thing; a language of emotion that needs no words. I could feel such warmth surrounding me, helping to give me the strength to hold it together.

Tears. I tried to speak. *More tears.* Please let me hold it together, I thought. Otherwise I'll sit here and cry for half an hour and I'll embarrass everyone and I mustn't do that. So I started.

'It's been an emotional rollercoaster.' My voice started to break and I looked over at Victoria again with her baby in her tummy, as she was willing me to do it, and I smiled and carried on.

I'm not very articulate today. I'm overwhelmed … incredibly happy. I want to say thank you to Theresa May, who made an incredibly brave decision. To stand up to another nation as strong and as powerful as America is rare and she had the guts to do it, and I always felt that it was she who had the strength to come through and do this, and to also change the extradition treaty to bring in forum, so that this hopefully won't happen to anyone else, is absolutely incredible.

I want to thank Paul Dacre of the *Daily Mail*, who stood up for Gary non-stop for years, and Michael Seamark and James Slack, who have been amazing.

The media has been amazing, the support … without the support we could never ever have done it; we just couldn't.

Gary is here because of all this and David Burrowes has been amazing. He stood up for Gary with speech after speech in Parliament, never letting up for a minute. Karen ... from the very start every time they used to say we're at the end of the road, she'd say: 'We've been at the end of the road before, we'll carry on.'

And she would go in there and fight, and she would keep him here, and she never stopped ... and Edward Fitzgerald is just fantastic, amazing ... and Ben Cooper absolutely incredible ... I mean thank you to everyone and to Mark of the National Autistic Society, who helped us so much, and Shami is, oh, astounding. She stands up for everyone and everything in every walk of life, she's just amazing ... she should get the human rights award because she deserves it.

There are so many people to thank and I hope I haven't forgotten anyone ... Duncan Campbell as well, he's amazing and his wife, Julie Christie ... David Gilmour ... oh, David Gilmour has been a godsend, he's done so much for us in so many ways, paid for psychiatrists, he's helped out in so many ways. He did a song with Chrissie Hynde and Bob Geldof. We've had so much support and without people power of all the different people together there's no way Gary would have stayed here. Us, all together, we've done it! ... We've won for the little person, not just the elite or the privileged but for the little person and that is an incredible achievement and thank you to everybody here because you've all done it, every one of you. Thank you.

Question: Can I ask how is Gary doing? How did he react to the happy news today?
He's still incredibly emotional – he couldn't speak, he actually literally couldn't speak and then he cried and then he hugged and he cried. It's been hugging and crying, it's so emotional. I know it seems odd that I'm tearful now but it's a culmination

of ten years and seven months and it's just so emotional. It'll take time to get back to having a normal life, really.

Question: He's got a future to look forward to now.
Absolutely, he said that he felt like a dead person, he said he was dead and that he had no job, he had no children, he doesn't go on holiday, he doesn't leave the house. He had no conversation. He had nothing, and he felt he was worthless; and I'm hoping that because the extradition treaty is getting changed and forum is being brought in, that he'll feel at least that ten years and seven months has brought about something that is going to help everyone, so it's not just … it's not been a waste, its achieved something, and I hope that will give him a bit of self-respect because he's got such low self-esteem.

Question: If Gary had been here today, what do think he would've said?
I think he'd find it difficult to speak. He's very articulate, but I think at this moment in time he would just be full and tearful and say thank you and he would thank all the same people as I have, everyone.

I'm bound to have left a million people out. Trudie Styler has been amazing, she's come to court with me, flown in from New York to stand by our side, and Melanie Riley is another incredible person who's fought tooth and nail for this extradition treaty to be changed. She never stopped, she's amazing, that's Friends Extradited … But there's so many people, I'll kick myself because I know I'll have forgotten a million of them.

Question: Janis, do you believe this has been literally a life-saving decision?
I know it's been a life-saving decision, because Gary doesn't

travel abroad, he doesn't go on holiday, he very rarely leaves north London, and to be taken from everything you know, your family, everything, thousands of miles away, it's so terrifying to him and I can understand that he would rather be dead. But also everyone thinks it's just Asperger's: it's not. Gary has a grandmother who had schizophrenia, lifelong schizophrenia.

His great-grandmother was in a mental institution for fifty years and died there. Gary was taken to a neurologist when he was sixteen because he was losing his mental faculties.

There's a lot in Gary's mental health history that is … no one knows about, so the Home Secretary obviously looked at all of that, but there's so much more to it. And the Asperger's syndrome is a very important part of that because logically it's not based on emotion; logically, his best decision would have been to take his own life than to leave everything he knows, it's absolute logic.

Question: And he still faces the potential of a prosecution here, has he said anything about that? How he might cope with that?
We can deal with that because we're here; it's all we've ever asked for. He has his family around him, we can visit him, he has his support. We'll deal with that. That's the only thing we've asked for is for Gary to be tried here.

He's actually lost ten years of his youth; he's lost ten years of his life. If this happens as well, we'll deal with it, but at least the actual release of knowing that he's here is just incredible, it's such a huge weight off our shoulders, it really is.

Question: As a mother, what's it like for you to watch your son go through this for ten years?
It's horrendous because basically he would just sit in the dark

all the time. He's a really good musician but he hasn't touched an instrument for years because he couldn't deal with what it would bring to the surface. He isn't allowed to go online, he didn't have an outlet. He used to go out and run and he stopped doing that, so we watched him shut down and my fear also was, with people with Asperger's it can become catatonia and once you're catatonic it's not very easy to reverse that and just the waste of talent ... ten years.

John Arquilla, an adviser to President Obama, came out last month or the month before and said that to prosecute Gary would be ridiculous, that he should be hired here and really they have to look at all sorts of people, hackers and people with Asperger's and channel that, because they are such an incredible asset and such amazing people and they would work so hard, they really would.

So it's been awful watching Gary go downhill so badly ... but such a relief to see him smile for the first time in many years. It's amazing.

After the press conference was over, individual TV interviews took place in the room. I spoke to Kay Burley on Sky News and Kay asked me what I thought of what Alan Johnson had said about Gary. The former Home Secretary came across as quite brutal and personally angry that Gary had not been extradited. I said:

I actually believed in Alan Johnson. I thought he would do the right thing and I was surprised that he didn't. I think the problem is that advisers often see politicians as new faces for the adviser's policies and that all too often seems to be the case.

Someone who leads the country has to stand up and say, 'You advise! I decide!'

The politicians have to be the decision makers, because the advisers were there through all of the different five or six Home Secretaries we've had, giving them all the same advice. We haven't elected them! So the people we elect, they have to be the ones who lead and who make the decisions.

It's fine to listen to advisers, but Home Secretaries have to look at all the evidence themselves, not only selected parts of it that they [the advisers] perhaps want them to see, but the full scenario! ... and that's really what makes a leader.

Any MP worth their salt knows when to unite over a good decision and Alan Johnson's bitter comments reflected badly on him. When I had written to him he rightly said that Gary's case was no longer anything to do with him; yet he seemed personally outraged when extradition was refused, in spite of the fact that he was no longer even shadow Home Secretary.

I was really surprised that the mild-mannered Michael Portillo had wanted Gary to be extradited and said on TV that Theresa May had made the wrong decision. I thanked our lucky stars that it was David Burrowes who was Gary's MP and not Michael Portillo, a one-time MP for the same borough. David Burrowes is a good man who fights the good fight and is not intimidated by anyone, no matter how powerful.

On the day of her announcement, when Theresa May informed the advisers of her decision, a few of the 'unelected' advisers were apparently sitting in Parliament with their arms folded, absolutely seething that the Home Secretary had dared to make a decision they did not want.

It puzzled me that Gary incurred such wrath, when a convicted 'most wanted' American paedophile whose extradition to the US was refused seemed to have brought not a murmur from the same quarters.

Theresa May had taken legal advice from multiple eminent professionals. As an elected minister, she had the strength and wherewithal to make her own decisions.

While being interviewed, one of the radio stations told me that they had just interviewed Professor John Arquilla, the expert on cyber-warfare and adviser to the US government, and that he had expressed his support for Theresa May's decision. It was so decent and courageous of Professor Arquilla to have said this, and so much respect to him for that.

A constant round of radio and TV interviews went on until late that evening but I was more than happy to repay the media for their support, as without them the outcome might have been very different for Gary.

Michael Seamark from the *Daily Mail* said that after I had thanked him by name during the press conference his daughter told him that he was trending on Twitter and Michael's wife said, 'What's "trending"?' Michael laughed and explained.

We eventually got home and emails had flooded in.

An eminent psychologist told us that he wept when he heard the news while he was travelling on the tube.

Nurses said that huge screams rang out in the wards when they heard Theresa May's decision.

A crowd in Saudi Arabia cheered loudly when the news was broadcast on TV in their club restaurant.

London taxi drivers were cheering and beeping their horns when they heard the news and even people in Australia and in Singapore were cheering and crying. Twitter was buzzing with people in Germany tweeting that they were laughing, crying and dancing when they heard the news, as were people in Israel and, yes, in America too.

Teachers in schools across the country wept when the news

came through on their mobiles. And the whole village where Gary's solicitor Karen lives held a party to celebrate.

This was a truly international celebration of how the good in people could lead to justice for an ordinary, yet extraordinary, man.

The phone was ringing continuously. I picked it up and a familiar voice on the other end exclaimed passionately, 'Janis! You've done it! You've f***ing done it!' It was Trudie Styler. 'And not only have you done it! But you've changed the f***ing law!'

As well as being hugely relieved that Gary wouldn't be going anywhere, Trudie was jubilant about Theresa May's decision to bring in forum to prevent other people who had never left the UK from being extradited.

She was about to go back on stage in New York, in a play called *The Exonerated*, depicting the true-life experiences of exonerated death row prisoners ultimately proved to be innocent.

As Gary's extreme suicide risk and decade of virtual house arrest was akin to being on death row, this was a fitting end to an extraordinary day.

CHAPTER 24

HOW IT FEELS TO BE FREE

Wilson and I had to get up at 5 a.m. the next day as more TV crews were coming to the house for interviews. Several large satellite vans took up residence in the street and masses of electrical cables were fed into our house and across the living room floor. We'd had barely any sleep but we were so happy. It was over. The nightmare was finally over.

Everyone asked us how we had celebrated and I had to tell them that we had been doing interviews up until the night.

Later, a young woman tweeted me to say, 'So happy to hear the news, how are you feeling now?'

'Much better than you,' I replied.

Luckily she was sharp enough to realise right away that I had meant to write 'much better thank you' but had mistakenly missed out the 'k' in the word 'thank'.

Lord Maginnis rang to say how happy he was about the decision – a decision he had worked so very hard for. Endless emails were still arriving, including from another one of our supporters, Baroness Browning, who had championed Gary's case both in and out of the Home Office.

We expected life to be quiet now but interview requests still came thick and fast and the lovely Michael Seamark continued to take us out for lunch, which was so much more enjoyable now that the fear had gone.

Armed with gifts of bottles of champagne, we went into Doughty Street Chambers to have a celebratory conference with Karen Todner, Ben Cooper and Edward Fitzgerald, Gary's astounding legal team.

Gary was very quiet and was still finding it difficult to believe that his almost eleven-year nightmare really was over. He was seeing Professor Digby Tantam and then Professor Emmy van Deurzen on a regular basis. Emmy is ideal for Gary and is helping him learn how to start living again. It is clear that this will take a long time.

On 7 November Barack Obama was re-elected as President of America.

• • •

Liberty asked me to co-present a human rights award on 19 November. Shami was as welcoming as always. Comedienne Sandi Toksvig was hosting the show, and asked me who I was when I was led into the green room. I told her my name, but was feeling a bit shy and didn't explain that I was Gary's mum, which I should have. She said, 'I know who you are,' although I'm not sure she did.

Lieutenant Colonel Nicholas Mercer, the army's former chief legal adviser in Iraq, now an Anglican priest, was in the green room. He spoke to me at length and really put me at my ease. He is the most wonderful man, filled with warmth and humanity.

Later, when I was sitting on my own, Kevin Maguire and Yasmin Alibhai-Brown were sitting opposite me. I had seen Yasmin speaking up for Gary on many occasions, so I introduced myself and thanked her. Yasmin was lovely and immediately made me feel at home.

We met up with Julia O'Dwyer, a wonderful woman I got to know when her son Richard was fighting extradition to the US for alleged copyright infringement. Julia joined us on Twitter to campaign against the 2003 extradition treaty and was an awesome fighter for her son and against injustice. Jimmy Wales also championed Richard's cause.

I went back to my seat in the green room and was sitting quietly and feeling a bit lost when suddenly this friendly voice called out 'Janis', as if they'd known me for years. It was Benedict Cumberbatch. I had never met him before but everyone thought that in his role of Sherlock he looked and sounded like Gary, as did I. Benedict chatted for quite a while and I found him easy to talk to, not only because of his similarities to Gary but because his conversation was so interesting.

I co-presented the award with Tim Farron MP and there were two joint winners, the Open Rights Group and 38 Degrees, which I thought was great.

Gary's barrister, Ben Cooper, won the Human Rights Lawyer of the Year Award and it was presented to him by none other than Benedict Cumberbatch.

After the presentations Shami came on stage to announce that they had a surprise. They wheeled a piano on stage, Emeli Sandé appeared and I could hardly believe it when she started singing 'I Wish I Knew How It Would Feel to Be Free'.

This was Gary's song, and now it was being sung at the Liberty Human Rights awards and Gary was free.

Yasmin Alibhai-Brown was sitting next to Wilson and me in the audience and I was telling her how this song relates to Gary. I was smiling from ear to ear and probably not making much sense, but I was just so happy. I had waited so long for moments like this.

I met Diane Blood at the reception that was held afterwards. Diane is such an inspirational woman and although I knew the story of her fight to use her dead husband's frozen sperm to have children, it was great to hear the details of her hard-won fight. I also hadn't realised that Diane's children were autistic.

We caught our train home in the nick of time. Our entire lives seem to be last minute, and constantly hanging from a cliff edge loses its appeal after a while.

The following day I took Gary to his appointment with Professor van Deurzen. Gary was nervous and stressed and wanted to stay at home, but afterwards he said that it had been helpful and he was glad he had gone.

Trudie Styler had arranged a party for Gary at her London home on Thanksgiving Day, 22 November. I started sending out invitations and got a lovely email from Graham Nash, another person who had done so much to help Gary, explaining why he wouldn't be coming:

> Thank you so much for the invitation, Janis … but … I'm here on the island where I live … 2,000 miles in the Pacific…
>
> Just finished 87 shows with the lads and I'm staying here until I'm forced to leave…
>
> Please give Trudie and Sting my very best … great news about Gary … again, thanks.
>
> Graham

Jacqui Smith had approved extradition on Thanksgiving Day 2008. Four years later we were celebrating Gary's freedom from extradition on Thanksgiving Day 2012.

I knew he was nervous, but eventually Gary was persuaded to

come along with Wilson, Lucy and me. I wished that Karl Watkin, a friend of Trudie's, could have been there too, as along with Melanie he has done so much to fight the 2003 extradition treaty.

As soon as we walked in to Trudie's house the atmosphere was good. Trudie was there to greet everyone and was so welcoming and kind. Sting's sister Anita was there too and is a genuinely lovely person, and I think a little bit shy.

Trudie's daughter Eliot Paulina, nicknamed Coco by her family, joined the party a bit later. Eliot looks younger than her age and has a real innocence and openness about her. She's a first-class vocalist and has a band named I Blame Coco.

I'm amazed that Coco isn't already as well known as Sting, because she is just as talented as her dad. I'm sure her new album will reach an even wider audience than it already has.

Our friend Joe Winnington and his wife, and Joe's sister Polly and her husband – Pink Floyd's David Gilmour – weren't able to be there as Polly and Joe's father was dying. It was poignant to think of them saying goodbye just as we were celebrating not having to say goodbye.

Politicians, peers, journalists, musicians, artists, doctors and tweeters, some with Asperger's and Tourette's, all mixed well and everyone had the most amazing time. So many people we know commented on how fascinating and exceptionally intelligent Dr Jan Vermeulen and his wife were. Everyone enjoyed talking to them as they were so interesting and such genuinely nice people.

The French doors in the living room opened onto the garden, and the warmth in our hearts made the winter feel more akin to a warm summer's night. Duncan Campbell was also a huge hit with everyone.

Coco later took Claire Simmons, my right-hand person in the campaign, to a club called Chinawhite. She was really impressed and hoped she didn't embarrass Coco by being too uncool.

Trudie sent me an email after the party:

Dearest Janis,

How wonderful the journey's end, personified in a radiant Gary surrounded by supporters, loved ones and friends for life.

I am here for you and your family, always and forever.

Trudie

It was now December and I thought everything was all over when suddenly I started dreaming that lots of camera crews and journalists were in our house again. In one dream there was a young pregnant journalist from the *Daily Mail*.

I also dreamed of looking out of the window and seeing my mum walking away down the garden and across the fields. I waved to her and called for her to come into the house but she looked up, waved back and then walked away.

I was scared again: I thought my mum was telling me that something bad was going to happen. But Wilson and our friends thought my mum was waving goodbye, as she had been with me in spirit to help Gary and was leaving as he was now going to be OK.

It was 13 December and Biba, our old dog, had died the day before. Wilson dreamed that night that Biba came and dropped our diary at his feet and that it opened at the page dated 14 December – my birthday.

The next day we were out when we got a call from Karen to say that the CPS had been in touch and were announcing their decision that afternoon, on my birthday, about whether to prosecute Gary. We rushed home and all the TV crews and press started arriving – including a young pregnant woman from the *Mail*, just as I had dreamed.

Here we were again, waiting for news, but I wasn't really worried this time. I knew that the CPS had no evidence of the damage that had been alleged by the US and that Gary had always denied.

The CPS announced their decision on TV: they did not have evidence that they felt could lead to a conviction. Due to such a low prospect of conviction, and due to the 'passage of time', they were not going to prosecute. Absolute finality, at last.

We recognised most of the TV crews as I'd done so many interviews over the years, but this time I wasn't pleading for Gary's life; I was thanking everyone for his freedom. Harry Smith from ITV said it was a rare pleasure to cover a story of this type with a happy ending.

Trudie emailed:

Dearest Janis and Gary,
    Victory!
    The day has come.
    What a Christmas this will be.
    I'm thrilled as I sit at NY Kennedy airport waiting to come back to UK for the Christmas holidays.
    Justice at last – sleep soundly in your beds, dearests – the nightmare over – only sweet dreams from now on.
    Trudie
    Happy Birthday dearest Janis – the best one ever, eh?
    Love tx

Such a lovely message and such a perfect birthday.

Had Gary been tried in the UK, I believe we could have proved that no evidence of damage existed and complete closure would have been attained. However, in truth, Gary wasn't up to more pressure being inflicted on him that might well have lasted for many more years. Dr Vermeulen had also stated that Gary was unfit for trial.

Our nightmare had ended with Theresa May's decision; that was the important one. I later read an interview she did with Allison Pearson. When the Home Secretary was asked about never having had children, she said quietly, 'It just didn't happen,' and admitted to a sense of loss when looking at families. I felt sad that the woman who had saved my child's life didn't have any of her own, but I was comforted to read that she has a happy marriage.

The CPS decision on Gary gave us closure on this side of the pond. The end of the Mayan calendar that many thought signified the end of the world brought an end to our ten-year nightmare and a new beginning for Gary ... but here's the sting in the tail.

The sad part of this happy ending is that Gary can never go to Scotland, the land of his birth. If he leaves England or Wales the US could have him arrested and could possibly start the extradition request all over again.

Gary is very close to his dad, but if Charlie ever becomes seriously ill Gary will be unable to visit him in Glasgow, and if his dad dies Gary will not be able to attend the funeral. America has not lifted its request for extradition but has left it hanging over Gary's head like the sword of Damocles. Nonetheless, Gary is free, and for that we are eternally grateful.

EPILOGUE

Shortly after Theresa May's announcement, it was brought to my attention that the five young siblings we fostered remain together and are apparently happy with their adopted parents. We were overjoyed to hear this and it gave Wilson and me closure to yet another chapter of our lives.

I hope with all my heart that the adopters and the children are truly happy together. Huge respect to the couple for working through what must have been difficult times, and for managing to unite and to keep their family together.

I was reminded when we watched the film *Despicable Me* of the words of a wise woman who said to me: 'Don't forget that children change the adults'. This comforted me.

The children's birth mother never had any more children as her heart was broken when they were placed for adoption. She is now in a long-term and happy relationship with a good man. Her hope is that her children are loved and cherished by their adopters and that one day she will meet them and be reunited with the children.

On 11 January 2013 a young Jewish American computer genius named Aaron Swartz took his own life because he was so afraid of the 35-year sentence proposed by US DOJ prosecutors for alleged computer offences.

Professors throughout the US downloaded their academic research and research papers onto the internet for free in protest at the treatment of Aaron by prosecutors, which Aaron's partner and his family say led to his suicide.

At the age of fourteen Aaron was involved in the development of the web-feed format RSS and later the social news site REDDIT. He hanged himself in his Brooklyn apartment.

This is not the first loss of a gifted young computer pioneer's life when facing prosecution and a ludicrous prison sentence.

How many more exceptional young men will we lose through suicide or by being locked up in a violent prison system for years on end, as a punishment for their desire to explore boundaries and push forward frontiers that may, in the end, lead to our planet's very survival?

AFTERWORD BY GARY MCKINNON

In the year 2000, my long-term interests in computers and the proven government secrecy surrounding the UFO phenomenon culminated in actions on my part that would lead my family, loved ones and me down a long and difficult road. Using basic IT knowledge and an old PC on a 56K dial-up modem, I searched US government and NASA computers for evidence of UFO truth. What I was to find was astounding, and not just in terms of UFOs but also in terms of computer security, or the lack of it.

More than half of the computers had no password set: this meant you could just type a username, leaving the password field blank, and you would be logged onto the system. I was greatly concerned about the lack of security and began to leave messages on all these insecure computers, highlighting the lack of security as well as leaving political diatribes. My activities didn't last long and I was soon caught.

I was told by the National Hi-Tech Crime Unit that as I had not sent any malicious code I would probably get six months' community service for unauthorised access. Later that year, when the US requested extradition, the potential six-month sentence in Britain suddenly became a maximum sixty-year sentence in America. This news was like a huge hammer falling on us all. Sixty years in a foreign jail is a far cry from six months' community service in your own country. Even if this figure was reduced by plea bargaining it would still be highly excessive in comparison to the punishment under UK law.

The next year, 2003, a new UK–US extradition treaty was passed, using ancient and undemocratic devices known as 'orders in council' and 'royal prerogative'. The treaty is imbalanced, since US citizens are protected by their constitution whereas UK citizens can be handed over to the US without any evidence at all. The figures bear this out if you look at the number of US nationals getting extradited to the UK versus the number of UK nationals getting extradited to the US.

I began a huge slide downward into depression. It looked like we had a fight on our hands that we couldn't win. The UK judiciary's hands seemed to be tied; working within the confines of this one-sided treaty gave little room for manoeuvre. In 2005 I was rearrested as the result of a US arrest warrant that described me as a 'fugitive', as if I had committed a crime in America and then run away to the UK. I was not a fugitive and have lived my entire life in the UK.

My mental state grew steadily worse as I tried to grasp how and why this was escalating out of all proportion and where this was all leading to.

Over the next few years we had many extradition hearings and judicial reviews and my mum gained support from celebrities and politicians alike. Come 2008 we were waiting in hope for the European Court of Human Rights to hear our case. But our hopes were dashed; they threw the case out so quickly I wondered if they had even considered it. I was losing all hope. Another year in this terrifying limbo and then our hopes were smashed again, this time by the new UK Supreme Court, who would not even consider the case. I did one last interview with *London Tonight*, my girlfriend Lucy in tears in the studio, then we went home. If it weren't for my mum and Lucy, there were many days I would never have survived.

At that point I stopped hoping. Everything we tried seemed to fail and there was no point in going on. I wouldn't wash, dress or eat and the worry was eating away at me. It was at that point that my mother, Janis, took over. I couldn't do it anymore, I just couldn't handle it. Years of mental attrition was taking its toll. My mum stepped up when I fell down. This normally quite shy woman was suddenly at the forefront of the interviews, the hearings, the demonstrations and the political meetings. Sitting at a PC, somehow gathering support from all walks of life, I think she got through about seven keyboards in five years!

My mum and I are very close and our family are fiercely loyal to each other. Janis made sure the right people got the right information; where most people would have thought they had done more than enough to secure their goal, she would push it even further. She breathed, slept and ate the fight for me. She was not alone: my stepfather, Wilson, looked after Janis while she looked after my future.

The support didn't end there. My mum garnered the support of many musicians who were sympathetic to our plight, including David Gilmour of Pink Floyd, Graham Nash of Crosby, Stills, Nash & Young and Trudie Styler, another amazing woman. Trudie is married to Sting and they both wrote to Jacqui Smith asking her to refuse extradition. David Gilmour also brought Chrissie Hynde and The Orb on board and they were also very supportive.

We had the support of many MPs, particularly my MP, David Burrowes, who was tireless in his activities and even threatened to resign if extradition was ordered. Keith Vaz, Lucy's parents'

MP, along with the Home Affairs Select Committee that he chaired, fought relentlessly for the amendment of the one-sided extradition treaty and for the victims of it.

The UK press was incredibly supportive; the *Daily Mail* ran a long and intense campaign against my extradition and the imbalanced treaty. Duncan Campbell of *The Guardian* was tireless in keeping our story alive, and his incredible wife, Julie Christie, also pledged her support. Virtually every other British newspaper and computer mag highlighted my case and the unfairness of the 2003 extradition treaty. Worthy of special mention is Tom Bradby, who kept asking the questions that contributed to President Obama and Prime Minister Cameron discussing my case twice in front of the world.

A twist of fate was to garner us more aid as well as leading to me having a deeper understanding of myself and of the many problems I had over the years. After the last interview I had on *London Tonight*, half a dozen people, including experts on autism, called and emailed to say that they thought I had Asperger's syndrome, a form of autism, because of my mannerisms, lack of facial expression and the nature of my answers on the programme. This was to lead to me being assessed for autistic spectrum disorder.

I had always felt different from everyone else and never fitted in but I always assumed that I was just very different rather than abnormal. It turned out that the reason I was very different from what autism sufferers term 'neuro-typical' people is that I had ASD. After seeking five separate diagnoses from top people in mental health, I was unanimously diagnosed as having Asperger's syndrome.

We have had so much support from the National Autistic Society and I'm glad to say that our problems have helped to raise awareness of Asperger's syndrome and other autistic spectrum disorders.

In May of 2010 a new Home Secretary was appointed. This was Theresa May, a tough politician who bettered a few of her recent predecessors in my opinion. With a fresh Cabinet came a fresh hope. We also had fresh medical evidence, including a history of mental illness in at least three generations of my family.

I had undergone so many assessments I began to feel like a lab rat outside of home as well as in it. I had to cope with learning that the reason I am as I am is because I have a brain that is wired differently to whatever 'normal' is – while already undergoing severe depression and no longer having the will to live. But thankfully, through the efforts of my mum and the care of the doctors and having Lucy by my side, I somehow survived to live another day.

After two more years of tests, discussions and hearings, and nearly eleven years in total of having our heads on the block, Theresa May announced that she would block the extradition on the grounds of my medical evidence and the specific details surrounding my mental health.

I can only hope that my mother's story will inspire others who are facing the sharp end of bad legislation. As I write this, it's Mother's Day. The first free Mother's Day my mum has had in eleven years. Words really aren't enough x x x

ACKNOWLEDGEMENTS

Michael Seamark, without whom this book would never have been written – and whose wit, charm and conversation lightened the darkest of days.

Rebecca Winfield, without whom this book would never have been published – and whose wisdom and unique way of pulling people and purpose together has been invaluable.

Iain Dale, whose enthusiasm and instant decision making were truly awesome.

Sam Carter, Editor, for his first-class attitude and consummate professionalism.

Suzanne Sangster, Publicity Director, for her warmth, ingenuity, organisation and flexibility.

Solicitor Karen Todner, our avenging angel, who fought with undying passion and fortitude until freedom was won.

Barrister Ben Cooper, for his warmth and humanity and for pursuing every legal remedy available.

Edward Fitzgerald QC, a man of the people for the people, who never took slight no matter how much I argued my point. Edward's intelligence and unique way of delivering argument to a court is truly inspirational.

David Burrowes, for being the man that he is and the best

324   SAVING GARY MCKINNON

MP Gary could ever have had, and whose determination, eloquence and tenacity revitalised the very heart of democracy.

Grant Shapps, my amazing MP, for his never-ending help and for being there in an instant whenever I needed to speak to him.

Katerina Allen, for passing on my endless letters.

Paul Dacre and the *Daily Mail*, for another outstanding campaign giving voice to the people, which resonated throughout society until justice was done.

Home Secretary Theresa May, an extraordinary woman, for her courage, compassion and wisdom, without whom this ending could never have been achieved.

Prime Minister David Cameron, for having the courage and wherewithal to twice raise Gary's case on the world stage with President Obama, and for giving Theresa May his full backing.

Nick Clegg and team, for joining our demonstration on a cold December day outside the Home Office and for giving Theresa May his full backing for her decision on Gary.

Gordon and Sarah Brown, for their commendable efforts in trying to help Gary.

Trudie Styler and Sting, Duncan Campbell and Julie Christie, Graham Nash, Chrissie Hynde, Anita Sumner, Alex Paterson of The Orb, Peter Howson, Paul Loasby, Bob Geldof, David Gilmour and Polly Samson, all of whom I can never repay for all they have done for Gary and me, and to Polly's brother Joe Winnington, an amazing man and a better friend than anyone could wish for, who despite not having seen us for years pulled out all the stops to help us when things were at their bleakest.

Mark Dziecielewski, a mine of information who worked tirelessly for ten years to inform and support Gary and me and all who joined the campaign.

Karl Watkin and Melanie Riley, a force to be reckoned with,

whose support for Gary and others and fight for the revision of the 2003 extradition treaty have been truly awesome.

Shami Chakrabarti and all at Liberty, who fight every day of their lives for justice.

Richard Mills of Research Autism, Professor Simon Baron-Cohen of the Autistic Research Trust, Dr Thomas Berney, Professor Jeremy Turk and Dr Jan Vermeulen, for saving Gary's life.

Professor Digby Tantam and Professor Emmy van Deurzen, for helping put it back together again.

Kevin Healey, SAAS campaigner extraordinare, Dr Luke Beardon, Matthew Downie, Mark Lever, Tom Madders and the National Autistic Society.

Michael Darwyne, a dear friend I have never met in person, whose endless support, knowledge, insight and way of seeing were inspirational.

The Rt Hon. Keith Vaz and the Home Affairs Select Committee, whose fight for right goes on.

Baron Maginnis of Drumglass, whose compassion and spirited fight to see Gary tried in the UK never waned.

Dominic Raab, Kate Hoey, Lord Carlile, David Davis, Caroline Lucas, Michael Meacher, Chris Huhne, Boris Johnson, Dennis Skinner and Alistair Carmichael.

Sally Bercow, a woman who speaks her mind and doesn't pull her punches, and John Bercow, a man who does the same.

Claire Simmons, an angel who appeared from the blue in a time of need, and John Davies, a dear friend of Storm Thogerson and long-time friend of ours who did the same.

Nadine Stavonina, a remarkable woman, campaigner and speaker on all things autism, for her knowledge, wisdom and tenacity in helping Gary and others with ASD.

Danny Alexander, Peter Hain, Fair Trials International, Menzies

Campbell, Julian Huppert, Peter Oborne, Hywel Francis, the joint parliamentary committee on human rights and the American Civil Liberties Union.

Professor John Arquilla, an American intellectual and presidential adviser on cyber-warfare, for showing us the compassionate face of America and having the courage to raise his head above the parapet to uphold traditional American values.

James Slack, Christopher Hope, Martin Beckford, Rory Carroll, Euan Duguid, Ben Boreland, Mary McConnell, James Murray, Michael Frith, John Leyden, Tom Espiner, Dave Neal and Mark Ballard, journalists who fight for right, and online and offline friends who do the same.

Ian Macleod, Lorna Scott, John and Jill Sharp, Charlie and Jeanna McKinnon, Mark and Ofer, Josie Betan, Jim and Helen Litherland, Oliviea and Johnnie, Pauline and Steve, Tamsin and family, Dhiren Shah, and all the wonderful children who were part of our lives, because family and friends matter.

Mike Garrick, Cliff Sullivan, Julia O'Dwyer, Ben Scotchbrook, @Harlechnnorfolk, Paul Stevenson, Les Floyd, Alex Magill, Jerry Pippin, Kerry Cassidy, Dan Bull and so many others who, because of limited space, I was unable to include.

My eternal thanks to all those already mentioned in this book and to those not mentioned, for every email written, letter sent, speech delivered, tweet tweeted, FreeGary avatar donned, article written, video aired, song written and voice spoken in support of Gary being kept in the UK.

Thank you for helping to save Gary.

INDEX

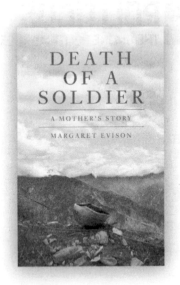